The Revolutionary War Era

The Revolutionary War Era

Randall Huff

American Popular Culture Through History
Ray B. Browne, Series Editor

GREENWOOD PRESS
Westport, Connecticut • London

Library of Congress Cataloging-in-Publication Data

Huff, Randall.
    The Revolutionary War Era / Randall Huff.
        p. cm. — (American popular culture through history)
    Includes bibliographical references (p.) and index.
    ISBN 0–313–32262–7 (alk. paper)
        1. United States—Civilization—To 1783. 2. United States—History—Colonial period,
    ca. 1600–1775.   3. United States—History—Revolution, 1775–1783.   4. Popular Culture
    —United States—History—18th century. I. Title. II. Series.
    E163.H84   2004
    973.3—dc22   2004042484

British Library Cataloguing in Publication Data is available.

Library of Congress Catalog Card Number: 2004042484
ISBN: 0–313–32262–7

First published in 2004

Greenwood Press, 88 Post Road West, Westport, CT 06881
An imprint of Greenwood Publishing Group, Inc.
www.greenwood.com

Printed in the United States of America

The paper used in this book complies with the
Permanent Paper Standard issued by the National
Information Standards Organization (Z39.48–1984).

10 9 8 7 6 5 4 3 2 1

For Robert Dean Huff,
a true patriot

Contents

Contents

Series Foreword

Popular culture is the system of attitudes, behavior, beliefs, customs, and tastes that define the people of any society. It is the entertainments, diversions, icons, rituals, and actions that shape the everyday world. It is what we do while we are awake and what we dream about while we are asleep. It is the way of life we inherit, practice, change, and then pass on to our descendants.

Popular culture is an extension of folk culture, the culture of the people. With the rise of electronic media and the increase in communication in American culture, folk culture expanded into popular culture—the daily way of life as shaped by the *popular majority* of society. Especially in a democracy like the United States, popular culture has become both the voice of the people and the force that shapes the nation. In 1782, the French commentator Hector St. Jean de Crèvecoeur asked in his *Letters from an American Farmer*, "What is an American?" He answered that such a person is the creation of America and is in turn the creator of the country's culture. Indeed, notions of the American Dream have been long grounded in the dream of democracy—that is, government by the people, or popular rule. Thus, popular culture is tied fundamentally to America and the dreams of its people.

Historically, culture analysts have tried to fine-tune culture into two categories: "elite"—the elements of culture (fine art, literature, classical music, gourmet food, etc.) that supposedly define the best of society—and "popular"—the elements of culture (comic strips, bestsellers, pop music, fast food, etc.) that appeal to society's lowest common denominator. The so-called "educated" person approved of elite culture and scoffed at popular culture. This schism first began to develop in Western Europe in the fifteenth century when the privileged classes tried to discover and develop differences in societies based on class, money, privilege and life styles. Like many aspects of European society, the debate between elite and popular cultures came to the United States. The upper class in America, for example, supported museums and galleries that would exhibit "the finer things in life," that would "elevate" people. As the twenty-first century emerges, however, the distinctions between popular culture and elitist culture have blurred. The blues songs (once denigrated as "race music") of Robert Johnson are now revered by musicologists; architectural students study buildings in Las Vegas as examples of what Robert Venturi called the "kitsch of high capitalism"; sportswriter Gay Talese and heavyweight boxing champ Floyd Patterson were co-panelists at a 1992 SUNY New Paltz symposium on Literature and Sport. The examples go on and on, but the one commonality that emerges is the role of popular culture as a model for the American Dream, the dream to pursue happiness and a better, more interesting life.

To trace the numerous ways in which popular culture has evolved throughout American history, we have divided the volumes in this series into chronological periods—historical eras until the twentieth century, decades between 1900 and 2000. In each volume, the author explores the specific details of popular culture that reflect and inform the general undercurrents of the time. Our purpose, then, is to present historical and analytical panoramas that reach both backward into America's past and forward to her collective future. In viewing these panoramas, we can trace a very fundamental part of American society. The American Popular Culture Through History series presents the multi-faceted parts of a popular culture in a nation that is both grown and still growing.

Ray B. Browne
Secretary-Treasurer
Popular Culture Association
American Culture Association

Introduction

The twenty years from 1763 to 1783, during which America conceived the possibility of liberty and successfully defended it against the greatest military power on earth, were more difficult and dangerous than those of any similar period in the nation's history. A succession of political crises led to the bloodshed of the Boston Massacre, the unexpected colonial successes at Concord and Bunker Hill, and eight more years of frequently disastrous combat, during which the Continental Congress, colonial legislatures, and local committees of public safety conducted governmental business despite their questionable legal right to do so. A series of prewar diplomatic failures left the British Parliament and the representatives sent by American colonies unable to reconcile their differences; the biggest diplomatic challenge of the new government was to gain recognition by the royal regimes of other European nations. Exacerbating all of these crises were the financial woes of the Continental Congress, which had few options when it came to raising the means to fulfill its military, political, and diplomatic ends. Without the legal authority to levy taxes directly, Congress could only petition and cajole the separate states for money, borrow the necessary funds from friendly foreign kings, and print massive quantities of unbacked currency, which consistently lost value during the war until it verged on becoming worthless.

Despite Thomas Jefferson's bold assertion in the Declaration of Independence, the premise that all men were created equal was anything but self-evident to anyone raised beneath a king's scepter, to those directly benefiting from an entrenched hereditary aristocracy like the men who controlled Parliament, or to the titled nobility they sent out with royal commissions to serve as royal governors. Most leaders in the initial political fight for independence were anything but dedicated to that proposition of political and social equality so eloquently suggested at the nation's birth; even such a prominent radical as John Adams frequently expressed his fear of mob rule even as he labored to destroy the established order. For those destined to remain in hereditary slavery for another three generations after the successful conclusion of the conflict, the rhetoric of the War for Independence was most remarkable for its unfulfilled promises of freedom.

America's ultimate victory in the Revolutionary War was never certain until the brilliant French and American military success of Yorktown in 1781 complemented a series of equally brilliant diplomatic successes and ultimately led to the Treaty of Paris in 1783. Throughout the decade of suffering before 1783, however, the sterling character of the emerging colonial leadership constituted the brightest hope for the nation, even in its darkest hours. Somehow, Congress continued to function despite the whirl of interconnected, seemingly insolvable problems that inundated them. The Continental Congress did not lose faith in George Washington's military leadership even as they were forced to flee from Philadelphia, first before an occupying British army and then before a mob of their own outraged soldiers who demanded back pay and undelivered bonuses. Washington continued to lead the army despite such major setbacks as the debacle on Long Island and seemingly insurmountable odds posed by a better-trained and continually better-supplied foe. Ultimately, however, America won the war because enough soldiers and civilians were willing to support the cause even when it meant years of painful and sometimes deadly service and virtual penury for many of them.

Serious study of the popular culture of the American Revolution can further our appreciation of the enormous risks undertaken by the Revolutionary generation. It can substantiate John Adams's claim that the American people embraced independence in their hearts and minds before the fighting even started; certain artifacts of the era can be used to determine such political tide lines, enabling scholars to fathom the depths and intensity of public sentiment in given areas at critical times in America's earliest national history. Popular culture can also provide perspective on the intentions of the founding fathers—a term often evoked even by Supreme Court justices as they apply the Constitution's eighteenth-century language to twenty-first century circumstances, as well as by extremists at both ends of the modern American political spectrum attempting to validate their opinions by connecting them with the statements of their Revolutionary-era predecessors. Best of all, however, the iconography of popular culture can make history come alive, a service of special merit for the insight it gives into the daily lives of groups of people so marginalized that their contributions to American culture have largely been overlooked by more traditional histories.

The standard histories of the American Revolution faithfully record the battlefield successes and diplomatic victories of the Patriot leaders, but a history of popular culture can come closer to revealing what life was really like for the founding fathers and mothers, their children, and their slaves. In order to understand the impact of the War for Independence on the American psyche, it is necessary to examine far more artifacts of early American culture than its political tracts and military history. Many of the major historical events of the era were shaped by popular culture, and certain of the personalities who shaped them eventually came to be chronicled and celebrated in folk and decorative arts, American music, and even architecture, to the point that in some cases the historical record has been irreversibly blurred.

The most pervasive images of the American Revolution as they appear in the popular culture of the twenty-first century come to us from later eras and had their origins not in popular culture but in the high cultural aspirations of academically trained painters who helped fill a nation's nostalgic desire to embrace the victorious cause. Moreover, most of the artifacts preserved from the era itself and usually haphazardly grouped under the broad heading of popular culture are in fact more indicative of the broader state of civilization than of a popular contemporary trend. As an example, a simple wooden plate laboriously carved by a frontiersman in his isolated cabin so that he will have something upon which to eat his food is more interesting to the cultural historian if its shape mimics the elegance of a popular pattern of porcelain china or if its wood was chosen in compliance with a colonial boycott on imported goods, or if its decoration reflects other aspects of the popular culture of the time. In the aggregate, the objects preserved from that era to the twenty-first century reveal an initial celebration of the connection with England and some occasional expressions of pride in a specific colony, a pride that gradually gave way to an assertion of American identity embracing all the colonies despite the vast differences in their religious as well as secular development.

For most historians, the most exciting developments in the popular culture of the American Revolution were its responses to a succession of burning political issues. Although a wide spectrum of practical considerations made possible independence from Great Britain gradually the most pressing concern for many colonists, a series of political crises initially felt by only a few individuals eventually encouraged the best minds of the generation to become political theorists. While these giants declared themselves members of an independent state and argued among themselves over the destiny of the fledgling nation, they were dependent upon the limited media of the eighteenth century to create the popular support that their ideas would need if they were to shape the political life of the new country. To a remarkable extent, the popular culture of the American

Revolutionary War shaped historical events even as it chronicled them. The best contemporary newspapers tried to keep their various audiences current on the day's events; the speeches, topical essays, and political cartoons that found their way into print were often designed to motivate the people to take action. Print media frequently provided the only forums available for political discussions throughout the colonies. Locally, the same sentiments could be voiced in a variety of public and private venues, and in more private settings they found expression in politically motivated consumer choices and the engraving or inscribing of sentiments on items of everyday use.

In 1763, the elite culture of the propertied classes was largely devoted to European, especially British, forms and fashions, and the popular culture that reflected the tastes of the masses was slavishly dedicated to emulating their betters. The political dimension of the popular-culture war waged by colonial propagandists was, at first, exclusively economic in nature, but the principles of political independence and legal equality had such broad popular appeal that the taxation issues over which the first rhetorical skirmishes were fought ultimately seemed rather inconsequential. This became especially apparent when the new Continental government was reduced to attempting several of the same taxation measures that had led to the conflict in the first place.

With the Stamp Act in 1765, Parliament sought to force the American colonies to pay for their own defense, but the colonists knew that their own militias were superior to the disorganized Indian forces, the only immediate military threats they now faced. It was not long before first-class propagandists like Samuel Adams and James Otis were attacking not only the tax and the reasons for it but even Parliament's right to tax at all. The new patriots gradually used popular culture to politicize the countryside, effectively spreading the call for independence and eventually disseminating the seeds of a uniquely American consciousness throughout the colonies. A new American iconography was developing at the same time that shortages in manufactured goods from England were exacerbated by, first, a series of boycotts and then occupation and blockades by enemy forces. As arguments over the form of the new government were developed, popular culture began serving this nation-building function.

Popular culture encouraged men to take the country's future into their own hands by taking up their pens, by joining public protests for one side or the other, and ultimately by prompting those of sufficient courage to enlist in their local militias or the Continental Army. There they were asked to withstand cannonades, volleys of musket fire, and bayonet charges from the most fearful army of the day. Their political opponents—who later joined Loyalist militias, usually serving in auxiliary or support roles for the regular British Army—gradually found their livestock, their homes, and even their persons increasingly at risk when they ventured to express their beliefs in any public forum. The political manifestations of popular culture grew in scope from sermons, songs, broadsides, and pamphlets to encompass such new phenomena as war material drives. Popular culture helped reconcile men to the differences naturally occurring among their friends and allies, and led them to revile their enemies to the point where sometimes not even the threat of capital punishment could keep enraged citizens and soldiers from wrecking havoc on their propagandistically dehumanized foes. Popular culture helped keep men fighting in the Continental Army and in the state militias despite long seasons of continual defeat in the field, chronic shortages of clothing and even food, and years of the most hazardous service without pay. Finally, popular culture consecrated the contributions of the men who had dedicated themselves to the enormous task of nation building by glorifying the battles of the Revolution and celebrating the individual military leaders, especially George Washington.

Timeline of the Revolutionary War Era

1763

Treaty of Paris ends French and Indian War (begun in 1754)

Royal Proclamation of 1763 forbids American colonial settlement west of Allegheny Mountains.

1764

Sugar Act (taxes sugar, indigo, coffee, pimento, wine, and textiles)

Currency Act (taxes to be paid in silver, not American paper money)

1765

Stamp Act passed by Parliament (taxes legal documents, newspapers, cards, and dice)

Sons of Liberty, founded in response to Stamp Act, advocate boycotts of British goods and anything requiring tax stamps

Forced resignations of tax collectors in several colonies

1766

Parliament repeals Stamp Act but passes Declaratory Act (Parliament's right to pass American laws confirmed)

1767

Townshend Acts (tax tea, glass, wine, oil and paint; royal officers could search colonial homes without demonstrating legal cause)

1768

British establish small garrison in Boston to force compliance with tax laws

1769

Monthly mail packet connects New York City and Charlestown, South Carolina

1770

All Townshend Acts repealed except tax on tea

Boston Massacre (March 5; aggressive mob quelled by British soldiers' volley, four killed)

1771

Benjamin Franklin writes first part of his *Autobiography*

1772

British revenue cutter *Gaspee* burned in Rhode Island

Charles Willson Peale paints first of his portraits of George Washington

1773

Phillis Wheatley's *Poems on Various Subjects, Religious and Moral* published

First public art museum in colonies opened (Charlestown, South Carolina)

Boston Tea Party (December 16, around 150 Bostonians dump an entire ship's cargo of tea into the harbor)

1774

John Woolman's *Journal* published

Boston Harbor closed to all shipping; ten thousand British soldiers arrive

First Continental Congress meets in Philadelphia (fifty-two prominent men representing all the colonies except Georgia)

1775

Paul Revere and other messengers gallop through the countryside to alert colonial militia that units of the British Army are advancing upon them from Boston

Lexington and Concord battles (April 19, beginning of continuous warfare in the colonies)

Boston siege begins (American militia keep British Army restricted to Boston)

Congress creates the Continental Army out of the militia forces around Boston (May 31)

Washington named commander in chief by Congress (June 15)

Bunker Hill battle near Boston (June 17)

Fort Ticonderoga captured by Colonial soldiers led by Benedict Arnold and Ethan Allen

Colonial invasion of Canada ends with unsuccessful attack on Quebec

Second Continental Congress meets in Philadelphia

Continental Navy formed by congressional resolution (October 13, birthday of U.S. Navy; by war's end, over forty armed vessels will be commissioned)

Continental Marine Corps formed by Congress (November 10, birthday of U.S. Marine Corps)

1776

Thomas Paine publishes *Common Sense*, an immediate best seller advocating American independence

British Army evacuates Boston

Declaration of Independence passed by Congress and signed by John Hancock (July 4, other delegates would add their signatures over the next six months)

American army driven from Long Island and New York City

Thomas Paine publishes first of sixteen pamphlets on *The American Crisis* urging Americans to persevere in their military struggle despite setbacks

Washington's surprise attack on Trenton, New Jersey, captures a thousand Hessians (December 26)

1777

Americans win Battle of Princeton (January 3)

Gilbert Stuart, later famous for his portraits of George Washington, begins studying at London studio of fellow American Benjamin West

Philadelphia occupied by British (September 26); Continental Congress again retreats to Baltimore

British General Burgoyne and his army captured at the Battle of Saratoga

American army takes up winter quarters at Valley Forge

1778

British abandon Philadelphia, are attacked by Washington's army at Monmouth but escape to New York City

Treaty establishes French and American alliance

First Battle of Savannah leaves most of Georgia in British hands

1779

H. E. Brackenridge begins publishing *United States Magazine*

British victory at Second Battle of Savannah secures Georgia

Spain declares war on Great Britain

British attack coasts of Virginia and Carolina

Americans under General Anthony Wayne capture Stony Point, New York

John Paul Jones, captain of the *Bonhomme Richard*, captures the *Serapis* after a pitched battle

1780

British victories at Charleston and Waxhalls, South Carolina, keep southern states loyal

French troops unite with Washington (July 11)

American general Horatio Gates is soundly defeated at Camden, South Carolina

At Kings Mountain, South Carolina, Patriot militia units rout their Loyalist counterparts

American general Greene begins a southern campaign that diverts British resources in a prolonged and fruitless chase

The Netherlands declare war on Great Britain

General Benedict Arnold defects to the British

1781

Benedict Arnold, now a British general, attacks southern cities and resources

British lose to Americans at Cowpens, South Carolina, in European-style battle

British general Cornwallis fortifies Yorktown, Virginia, and awaits evacuation by sea

French fleet enters Chesapeake Bay, Virginia, preventing British evacuation

General Washington and his French allies successfully besiege Yorktown; General Cornwallis surrenders (October 20)

1782

The Netherlands officially recognize American independence

General Anthony Wayne defeats British in Georgia

British evacuate Charlestown and Savannah

Jean de Crèvecoeur's *Letters from an American Farmer* published

Charles Willson Peale begins exhibiting his portrait gallery to the public

1783

Treaty of Paris officially ends Revolutionary War (September 3)

British troops evacuate New York City; American troops under Washington enter the city in triumph (November)

Part I

Life and Youth During the Revolutionary War Era

1

Everyday America

By 1763, the conditions of everyday life in British America were largely determined by the circumstances into which one was born. The average American colonist never traveled more than thirty miles from his birthplace; his entire life was conducted in response to the economic opportunities, religious and secular authorities, and agricultural or maritime possibilities of the terrain surrounding the family's farm or the nearby towns. Almost everyone lived close to the Atlantic coast, upon which all were dependent for manufactured goods imported from Europe and news from the other colonies as well as the rest of the outside world. They had been raised with the characteristically European consciousness that just across the border were the lands of traditional national enemies; in their case, these were the Native Americans and the French. The extensive French claims to North America extended from the Allegheny Mountains to the east and to the Mississippi River in the west. Victory in the French and Indian War removed this French obstacle and initially promised unhampered access to the fertile lands of the Ohio and other river valleys all the way to the Mississippi. The only major political obstacle that seemed to remain was the land's prior occupation by various Indian tribes, especially the Iroquois federation in the north and the Creek in the South. The French and Indian War had exposed the military weakness of the tribes, the fertility of their lands, and to many European settlers, the folly of letting such bloodthirsty savages inhabit adjacent territories. Of course, many of the Indian tribes had by this time learned of the blood thirst and land hunger of the settlers, but they could do nothing effective to stop the encroachments.

For over a century, the European colonists had been increasing their military might along the seaboard, a fact that placed unceasing pressure on the tribes they encountered. A century's natural increase in numbers and constant immigration from Europe combined with a precipitous decline in Native American numbers to make the westward expansion of the colonies almost inevitable. The cultural heritage of anyone whose family had been living in the colonies since the prior century included lurid tales of fighting the tribes along the coast and sometimes painful encounters with the Indians of the interior forests. Fear of massacre by the Indians helped keep the average American in or near his colonial birthplace, but the French and Indian War demonstrated the vulnerability of the most powerful tribes even when they acted in alliance with a major European power. The Europeans' ultimate success in every prior war with the Indians and a century's experience in dispossessing them of their ancestral homes emboldened everyone whose war or surveying experience had exposed them to the interior, some of the richest farming lands in the world.

REGIONAL DIFFERENCES IN EVERYDAY LIFE

By 1776, those born into some of the thriving American coastal towns were the beneficiaries of up to 150 years of European management of the land. Residents of Philadelphia, the largest city in British America, had been prodded into action by the many civic projects of Benjamin Franklin, the indefatigable spirit of urban boosterism. Even if not swept up in his street-cleaning campaign, they may have served in one of the many volunteer fire companies he helped organize. Certainly everyone benefited from his pavement, streetlight, and night watchman schemes. Franklin was not a man to neglect the intellectual and moral aspects of life, either. The men who would provide the city's leadership in the coming crisis of the Revolutionary War were already honing their skills in small *juntos*. Franklin propagated these fraternal circles for the mutual benefit of all their members, and through their agency many men became as dedicated to the betterment of their society as they were to their personal development. With Franklin's extraordinary industriousness and exemplary commercial diligence constantly before their eyes, most merchants strove to better their trades in the thriving city. Philadelphians had little time to waste on unproductive men regardless of their ancestry; what mattered most were the contributions an individual could make to the general prosperity. Despite having just twenty thousand inhabitants, Philadelphia was second only to London as the most populous British city.

New York already claimed the second-highest population and the most cultural diversity of any city in America. Apart from the residents of a few relatively densely populated areas like Philadelphia, New York City, and

Most American colonists were still tied to the soil in 1761, when this
representation of their rural progress was printed in London.
Courtesy of the Library of Congress.

Boston, however, the overwhelming majority of colonial Americans were
engaged in agriculture on private farms. Because the industrial revolution had not yet arrived, most people throughout the British Empire were
still small farmers. Alexander Hamilton, a New York lawyer attempting
to get the colonists to realize their potential strength as a nation, estimated
that the British colonies contained over three million people in 1774.[1] Their
livelihoods depended on industries as disparate as whaling in Nantucket,
Massachusetts, and tobacco farming by South Carolinian plantation owners and their slaves, but soon political events would force everyone to
come to terms with the implications of their being Americans as well as
British colonists.

Tobacco and cotton were the chief export crops of the southern colonies, the former being so valuable as to be almost the principal salvation of the Revolution. As early as 1765, two hundred large ships were
filled with the estimated forty million pounds of tobacco that were being exported yearly from Virginia and Maryland.[2] During the Revolutionary War, the Continental Congress, having exhausted its credit,
reached the point where its currency was practically valueless; it was
reduced to selling tobacco in European markets to procure the cash,

credit, and merchandise needed in America. Both sides quickly recognized tobacco's value in this connection, and when the British unleashed Benedict Arnold in the South in 1780, the tons of tobacco he destroyed were given almost as much prominence in his battlefield reports as if they had been cities leveled and men killed.

Hemp, the fiber produced from marijuana plants, was also an important commodity because it was used in the manufacture of ropes and the production of oakum. Both of these products were indispensable for the sailing ships of the era. To make oakum, sailors dipped hemp or other fibers into tar and used it to plug between the wooden planks of the ship's hull.

ARISTOCRATIC PRETENSIONS

Aristocratic life along the tidal basins in Virginia and South Carolina most closely replicated the privileged life enjoyed by the social elite in Britain. By 1776, in some areas as many as six generations had devoted themselves to building up great estates, the nerve centers of which were often elaborate mansions surrounded by extensive gardens with tree-lined drives. Some of these buildings survive and still dominate their manors. In America's coastal colonies, success in the accumulation of enormous wealth often fell to those fortunate in large-scale commercial agriculture or transatlantic commerce. It was always important to the native-born social leaders of the provincial British colonies always to maintain the dress and manners of the class to which they aspired. While they sometimes busied themselves with the improvement of their estates, most were eager to join their wives, sons, and daughters in the social whirl of dances, private parties, and theatrical entertainment to which their wealth gave them entrée. Substantial men like George Washington and Thomas Jefferson flourished in that society, and their offspring frequently enjoyed leisured privilege and exceptional formal education. By the outbreak of the American Revolution most of them had a tremendous sense of entitlement. In the absence of direct genealogical links to the Old World aristocracy, it is easy to understand their willingness to justify their privileges as the fruits derived from the natural merits of their immediate ancestors. All men with money and property could agree that landed aristocrats like themselves should enjoy exalted places in society, if some naturally chafed at the precedence claimed by those with more distinguished lineages than their own.

Many of the wealthiest Americans attempted to acquire the luxuries available to their peers across the ocean. A few sent their sons abroad to study; these young men returned home with news of the fine quality of aristocratic British life and a keen sense of the latest fashions. Some of the newly rich American tradesmen had their factors (agents) scour British stores for the latest aristocratic tastes in clothing, furniture, and other accoutrements of success, and the American craftsmen modeled some of their own efforts on these imported items to meet the new demand. The elegant simplicity of the latest trends in home furnishings made them widely popular throughout the colonies; today the surviving pieces continue to command high prices, under the generic name of "Chippendale furniture." In the southern colonies, the men and women who first used such furniture were as proud of their stations in life as of their sumptuous furnishings; some of them even welcomed the traditional deference paid them as representatives of the propertied class by the most recent arrivals from England. Indeed, an extreme awareness of class distinctions seemed almost instinctive in all the products of the British political system who made their way to American shores, and even those whose families had by that time toiled among the same neighbors for over 150 years acknowledged that some bloodlines were more important than others, that some men were entitled to more opportunities in life by virtue of their family titles, and that the governance of their colonies was best left to those born to such advantages. It seemed natural for many men who possessed such beliefs to support the institution of slavery, which was found throughout the colonies, and for some of them to be so fixated on acquiring and maintaining the accoutrements of nobility that they were blind to the innate nobility of every man, and even to the best things that resided in their own natures.

If some people in colonial society attempted to replicate the rigid class consciousness of Great Britain, they had to be more flexible in admitting men of sufficient wealth to the privileged rank of gentry. Far greater distinctions were made between men of different social and economic classes in all the British colonies than would be the case in post-Revolutionary America. Wealth and property determined if one was driven in an elegant carriage attended by liveried footmen or was forced to walk through the streets. Boston was small enough that even the wealthiest men (and John Hancock, the wealthiest man in British America, lived in one of its Beacon Hill mansions) often found themselves among men of all classes. At the same time, the power and privilege of rank were so great that the propertied classes took great pains to distinguish themselves from other men. A few well-educated and socially prominent men aspired to the rank, power, and status positions of their colonial governments, but the highest position, that of royal governor, was usually reserved for titled British nobility with impeccable bloodlines. The fact the even the best-intentioned efforts of the colonial legislatures could be subject to the arbitrary will of a royal governor was a constant irritant to the most important men of some colonies.

A LACK OF SOCIAL PROGRAMS

The very wealthy not only dressed better but drank and even ate far more sumptuously than their average contemporaries. Gout and dyspepsia, the natural consequences of a too-rich diet, were almost fashionable disorders. The best-trained doctors would be summoned to the "quality," while the poorest inhabitants were dependent upon the care of relatives even for childbirth, serious injury, or life-threatening illness. Bleeding, the drainage of blood to restore the proper balance of "humors" in a patient, was widely practiced by doctors and, especially, barbers as the specific cure for a variety of ills. The red and white stripes on the traditional barber pole originally advertised that bloodletting was available on the premises. Of course, the practice had little effect on most diseases, and colonial doctors frequently found themselves powerless in the face of smallpox or yellow fever epidemics. The colonists were so well acquainted with rabies, an inevitably fatal disease at the time, that the termagant wife in an early Revolutionary drama need only mention the symptoms of biting, foaming, and slavering; the audience would appreciate the gallows humor behind the implication that her husband was mad for participating in the Continental Congress. More than another century and a half would pass before government assistance was routinely available for the elderly and infirm, and government-backed unemployment insurance and workman's compensation provided laborers with a financial safety net only in the twentieth century.

When one fully realizes the lack of social services in pre-Revolutionary America, the courage of its citizen soldiers becomes all the more remarkable. A crippling battlefield injury could completely deprive them of any means of making a living, burdening their closest relatives with their care for the rest of their lives. Thanks to the efforts of Benjamin Franklin and other civic leaders, Philadelphia had a hospital. Most other places did not. In colonial America, a serious injury sustained in the workplace could result in dismissal from employment regardless of whose fault the accident had been. The average man went about making his living as best he could, while the educated elite focused their attention on accumulating wealth and power. Collective bargaining had little footing in a legal system still largely feudal in temperament, and such niceties as sick leave or vacation pay had yet to be invented.

In sharp contrast to the thriving commerce evident in a few cities along the coast, elsewhere a poorly developed infrastructure of roads between the colonies, an executive branch of colonial government largely administered or appointed by authorities an ocean away, and continual migration of colonists to the western frontier hampered economic development. The fact that it took two weeks for a letter to arrive in Boston from New York suggests the primitive conditions of the roads. Regular (twice monthly) mail service did not connect New York City with the important southern city of Charlestown, South Carolina, until 1770. Until then, local letters frequently had to be entrusted to the care of people traveling in the right direction; it could be safer to ferry mail between the northern and southern colonies twice across the Atlantic. The situation improved remarkably with the appointment of Benjamin Franklin as postmaster general of the northern colonies. He standardized the routes and delivery schedules, in some cases personally measuring the distances between towns and placing milestones along the route. For the first time carrying the mail turned profitable; Franklin remained in the office until dismissed for his role in the publication in the colonies of the royal governor's reports back to England. These were allegedly acquired by tampering with the mail, but Franklin eventually had the last say when his colleagues in the Continental Congress named him their first postmaster general. The post had become necessary because letters were being stolen from the royal post and published to the embarrassment of members of the Congress.

If one wanted to keep acquainted with one's family and maintain an active hand in one's business, it was necessary to live and work within a relatively few miles of home; accordingly, most people rarely traveled far. The frontier, where all were entirely dependent upon their own resources, with no potential aid from any established governmental or social institution, was not across the Sierras, the Rockies, or even across the Mississippi; it was as close as western Pennsylvania. On the more isolated farms you ate what you grew and wore what you or your family were able to make; however, the typical eighteenth-century laborer was far more skillful at creating the things he needed than his descendents would be. Life could progress at an oxen's pace following the plow for days on end, but there was ample time in the dead of winter to add decorative touches with a carving knife to the objects surrounding one. If you were young, your thoughts might turn on the prior Sunday's Bible lesson, your chances of again seeing your neighbor's son or daughter, or the cosmic injustice that had brought you under the tyranny of your father. With advancing years came the necessity of providing for all of one's own family's needs. The church could inculcate resignation to one's fate, and the tavern could provide the latest news, albeit at a stiff price.

MEETING YOUR EVERY NEED

By 1774, a European or colonial traveler approaching any of the prosperous cities and towns along the Atlantic coast would have had no trouble in securing the food, clothing, shelter, and transportation he needed to continue his journey if he had sufficient funds with which to pay for them. While this fact may not impress the reader of a later day, it should be remembered that European occupation of most places in the colonies was less than a century old. Earlier travelers would have been left to their own devices in searching for adequate nutrition, would have slept outside in all weathers, and gradually would have worn their clothing to rags unless willing and able to process buckskin from the deer they killed as a substitute for manufactured cloth. British pounds sterling could now purchase value on the spot, and some of the places an eighteenth-century traveler might take his rest were so aesthetically pleasing that they have been preserved in the twenty-first century. While horses still provided the readiest transportation throughout the colonies, rudimentary roads accommodated wagons and carriages between others. One might book passage on a private schooner to travel even more comfortably from one colony to another, although the wait for such transportation to become available could seem interminable.

As most towns had not been founded for religious purposes, taverns began springing up like dandelions along the roadways, and many offered a weary traveler a bed for the night at a reasonable price. By 1778, the German major general von Riedesel thought that a majority of the inhabitants of even the rural districts surrounding Boston had opened taverns or small stores, by which means they gained easy livelihoods.[3] Sometimes complete strangers would be asked to share the only available bed; once even Benjamin Franklin and John Adams, traveling together on official business, had to be accommodated in this fashion. Food and wine could be plentiful at some such inns. It was common practice to drink alcohol instead of water, because the latter, although plentiful, sometimes contained harmful bacteria and other impurities.

For amusement, a traveler might chance to hear local amateur musicians play or, if he happened to land in someplace like Charleston at the right time, even a theatrical performance. He might hear spirited discussions of current events in the taverns, although as the Revolution neared he would be wise not to reveal any political opinions of his own. Table fare at such places was typically coarse, lighting was often supplied by candle-light instead of the more expensive options of whale oil or kerosene lamps, and only a commode bucket and water pitcher in the room could save one a trip to the outhouse—indoor plumbing was not an option.

The traveler would have found his circumstances much less promising had he run out of money, however. If he had reached the journeyman level in some craft, such as printing, joinery, or blacksmithing, he might have been well advised to continue traveling until he reached a city large enough to support such trades. While it is true that there was a demand for skilled labor throughout the colonies, ready money to pay for it was already short before war debts and other uncertainties destabilized colonial currencies.

PREWAR AMERICAN MANUFACTURING

By the second half of the eighteenth century, colonial American found-ries had begun to turn out iron pots, kettles, plowshares, guns, and swords, which had previously been ferried across the Atlantic. Water mills, and less frequently windmills, were being built to grind grain. At least one water mill was being used to process wool for clothing in 1776;[4] a foundry was producing cannon in Rhode Island in 1777, despite the presence of a large British army in the neighborhood. In direct contravention of British laws aimed at protecting English manufactures against colonial as well as foreign competition, ships from other European states found ready markets for their cargoes in American ports.

For the most part, however, the poorest Americans had to continue to make the best out of materials at hand. There are in many of the artifacts from the era clear demonstrations of the grace and elegance of a purely functional apparatus. This can be seen in the few wooden plates that have survived, as well as in the more common pottery. Sometimes, in idle moments that might be turned to account, one's hand might be turned to the decorative arts. Furniture, gunstocks and gun barrels, virtually every available surface, might lend itself to quick carving and scrawls. The popular culture of the Revolutionary era inspired and directed such craftsmen's artistic expression, although the relatively primitive state of industrial development in British America meant that goods of the high-est quality still had to be imported. Such merchandise, however, brought with it either the taxes, risks, and transportation costs of a transatlantic voyage from England or the stigma of contraband as the illegally smuggled goods of other European nations.

Most southern factories were small-scale affairs, originally developed to supply the immediate needs of the plantation or to prepare its produce for market. One plantation in North Carolina boasted its own rice and tim-ber mills and an indigo factory.[5] Tar and turpentine were also manufac-tured locally, but tobacco was the cash crop of most importance from Maryland south at this time.

WORK AND FAMILY

Work and family were the centers of the typical colonial American's life in the period following the French and Indian Wars. The extent to which these institutions were shaped by religious practice varied greatly from colony to colony and, increasingly, even from house to house. In the middle colonies, especially Rhode Island, Pennsylvania, and New York, and on the frontier, a de facto religious tolerance was becoming engrained as families found themselves the neighbors of people of different faiths and nationalities. Most colonial denominations tended to reinforce one's role within the family, the church providing opportunities for social interaction, intellectual stimulation, and spiritual comfort. Membership in the Anglican Church, the state church of England, reinforced one's identity as a British subject and one's loyalty to the sovereign. Quaker, Puritan, or Catholic lineage not only distanced one from dominant English society, it tended to make one aware of the long history of religious independence in America.

This freedom of worship was largely dependent upon colonial self-governance, which most American colonists had experienced since their first arrival on the continent. Colonial assemblies usually were left to their own devices in deciding how to raise the necessary funds to govern and develop their colonies, in accordance with royal or gubernatorial decrees.

Because the majority of American colonists were still engaged in agriculture, work consumed a greater portion of daily life than would later be the case. There was always land to clear and improve for subsistence agriculture on the frontier, where it was necessary for farmers and their wives to strain mightily to feed their growing families. Balanced against this constant struggle to survive was the freedom from oppression that was justly celebrated by such contemporary writers as Michel Guillaume Jean de Crèvecoeur and Thomas Jefferson. In his *Letters from an American Farmer*, the former recalled his delight in exposing his small son to the fresh air behind the plow; Jefferson, for his part, envisioned a nation of small farmers whose very independence lent them the freedom and leisure to develop their own interests. Real freedom in his time, though, was reserved for those of his own set; it was his servants who made it possible for him to indulge his varied studies.

In the spring of each year, many men of other classes would guide plows all day behind their oxen or horses, physical labor that involved keeping pace with animals on often newly broken ground, having to lift the entire rear of the plow when rocks were encountered, and being forced to jerk it into position at the beginning of a row. Pigs were kept all summer, but the slaughter of the biggest and heaviest hogs in the fall was a prodigious task. Wood had to be chopped to ensure an adequate supply for cooking throughout the year and for heating in the winter. The livestock also had to be maintained throughout the year, and sufficient forage had to be grown and harvested to sustain them from fall one year to mid-spring the next, when grazing could resume. Cows had to be milked every day. Chickens and the remaining hogs had to be fed, and the fences and buildings had to be maintained throughout the year. Such produce as could be sold at market had to be carried or ferried there, another strenuous undertaking.

Most Revolutionary-era colonial women were kept as busy rendering the crops and meats edible as their husbands and sons were by growing and hunting them. Cooking and cleaning required water, which had to be fetched from a nearby stream or brought up from a well in buckets and carried by hand into the house. Chunks of wood for the kitchen stove had to be brought inside, in all seasons and in all weather. Several preliminary steps were required before some agricultural products could become digestible for humans, let alone palatable. Salt was the principal preservative of the eighteenth century, with smoking and boiling sometimes also being used. Although there was still no awareness of germs and bacteria at that time, it was understood that boiling fruits and vegetables before pouring them into containers and sealing them with wax kept them preserved long after untreated produce would have rotted. Cream could be churned by hand to create butter. Women were kept busy at such seasonal tasks for days on end each year, and such necessary chores had to be performed in addition to the cooking, cleaning, sewing, and mending that normally consumed their days.

Knowledge of family planning was not widely disseminated in America until a century after the American Revolution, so many married women were frequently pregnant. All pregnancies were extremely risky due to the complete absence of the sterile delivery rooms and surgical interventions which would be developed in a later century. Much of a married woman's time was taken up by nursing and tending to infants, and by providing their young sons and daughters with rudimentary educations and moral instruction. Care for sick or wounded children as well as infirm, injured, or elderly adults sometimes burdened the colonial housewife even more. Religious fervor may have been only one of the motivating factors that sent colonial men and women to church on Sundays; church services could bring them into contact with a college-educated minister, intellectual stimulation through reading the Bible, and intimate contact with other wives and husbands. A couple hours free from the arduous labor that otherwise filled their days must have been a powerful attraction of active church membership.

Other chances for social interaction outside the towns of colonial America included the quilting and sewing bees organized by women to provide company in what otherwise could become a too-cloistered environment. Sometimes they also supplied an opportunity for sharing news and opinions on the events of the day, commentary that the uninitiated sometimes dismissed as gossip. Other opportunities for social interaction including house and barn-raisings, which entire families and even neighborhoods might attend, or militia drills, which brought the men together. The colonists drew strength from their communities.

BRITISH SANCTIONS AGAINST AMERICAN EXPANSION

The colonial enterprise as a whole was potentially enormously profitable for the British establishment. There was little chance, however, for

British profit in the propagation of small farms across the Appalachian Mountains, because the fresh produce raised there could not be preserved for sale in London markets. Only the larger plantations could support such labor-intensive export crops as tobacco, which lent itself to the transatlantic trade because it required long, hot summers for propagation; the drying required by its customary preparation also preserved it for shipping; and its addictive properties helped ensure a consistent demand. From an English perspective, it would be far better to keep the colonists bottled up on the Atlantic seaboard, where trade could be conducted directly with the mother country and on terms that she was in a position to dictate. Concentrating the population close to the shore had the added advantage of simplifying defense, because of the relative ease in that case with which the British navy could transport forces to meet either a foreign or Native American threat. Nonetheless, inducements like inexpensive land, increased chances for social mobility, and greater personal freedom that had lured many colonists to immigrate to America generally drew them on to less-developed areas. Debates about the proper role for England and the future of America within the British Empire soon enlivened political discussion up and down the coast.

Two novel developments across the Atlantic forced the issue. On October 7, 1763, a royal proclamation preserved the lands west of the existing colonies as Indian territory and closed them to European settlement. For most eighteenth-century American colonists, the right to settle in the new territory had been a military question, not a moral one. Everything had seemed ripe for western expansion, but now those who cared about British laws even when they were beyond the enforcement arm of the government were stopped in their tracks. Like many other measures designed by Parliament to keep the colonies from becoming too powerful, the proscription of western expansion was most frustrating to Americans near the very top of colonial society and those at the very bottom.

Nonetheless, life went on unchanged for most Americans as they continued to conduct their private lives, and the veterans returning from the French and Indian War tried to reintegrate themselves into social and economic life. Since most British citizens had the same degree of reverence for the king that twentieth-century Americans would hold for their flag, opposition to the Proclamation of 1763 was largely limited to grumbling in private quarters. From that moment on, however, political considerations had an increasing impact upon the conduct of everyday life in America. The bold political maneuver hit many of the most ambitious and rapacious Americans like a bolt of lightning from a clear sky. It was a serious blow to many veterans of the recently ended war, who had found no natural impediments to their acquisition of the rich farmlands they had fought over. It also frustrated the western land development schemes of such men as George Washington and Benjamin Franklin. The fact that these two prosperous men, who subsequently took leading roles in the Revolution, had earlier (but separately) worked to corner this potentially rich resource demonstrates how deeply an awareness of this new land had permeated the American consciousness. From a British perspective, preserving this land as Indian territory would permanently keep a potentially deadly enemy of the colonists as close as the French had been before the war, rendering them dependent upon British military assistance for the foreseeable future. Legions of independent backcountry men had streamed across the western frontier but still maintained their identities as British colonists. A few of them were now informed that their government did not support their claims to the new land.

A second problem arose from the war debts that the English had incurred in fighting the French. The usual import and export tariffs were woefully inadequate to overcome the double burdens of retiring the existing debt and maintaining adequate defenses along a two-thousand-mile frontier. In 1765, Parliament passed the Stamp Act to raise the necessary funds, and soon tax collectors were dispatched up and down the American coast to explain the new law and attempt to collect from people who had never been so directly taxed by England before. In addition to its economic impact, the law struck at the American pretensions of full citizenship as Englishmen. Since their inception, most American colonial governments had managed their own affairs within the framework of the executive powers exercised by the royal governors, who served as representatives of the king. By insisting on the sovereign right of Parliament to legislate colonial law, the British government was in effect denying the colonial gentry a full equality with the home aristocracy, the members of which held the privilege of electing their own governments. Many Americans dismissed the chief arguments advanced for such taxation as spurious, while British authorities argued that such steps were necessary to finance a substantial British army to guard the frontier as well as the coastal cities. Their colonial counterparts wondered at the purpose of such a military presence, since their militias could handle the Indians, the French had given up their American colonies, and no other international threat seemed realistic. The new revenue agents were roughly handled, sporadic rioting and other acts of protest broke out from Massachusetts all the way down to North Carolina, and the unenforceable law was repealed within a year.

Suddenly, a new topic of conversation began sweeping the American landscape. British authority, represented by the tax collectors, had been rendered ridiculous in part by the quaint custom of tarring and feathering. Such hilarity! The caricatures of the hapless victims preserved in the political cartoons of the day do not convey the physical agony attendant upon such torture, nor do they adequately convey the injustice of mob rule as a device for overcoming tyranny. Still, the indelible image of officialdom brought low gave people something to talk about on both sides of the Atlantic. The official British response took the form of a rapid series of increasingly repressive laws, all of which were deeply resented and widely resisted in the American colonies.

While most people living in the British colonies at the close of the French and Indian War considered themselves British citizens, it became increasing apparent that London considered them merely British *subjects*. Prior to the Revolutionary War, an unwavering loyalty to the king was a crucial part of the identity of everyone who prided himself on being a British citizen in the colonies. As Parliament began to assert its right to legislate all laws for the colonies without regard for locally elected legislatures, the colonists rightly saw that they would have no voice in such critical matters as their currency, their defense, and their taxes. At first, they thought that Parliament was usurping royal prerogatives as well as the power traditionally delegated to their locally elected officials. Hence the first Continental Congress created a petition to the king to intercede on their behalf and not allow Parliament to assert its authority over them. That the longest parts of the Declaration of Independence spell out the supposed transgressions of the king is in part of reflection of their disappointment upon learning that he sided with Parliament.

In the decade prior to the start of open warfare, questions about the benefits of maintaining a political connection with Great Britain occasioned increasingly heated and ever more frequent debates. Both sides availed themselves of the opportunities provided by popular culture to spread their chief arguments throughout the colonies. Before the Revolutionary War, the greatest harbingers of the coming crisis were the loud tavern arguments that steadily increased in number and intensity; the politics of the day were a great source of entertainment throughout the colonies. Public demonstrations increased in size and fervor; groups of colonists found diversion in occasionally tarring and feathering luckless customs agents or outspoken Tories who fell into their grasp, publicly hanging dummies as a surrogate for a particular royal governor or other official, and in destroying the property and attacking the persons of those who disagreed with them. Revolutionary hotheads were quick to use the frustrations of the common man to produce mobs intent on looting and burning the homes and businesses of the royal representatives. Even the royal governors were not safe.

On the night of March 5, 1770, five members of a taunting mob were killed by a volley from a detachment of British regulars. The soldiers were subsequently found innocent in a royal court, because in the confusion of the night and amid the shouts and snowballs hurled their way, they had thought they had been ordered to fire. The five victims of what became known as the "Boston Massacre" were immediately hailed as martyrs by the Patriot propagandists, and their fate was publicized throughout the colonies. The British revenue cutter *Gaspee* was boarded and burned in Rhode Island on June 9, 1772, and similar acts of treason took place in other colonies as well. Some members of Parliament hoped that a single demonstration of British military power and political resolve would intimidate the radical element and restore respect for their authority throughout the colonies; they waited for a suitable provocation to demonstrate their power. It was in keeping with the spirit of the times that on December 16, 1773, a group of Boston rebels disguised themselves as Indians and dumped an entire shipload of tea into the harbor in defiance of British taxes on the commodity. In response, in March 1774 Parliament closed the port of Boston; a naval blockade was imposed a few months later. The entire colony of Massachusetts was placed under military rule. Whatever inconveniences had been occasioned by boycotts up to this point were exacerbated a hundred times over, for the British fleet and three regiments of soldiers now threatened to take the fun and profit out of smuggling. Americans throughout the colonies were astounded at an escalation they perceived as an open act of war; all the colonies except Georgia sent delegates to the first Continental Congress, in August 1774, to coordinate an appropriate response.

Many colonists were intellectually stimulated by the profound changes in their economic and political relations with their government before the Revolution. Many of them were also severely pressed to find the hard currency required to pay all the new taxes, hampered as they were by regulations that forbade their production of manufactured goods or severely hampered their efforts. It was but a short step for the radical men in colonies up and down the coast to discover common ground in a wish for independence. Up to this point the colonists of South Carolina had had little knowledge of, and very few commercial ties with, their Massachusetts peers, but now it seemed their own government was turning on its citizens. Closing the port of Boston threatened the very existence of the Massachusetts colony, and men of substantial means even as far away as Charleston perceived the threat to their own property as well. Such men are quick to protect their interests. It should surprise no one that many of the delegates to both Continental Congresses held college degrees, at a time when even a secondary education was a luxury that most people could not afford, and that the delegates were among the richest men of their respective colonies. The chief motives behind their resistance to the new laws were financial as well as political, and the two themes were brilliantly combined in their slogan—that taxation without representation is tyranny—and in their calls for boycotts of British manufactures. Although the delegates to the First Continental Congress, in 1774, were not ready to declare their independence, it was clear that boycotts would cause serious shortages throughout the colonies even before their impact was felt by the London businessmen and manufacturers, whose protests the congress hoped to add to its own.

The British hope of bringing Boston to its knees was predicated on the effectiveness of its naval blockade and an increased army presence in the city, but these measures further aroused the countryside. The battles of Lexington and Concord, Massachusetts, on April 19, 1775, marked the beginning of continual fighting; these irregular engagements went fairly well for the rebels. Companies of British infantry had been dispatched to capture several rebel leaders and seize such military supplies as they could find. The colonial militias were able to drive these regulars back to Boston and cut off land access to the city, just as the British ships had blocked the port. The June 17, 1775, Battle of Bunker Hill further demonstrated the seriousness of the colonists' intentions.

However, everyday life in the colonies was adversely effected by the economic warfare that preceded the open combat and would continue until the war's end. As early as 1776, finished goods were in short supply by the British colonial standards of the day. As the war progressed, imported supplies dried up nearly completely. The rebels created courts of inspection for the purpose of enforcing their sanctions against British goods and shipping, an act of tyranny that at least one Tory writer, the dramatist known only as "Mary V.V.," compared to the Spanish Inquisition. She was probably referring, in this rather far-fetched comparison, to such public humiliations as forced oaths, the tarring and feathering of Tory sympathizers, and wanton destruction by mobs. It was not until the war reached the southern hill country that it turned truly murderous for civilians on both sides.

CHANGES IN EVERYDAY LIFE AFTER 1775

The advent of open warfare in 1775 had disastrous consequences for many Americans on both sides of the controversy. Individual liberties were suspended; the press—formerly censored, but ineffectively—was suppressed in rebel-held territories; and the exercise of freedom of speech was hazardous everywhere. The armies did collateral damage as they circled each other, and foraging parties sometimes were as much concerned with individual profits as with their obligation to feed the army. Fields in the enemy's probable path were burned to prevent grain from falling into enemy hands. On the actual battlefields, however, the relatively primitive state of the machines of war led to far fewer deaths and less permanent destruction than would be the case in subsequent wars. At sea, warships were occasionally sunk or burned after grounding. Commercial vessels were stopped on the high sea with increasing frequency as the Royal Navy's preoccupation with the war precluded its normal protection of mercantile shipping; with the breakdown of British authority, privateers came to be admired and rewarded for their depredations. Even the ships of the British navy gradually came to be feared; sometimes warships arrested crewmembers or passengers on other ships for treason or forced them to fill out their own crews. Such oppression was becoming commonplace on land; arriving in Wilmington, North Carolina, in the summer of 1775, Janet Schaw was surprised to find the most prominent men of the city crowded into a public square. They were held until the middle of the night because they refused to sign an oath against the king and were released only upon pledging to return the next morning.[6]

As the war progressed all aspects of personal safety became problematic, because both rival governments claimed political autonomy and authority. Under the old colonial system, a dissident could at least readily discover the proper authorities to whom to voice a complaint, and had some idea what to expect in response. It was inconvenient that the prewar government had been controlled, and the highest colonial authorities chosen, in far-off London, but the king's presence as the stable apex of British society seemed to guarantee the rights of all citizens. Revolutionary governments were more likely to be controlled on the local level, which provided an opportunity for settling old scores or passing legislation favorable to the cause or its supporters without regard for precedent under British common law. The Articles of Confederation were not ratified until March 1, 1781; until then, each of the states governed independently. Travelers and other strangers became increasingly suspect, and gangs of men sometimes terrorized even their neighbors under the color of loyalty to one government or the other.

As confusing as the political situation was, the economic situation was even worse. Finished goods were scarce, and hard currency with which to pay for them was even scarcer. Figuring out how much the various types of money in circulation were really worth had been a problem even before the Revolution. Local innkeepers could turn the confusion to their advantage by discounting whatever currency a customer used. Hence, in 1762, Benjamin Mifflin was upset when a tavern owner valued each of his coppers at only a penny.[7] Colonists had already tried several schemes to cope with their currency problems, including the issuance of paper money and the circulation of foreign as well as British coins. State governments were free to print their own money after political independence was declared, which added thirteen new currencies to the mix; the Continental Congress also began circulating its own promissory notes. As early as June 1777, state currencies were not accepted in other states.[8] All of these factors encouraged counterfeiting; in fact, large sums of fake currency were dumped on the colonies by agents of the British government as a destabilizing war measure. So much questionable money and the oscillating fortunes of the war encouraged speculation; ruinous inflation was to plague the new nation even after the war had been won. Boycotts and embargoes also interfered with normal commerce, and the heightened presence of British warships in American ports made smuggling much more hazardous.

As the war progressed, the new country's monetary problems worsened. The value of the Continental dollar fluctuated in accordance with the Continental Army's success in the field. It seemed to reach its nadir after the fall of Charleston in 1781, when sixty Continental dollars were worth only one of specie.[9] Even worse times were ahead. After the Pennsylvania mutiny, American paper fell to nearly one hundred to one and threatened to lose its entire value.[10] After it fell to a thousand to one, Congress was forced to completely annul its paper currency.[11] In May 1781, reports reached British officers in New York of riots in Philadelphia over the Continental currency; a mob had allegedly tarred a dog and covered it in Continental dollars before turning it loose in the Congress's chambers.[12] The phrase "not worth a continental" had real meaning at this time in the nation's financial history. The situation was so desperate that the Marquis de Lafayette, a French nobleman who served on Washington's staff as a general, thought everything had to be risked for a decisive military victory before the money ran out.[13] After the war, Washington had to use his influence to keep the Continental Army docile despite the fact that some units were owed nearly seven years' arrears of pay.[14]

Not until long after the conclusion of the Revolutionary War would the full political and economic benefits of independence be fully realized, but a few advantages had quickly became apparent. A generation of American men who had found their political voices in lobbying for independence and arguing about the proper course of action dutifully took the helm of the new state in the most perilous moments of its existence. In sharp contrast to the mutual ignorance between American colonies that had existed in 1763, the delegates to the Continental Congresses formed personal bonds and began to see the advantages of unity throughout the nation. Suddenly freed from London's sanctions against their production of finished goods, the former colonies were ready to embrace the industrial revolution fully, and no federal taxes dimmed their entrepreneurial spirits. Before the war, few common people traveled, but the war exposed thousands of soldiers to new lands and even new regions beyond their immediate neighborhoods. The frontier, with all its promises of continued growth and unlimited opportunity, was opened politically, as the new government did not recognize the Proclamation of 1763. The war also revealed the inability of the Indian tribes to defend the rich farmlands they inhabited east of the Mississippi, a weakness that the American people were quick to exploit aggressively.

THE TRUE NATURE OF AMERICAN LIBERTY

The notion of independence presented an interesting problem for most colonial Americans. The majority were certainly free of the servitude sometimes required of their European counterparts by Old World aristocrats or church officials upon whose property they chanced to have been born. Aside from the residents of a few religious communities, by 1763 most Americans were under no legal sanctions to support their churches financially, as many people had been in continental Europe. It was possible to labor on the frontier with no hindrance from any political authority whatsoever. For many Americans, however, true freedom was as distant on our shores as it had been across the seas.

To obtain passage from England, many of the poorer immigrants were forced by economic necessity to become indentured servants. The full weight of British authority kept them bound to their masters for terms that could span a decade. Sometimes they agreed to such terms in exchange for their passage across the sea; their ship's captains would sell their indentures once they reached America. Numerous advertisements in colonial newspapers suggest the frequency with which the servants tried to quit their masters before their times were served; on at least one occasion a group tried to rebel before their time had even begun. The *Providence Gazette* of November 3, 1764, mentioned the arrival of the brig *Colin* in Annapolis, Maryland, despite the attempt by forty indentured servants to make themselves masters of the vessel. Thousands more had been ordered into such service by criminal courts in England. During their contractual servitude they were forbidden to work for themselves unless they could obtain their masters' consent. In most labor disputes, British law tended to favor economic capital and political interests almost as much as ancestral rights. Even full-grown men and women sometimes had to bear the injustice of arbitrary corporal punishment with very little legal protection. In 1776, almost half of Philadelphia's population were (or had been) indentured servants.

Approximately a seventh of all the nonnative inhabitants of the British colonies were held in perpetual bondage. The international slave trade was in its heyday, financing much of the colonies' expansion by exploiting slaves captured in Africa, sometimes delivering them into the hands of men whose only interest was the accumulation of wealth by whatever means they could avail themselves. Some check on a slave owner's wrath derived from the need to protect one's property from the economic loss attendant upon neglect or extreme punishment. Other owners might have become more circumspect in their brutality as a consequence of the opposition to slavery that was becoming more vocal among the Quakers of Pennsylvania and other groups. Independence for individual slaves could usually only come from their masters, although an extraordinarily lucky few survived perilous flights from Georgia or South Carolina to Spanish Florida, or sometimes to the Indians beyond the frontier. For all but a miniscule portion of the slaves, however, this outlaw alternative was an impossible dream or simply unheard of. One of the terrible ironies of history is that while slavery was dying out in the British Empire, the success of the American Revolution kept the institution alive in the southern states long enough for the invention of the cotton gin to make it again enormously profitable in the early nineteenth century.

Yet a third class of Americans also worked under terms that might strike the modern observer as forced labor. Many young males became apprentices, essentially exchanging seven years of increasingly skilled labor in exchange for room, board, and training in their craft. The father of an apprentice typically paid a premium to a master craftsman at the start of the apprenticeship, thereby freeing himself from the burden of supporting the youth until the age of twenty-one. The extent to which parents would enter such agreements to rid themselves of problem children cannot be calculated. Here too the law favored the master's rights over those of people bound by contract to serve him. Much earlier in the century, the young Benjamin Franklin was physically punished by the older brother to whom he was apprenticed despite their close kinship; the extent to which a master might abuse an unrelated apprentice can be surmised.

Before the Revolutionary War, service in the militia was not as onerous as life in the standing armies of Europe. As militia service was entirely voluntary, individuals could leave a battle, intending to rejoin at a predetermined site or return home, at their own discretion, just as most Indian warriors were free to do. As the war progressed, Washington and his officers increasingly relied on corporal punishment to preserve order in the ranks; they even resorted to executions to prevent desertions. However, the average soldier in what became a well-disciplined Continental Army still remained more independent than the British regulars he faced.

Soldiers in the British Army were routinely subject to corporal punishments ranging from flogging for minor offenses to execution for desertion. The strain of marching through a hostile countryside in a bright red uniform, the knowledge that one was expected to stand still in ranks until ordered to discharge one's weapon or charge with the bayonet regardless of the enemy's fire, and the ease with which one might pass as a civilian, all combined to make the common soldier's duty in America less attractive than has generally been supposed. Entries from the diary of a British officer in Rhode Island provide important clues as to how difficult their service was. On July 5, 1777, he recorded that a soldier had deliberately drowned himself after leaving a suicide note in clothing left on the shore. The same day another soldier shot himself, the second to have availed himself of that means of killing himself, and a fourth soldier had earlier slashed his own wrists.[15] All four of these attempts had been made in the month and three days since the unit had set up camp in Rhode Island. Other soldiers had already deserted, a problem that grew until sentries were ordered to fire upon anyone seen making the attempt; several men were wounded and a couple were even killed under the new policy. Any illusions individual British soldiers may have sheltered as to their personal safety in camp in Rhode Island were completely dashed when their commanding officer, Gen. Richard Prescott, was abducted during the night of July 1, 1777.[16] More than twenty-five soldiers deserted in their first three months in Rhode Island.[17] The services of mercenaries were purchased from several German princes, who typically received large sums, while the individual soldiers were promised only regular British Army pay. Such men could hardly be expected to become devoted to their British masters or universally happy in their service, and their morale received major blows with the surrender of German regiments at Trenton in 1776 and the destruction of Lieutenant Colonel Baum's seven hundred Germans at Bennington, Vermont, in September 1777.

At sea, long tradition and British admiralty law granted nearly absolute power to the captains of naval, merchant, fishing, and whaling vessels. This gave these fortunate individuals far more independence and incalculably greater freedom of movement than most colonists enjoyed. The authority of commercial captains was so well established that even General Lafayette was forced to negotiate with the captain of a ship Lafayette personally owned; the captain was unwilling to take him directly to America in 1777 until the general purchased the goods that had been smuggled on board to be sold elsewhere.[18]

Ships of the Royal Navy still occasionally used press gangs to add forcibly to their crews whatever men fell into their clutches. On May 4, 1781, three hundred men who had been collected from the streets of New York the night before were assigned to various ships in the British fleet.[19] However on board, the crew of a British warship lacked any civil power to resist the captain's orders. Ashore, however, the pent-up frustrations of naval personnel as well as private sailors could tempt them to a licentious spree that the coarser sort could confuse with liberty.

Conditions were also harsh on the farm. Even the best and brightest colonial farm children were forced to labor, according to their strength, from a young age. Since agriculture on the frontier was practiced under relatively primitive conditions, human and animal labor provided the only means of getting everything done. Whatever individual interests and talents a farmer's son might have, chores had to come first. For six generations descendents of the *Mayflower* pilgrims had found themselves bound to the same land in that way.

Ideally, girls were taught the homemaking arts at their mothers' knees, eventually acquiring expertise in virtually all aspects of domestic life until they attained the age of sixteen. This was considered an age ripe for marriage; it was time for many of them to begin their own domestic management with their new husbands. Domestic tyranny was as prevalent in the eighteenth century as it was to be in later periods of American history, and the law greatly favored the husband's rights in most areas. Some few men and women did assert their independence, but the freedom of separation and divorce was paid for with a stigma even in those colonies where it was permitted.

The impossibility of closing all American ports to foreign shipping, as the British government mandated during the war, encouraged continued smuggling. It was clear to such writers as Alexander Hamilton that the colonies could easily be entirely self-sufficient in clothing as well as food through the cultivation of such crops as cotton, wool, flax, and hemp.[20] When resistance to British rule increasingly took the form of boycotting British goods and shipping, a wider and even more lucrative opportunity opened for smuggling up and down the coast. This provided an additional economic incentive for the American merchant class to resist the mother country, for unfettered access to world trade offered tremendous commercial advantages.

Any account of daily life in eighteenth-century colonial America must similarly consider the willingness of independent men to drop their daily concerns and present themselves for militia drills on the village greens and, on very rare occasions, for a march into the countryside in disordered columns to meet their foes. A century earlier in American history, the ever-present danger of Indian raids, sometimes instigated by their French trading partners, had forced many colonists to band together; they sometimes formed local militia companies for mutual protection. These provided immediate and effective military solutions to the threats posed by the Indians on the frontiers, essentially quelling armed resistance to their continued expansion by bringing more and better-armed men to the field than their opponents. They, or their descendents, continued to battle during the lengthy colonial wars as the British, French, and, far less frequently, the Spanish fought to see who would ultimately control America. The colonists had shared the risks of frontier fighting in the French and Indian War, and they deserved no small credit for the ultimate victory of English arms in the conflict. In the early years of the Revolution, militia units tackled the elite British companies sent to subdue them at Lexington and Concord, fought bravely at Bunker Hill, and chased the British from Boston after a lengthy siege. Though initially clinging to their identity with the areas that spawned them, several militias were combined to form the core of the Continental Army. At first, these units tended to melt away when facing concentrated British forces, but at Bennington and, astonishingly, at Saratoga, they defeated professional European armies. Later in the war, militia groups were instrumental in several pivotal battles, including Kings Mountain and Cowpens. Without the individual militiaman's personal commitment to their companies, it is unlikely that so many citizen soldiers would have risked so much for a cause predicated upon a liberty that their isolation and self-sufficiency had, in many cases, largely already given them.

TORIES AS LOYALISTS

Even by the end of the Revolution an estimated one-third of the entire population of the American colonies remained loyal to the British crown. These were more than British sympathizers. Although the name "Tory" seems completely alien to the modern American audience, its application to those who preferred to remain British subjects underscores their thoroughly British identity, because it associated them with a major party in Britain's Parliament. For most British citizens at the beginning of the 1770s, whether they lived in England or the British colonies, the appellation of "patriot," which the Americans who favored independence began applying to themselves, was equally problematic. The Patriots of the American Revolution were those whose increasing resistance to their king and country could rightly be called anything but patriotic. To the dismay of their Tory neighbors, the adoption of this name was the most effective stroke of the propaganda war in support of independence. Treason, the Tories might argue, had never flourished under a more inappropriate name. The Tories were Englishmen who valued that identity. Some of them directly benefited financially from their connections with England, and most were unwilling to sever their ties with the country of their birth or with the families they had left behind. For such people, the appellation "Loyalist" comes closer to their true feelings than "Tory," which has become pejorative. The Patriots were rebels in fact as well as in the mouths of their opponents, but their victory in the Revolution gave them and their descendents the prerogative of determining how each side would be designated.

Thousands of Loyalists did serve in the British Army or Tory militias, but many factors combined to keep them from organizing a more effective resistance to the Revolution. Loyalty to the crown meant that one supported the British colonial government and naturally looked to the royal governors and other officials for leadership. They tended to rely on the British Army and the Royal Navy for their defense, and their faith in the established authorities kept them from terrorizing and effectively silencing their opposition, as the unfettered rebels and their propagandists were sometimes able to do. After the war, many Tories were forced to migrate to Canada or England, and others willingly did so. Some may have feared the likely chaos as a newly freed people learned to govern themselves, while others may have sought to avoid the economic woes the new nation faced as it struggled to develop a new national currency and pay off its war debts. Tens of thousands of the most active Tories were expelled from the former colonies and had their estates confiscated for their roles in the war.

AMERICAN DIVERSITY

Although British control of the region kept America from being as heterogeneous as it would later become, the American colonies were already remarkable for the diversity of their inhabitants. In 1790, the first national census offered Americans the opportunity to identify their nationalities. Of the nearly four million people living in the eleven states that participated in the census, just over half classified themselves as English or Welsh. There were nearly seven hundred thousand slaves. Over a million people still identified themselves as Scotch, Irish, Dutch, French, German, or Hebrew—a large enough proportion of the population as a whole to suggest that their resistance to British sovereignty may have had other than purely economic origins. There were also indeterminate numbers of Indians, scattered in tribes with cultures even more diverse than were those of the separate British colonies. At least thirty distinct tribes lived in Virginia alone, but the colonists' overwhelming numbers, their better armaments, training and discipline, and their unrelenting ferocity now made their homes safer from Indian attacks than they had been throughout the prior century.

By the start of the Revolution, most of the eastern tribes had been so decimated that their participation was not decisive in any major engagement. Active Indian involvement with the British tended to inflame the local militias, typically swelling their ranks with ferocious colonists often bent on removing this threat forever. Galvanized into action, the colonists would mount punitive expeditions that were generally disastrous for their traditional foes, and that again demonstrated the Indians' inability to defend their lands once British support was removed.

The population of all the Indian tribes east of the Mississippi had long been declining as a consequence of their continual contact with superior European armaments, military organization, and microbes. They continued to be decimated by smallpox, yellow fever, and other diseases, which also reached epidemic proportions in some colonial American cities. Hundreds of settlers migrated westward as soon as it was discovered how weak the Indian tribes had become, a trend that would continue throughout the next century.

America was large enough to permit enclaves of ethnic or religious communities to flourish, and many new immigrants found solace in the company of their transplanted countrymen or fellow believers. Frontier living forced self-sufficiency on most of the new settlers, and their varied cultural backgrounds sometimes added unique ethnic stamps to the things they produced in answer to this challenge. Much of what we perceive today as the popular culture of the American Revolutionary era derives from the artifacts that served the private, especially domestic, aspects of life, but popular culture also had more public functions. It was the chief means by which the colonists expressed themselves, and it has provided an enduring answer to the question of what it means to be uniquely American.

2

World of Youth

In late eighteenth-century America, half the children did not reach their fifth birthday. Parents believed that sex was only for procreation, felt that they had an entire continent to populate, knew that they probably would not live past the age of forty, and had a great deal of work to do. As a result, large families continued to be the norm in pre-Revolutionary America as they had been from the earliest permanent colonies. This meant plenty of brothers and sisters with whom to play, but the addition of young children also increased the workload of the older ones, children who were asked to take care of them. Nearly a hundred years would pass before the British Victorians educated the world about the value of childhood as a special time of life, to be celebrated and cultivated. Revolutionary-era children were often treated as small adults; they were expected to behave rationally or face severe discipline.

The tyranny from which the colonists risked everything to escape was, in many cases, first observed in their domestic, scholastic, and apprentice environments. Most parents still felt it their duty to teach obedience to their children, a sense of obligation reinforced by both religious and secular authorities. Two centuries would pass before corporal punishment was outlawed in American schools and discouraged in the home; in this period most children received physical punishment for their transgressions. Spankings, canings, ear-twistings, and slaps in the face or across the back of the head could be administered by their parents, and children lucky enough to receive formal educations were often exposed to the same treatment at the hands of their schoolmasters. Many lessons were to be memorized, and failure to perform when called upon to recite could have immediate physical consequences. One colonial soldier considered the brutality he had experienced in school (which he even characterized as flogging), as having perhaps been necessary because only two school-masters had between two and three hundred pupils to tend.[1] Even in college a severe discipline was imposed; undergraduates were "subjected to despotic sway, [and] compelled all mandates to obey."[2]

Master craftsmen were sometimes less tolerant of horseplay in an apprentice of even tender years. Sometimes their wrath could be provoked by an apprentice's lack of skill as readily as by willful disobedience or deliberate inattention to duty. Youths who were sold into indentured servitude could feel their masters' anger on their backs as well as hear it in their ears. Corporal punishment was also considered useful in teaching slave children their proper place in life; while infants might escape notice, children as young as five could be gainfully employed in the planting and harvesting seasons. As field hands they came under the watchful eyes of overseers on the larger plantations. The term "slave driver" was not an empty phrase for these sometimes pitiless men; it signified their principal means of earning a living. Part of their job was to keep the slaves focused on their tasks, and brute force was the most immediate means of imposing their will upon their charges.

Even in times of peace, colonial children could be terrified by their parents' tales of Indian massacres on the frontier. From the windows of their rural cabins many children could see the woods in which, conceivably, a hundred Indians could be waiting to avenge the atrocities committed against their tribes and to reclaim their lands. Once the Revolutionary War began, tensions in frontier households went even higher as the war progressed to the hinterland, and England succeeded in enlisting the Iroquois and other tribes on their side in the conflict. In his *Letters from an American Farmer*, the writer Michel Guillaume Jean de Crèvecoeur imagined that the terror civilians in war zones felt as they sat by their firesides with their vulnerable families was a thousand times worse than that felt by soldiers engaged in the most severe combat, for the soldiers had at least the means of defending themselves.[3] After the fighting began, the entire household of his American farmer felt every night might be their last and were as wretched as criminals awaiting only their deaths.

Like recurrent peals of thunder, news of the war rolled through the colonies in advance of the armies. Not only were the western Indian tribes incited to violence, but large units of the British Army penetrated deep into the countryside from Canada. A second army marched out of New York, outflanked George Washington's soldiers, and captured Philadelphia. Finally a large British force with highly mobile cavalry chased an outmanned American army through the southern colonies. The hardships and tragedies the war brought were most real to those in the immediate area of the fighting, but news of the clashes must have given frightful dreams even to the children on the remote frontiers, as Crèvecoeur imagined.[4] When the Iroquois allied themselves with the British, the safety of a farmer's entire family seemed to rest on his decision as to which side to take in the dispute; those closest to the fighting could find their houses filled with refugees "just escaped from the flames and the scalping knife, telling of barbarities and murders that make human nature tremble."[5] Even the populous coastal cities, occupying lands from which the local Indians had been driven two generations earlier, were not havens from the nightmare of war. The British garrisons occupying New York City swelled after they drove out the colonial army, and the city remained their center of operations throughout the war. From there, entire regiments could be ferried to any other colony. Philadelphia was next in a succession of cities occupied and subsequently abandoned by the British. In addition, local militias occasionally opposed each other in the field even when the principal national armies were not on the scene.

Youthful exuberance had ways of exerting itself, however, no matter how narrowly circumscribed the circumstances. Like their peers in later generations, youth indulged in sleigh rides and snowball fights, kite-flying in fair weather, and raids on their neighbor's fruit trees or gardens. Impromptu wrestling matches and fistfights provided diversion for the strongest. Others could be driven to ecstasy or to tears by seemingly casual statements from their peers. Privately dressing in their parents' clothes and imagining themselves in their social roles was an experience rather foreign to their generation, however, because the clothes of the young were usually smaller replicas of adult clothing. Since children were usually expected to act like small adults, adopting their parents' clothing did not seem the leap into their own futures that was to make the experiment so humorous for their descendants.

Most people's lives were lived far closer to nature than would be the case as the nation became urbanized. Dogs were helpful guards, and certain breeds could be useful companions on hunts. Rural mornings would be announced by a rooster's crowing and by the protests of other animals, whose sunken stomachs or swollen udders told them it was time to be fed or milked. Swallows, phoebes, wrens, and sparrows would nest under the eaves of houses and barns. Northern farmers would keep a passenger pigeon, blinded like Samson to prevent escape attempts, caged beside their doors. During the twice-yearly migrations of his wild cousins, his song could lure sometimes thousands of his still wild kin to their deaths in nets hung from the trees. At dawn, or just before it, he would serenade the household each spring with warblings pleasant beyond description.[6] Robins, then as now the heralds of spring, as well as shrill catbirds, sublime thrushes, and woods full of other songbirds added their distinctive notes to the avian chorus. Endless adventure could begin at the doorstep of the rural home, inviting children of both genders to explore the constantly changing panorama of nature in bloom. All manner of hornets and wasps offered their diversions, and honeybees were brought to boxed hives close to the home.

But just as belonging to large families and being surrounded by so many animals, both wild and domestic, gave children of this era a greater familiarity with life than would later be the case, the same exposure also gave them an intimate acquaintance with death. Most children in Revolutionary America grew up on farms, where they would be witness to the complete life cycles of innumerable animals. As hunters, boys could contribute the game animals they killed to the family's diet. As they matured, children of both genders would become increasingly active participants in the slaughter of animals and the processing of their flesh as food.

They also became aware of their own mortality at a tender age. Epidemics, accidents ranging from falls from horses to drownings, and infections that could lead to lockjaw or gangrene decimated the children of many villages and brought lasting grief to many families. Even if by some miracle all their siblings managed to survive their early childhoods, they would likely be exposed to the decrepitude of old age, as their grandparents were taken into the home in their declining years. Among the colonies, Philadelphia was unique in starting to provide care for those too old or infirm to work; elsewhere they lived amid the bustle of their large families. The bodies of those who died typically did not await interment in a far-off mortuary but were buried near the very households in which they had breathed their last.

THE TRAINING OF GIRLS

Girls were typically trained in the domestic arts by their mothers. At an early age they might mimic the housekeeping chores of their mothers and older sisters until they were permitted to participate actively. Many were given scraps of cheap cloth on which to practice embroidery and other sewing skills until they acquired the dexterity needed to assist in the household sewing. It could seem a blessed day to a girl finally allowed to use her skill to mend something, like her father's work shirt, that would actually be worn by a family member. Much time was consumed in knitting new socks and darning old ones, and many girls were trained in all kinds of needlework. Some of their productions were elaborately rendered masterpieces of patterned symmetry, especially in the southern colonies.[7] At first they would be given simple household chores and perhaps a single dish to wash; as they became proficient in such tasks, responsibility for performing them all the time could be shifted onto their shoulders.

The most familiar objects in the Revolutionary home were the spinning wheel, the boiling pot, andirons that supported the burning logs, and fire irons (large tongs, a small shovel or a wrought-iron poker with which to tend the fire). It is no accident that all of these items were the means of domestic food or cloth manufacture and clothes production. It could take a long time for a girl whose parents did not own servants or import everything the family wore to master all aspects of cloth and clothes production; the spinning wheel has rightfully been called the most important piece of furniture in a country house.[8] The peace and tranquility we associate today with the colonial woman gracefully passing a winter's evening engaged with her spinning wheel beside the hearth belies the laborious process by which wool was processed from its native state to something people could wear. The process included five steps: the wool had to be washed, carded (combed to remove such impurities as broken twigs and to untangle individual strands), spun into string or yarn, dyed, and knitted or woven. Even this list oversimplifies the process; the lye soap used in the first stage of manufacture was often made at home by mixing cooking grease with ashes, and the making or preparing of dyes could involve considerable knowledge and effort as well. A discussion of the knowledge and labor involved before the man of the house sheared the sheep from which the wool came would be out of place here, except to note that wives, like some even in the twenty-first century, were often called upon to help with farmyard chores.

Most women had to prepare meals from scratch, which meant taking rough agricultural commodities, like hardened kernels of dry corn, and grinding them into corn flour or laboriously processing them by hand so they could be used as ingredients. The mistress of most Revolutionary households would undertake everything from cutting up the slaughtered animals to placing the sausage or mince-pies on the table.[9] Animal fat could be turned to good use in tallow candles, and some women learned to make heat-resistant myrtle berry wax candles, which gave off pleasant fragrances when extinguished.[10]

Many women were asked to prepare food in heavy pots suspended over open wood fires in the hearth, a process rendered difficult by the extreme heat sometimes projected into the room and by the uneven cooking temperatures. It was also necessary to carry water for human consumption, prepare the meals, and scrub the pots, dishes, and silverware. Refrigeration was not generally available for food preparation or storage, although some root cellars and, less frequently, ice caves might slow spoilage rates. Salt was the usual preservative for meat. Considerable canning and other preserving of fruits and vegetables had to be done if the household was to have palatable food throughout the winter and early spring. For the most part, the domestic practitioners of the culinary arts were asked to memorize all nuances of food preparation without the aid of cookbooks, which few women on the frontiers would have had the leisure to read or money to afford even if they had been widely available.

Crèvecoeur, emphasizing the difference between the happiness of a farmer whose wife was a great cook and the misery of one whose wife was not, boasts that Americans blessed with good wives lived better than any other people of comparable rank.[11] The implication that cooking skills alone determined whether a wife was a "good" one reveals the limits of his eighteenth-century thinking. He betrays a similar bias when he notes that the functions of a "great" farmer are still dependent upon his "good" wife. Earlier he mentions being brought to involuntary tears whenever he contemplated his own good wife by the fireside, "whether she spins, knits, darns or suckles our child."[12] Sometimes he delighted in inventing machines to simplify his wife's labor, but the thought of turning a hand to assist in her work evidently never entered his head, nor that she might have appreciate time for contemplative pursuits.[13]

Cooking, sewing, housekeeping, and other chores were performed in an unending cycle in the average girl's life. Extended formal schooling outside of the home was rare for girls of the era, but girls raised in genteel environments might be expected to learn to dance, sing, play musical instruments, and manage a household staff of servants.[14] Relatively shortly after attaining sexual maturity, a young girl could expect to be taken into marriage, whereupon she would put her acquired skills to good use. In time children would come, and the girls could be trained to help her, while the boys would take their turns behind the plow. Like the wife in an early drama, mothers were expected to teach their children to read. However, a woman's yearnings for high intellectual attainment, or simply more stimulating discussion at the dinner table, were likely to be dismissed as "prate," with which they were never to trouble their heads.[15]

Even in the poorest households, however, some women took pride in their sacrifices and lived surrounded by the love and admiration of their growing families. If cooking and cleaning arts can be seen as unenviable drudgery for the girls trapped by their gender into performing them all their lives, domestic chores also brought them closest to those who loved them most. The mother could provide small food rewards, or devise or remember from her own childhood games and pastimes to ensure the happiest possible childhoods for her offspring. Girls were fortunate in that their daily chores could bring them into constant contact with such angels, contact that prepared them to assume that role in households of their own as the need arose.

HOBBIES, PASTIMES, AND GAMES FOR GIRLS

Many girls' games of the eighteenth century had the hidden purpose of teaching skills needed in adult life. Most girls were given dolls at an early age with an eye toward developing the nurturing instincts the child would need as a wife and mother. Depending on her placement in the birth order, a girl might be entrusted with the care of younger siblings, and they could sometimes enter games of tag, hide and seek, and other traditional games with the boys. They could also test their mettle with a stick and hoop and with other toys and games, though exhibiting too-great exuberance in such pursuits could bring reprimands for unladylike behavior.

Things were much freer for girls in America than in Europe, however. In his journal, the German major general von Riedesel thought that the women of Boston were all well educated because they could write. They rode well on horseback and loved music, stylish imported dresses, and dancing, but they rarely worked. The Connecticut women dressed more modestly, in von Riedesel's opinion, and were better housekeepers.[16]

Because girls rarely left the communities in which they were raised, they had to be careful lest they unwittingly procure bad reputations. Benjamin Mifflin recalled that his uncle's second spouse had "had a slip in her youth" but was now a good and industrious wife.[17]

THE TRAINING OF BOYS

Urban boys were likely to receive more formal education than their rural counterparts, but many could expect to be apprenticed to a craftsman in one of the many practical trades often in great demand in the colonies. In 1716, Benjamin Franklin was put to work at the age of ten making candles for his father's chandlery. Within a year he was apprenticed to an older brother, a printer, for ten years. Having but two years of formal schooling at the time, Franklin nevertheless had the energy and intellectual curiosity to engage in a lifelong course of self-education. John Woolman was likewise hired by a shopkeeper but managed to improve his schooling on winter evenings and at other leisure times. Most men, however, lacked such energy and dedication and were unable to surmount the early handicap of inadequate education. Many boys also lacked fathers as sympathetic as Josiah Franklin, who exposed young Ben to a wide variety of trades and encouraged him to voice his preference. The makeup of a single artillery company of the Boston militia prior to the war hints at the wide diversity of occupations available in that colony. The captain was a carriage maker, and the men included two carpenters, a cobbler, a hatter, a tailor, two sail makers, a rope manufacturer, three coopers, a painter, a mason, a chair maker, and a butcher.[18]

Outside of the larger cities, however, the vocational choice was more likely dictated by which local craftsman had immediate openings for an apprentice. If two positions were available, the decision might be based on which craftsman offered the best deal to the boy's father.

One thing that most boys were not taught in Revolutionary times was dental hygiene. The toothbrush was a relatively recent innovation, and some people thought it effeminate for men to use them.[19] Because of their owner's prominence, much has been made of George Washington's false teeth, but in fact they were remarkable only because most men in the Revolutionary era died of natural causes before they needed dentures. Since life was more rugged, their childhoods more rough and tumble, and restorative techniques involving silver filings and porcelain crowns had not yet been developed, possession of a full set of teeth was far more rare among both genders as they approached their fortieth birthdays than it would later become. A mitigating factor was that food contained fewer refined sugars and processed flours; still, preventative dentistry was still largely unimagined.

The most famous accoutrements that survive from the men of the Revolutionary era comprise a confusing mixture of powdered wigs, coonskin caps, long rifles and their powder horns, homespun shirts, deerskin breeches, tricornered hats, and old plows with iron blades in wooden frames. This mishmash is entirely appropriate for such a transitional period. Approximately 95 percent of the people still lived on farms in 1770, and most boys learned about agriculture at their father's side. The most exciting development in agriculture was the cultivation of new crops and flowers on an experimental basis. No less a personage than Thomas Jefferson was a leader in trying new and rare species in his garden, and similar experiments elsewhere provided much more variety in the American diet than could be found in British homes of similar social and economic classes. Such practices as grafting limbs from one type of fruit tree onto a different type were yet another way for the colonists to broaden the produce available for their tables; a single tree could theoretically be brought to produce apples, pears, and other fruits by this method. It could take a long time for farm boys to learn animal husbandry and the proper cultivation of crops from their fathers. A few boys might succeed in landing a job like driving teams of horses; Crèvecoeur advised a new immigrant that his fourteen-year-old son could gain a dollar a month plus food and board for such service in Philadelphia in 1770.[20]

Perhaps the luckiest boys in America lived on Nantucket, in Massachusetts. Not only were their families on average rather rich by colonial American standards, but they had careers in the fishing and whaling industries as options along with anything one could do for a living on the mainland. Each day they could view the sea in its varied moods, each day the rocky shore was changed by the winds and waves, and nearly every day ships arrived from scouring the Atlantic Ocean for fish and whales. Very rarely in this period would a vessel have as many mysterious foreign crewmen or carry such exotic spices and clothing as whaling ships would in the middle of the next century, when the whaling industry established itself on a worldwide footing. Already, however, Indians, Quakers, and other inhabitants of the island were coming along into effective crews regardless of their diverse backgrounds. Crèvecoeur noted that the Quaker sailors had often learned to read and write in school before they were twelve. Some had been apprenticed to coopers (makers of barrels, for which the whaling industry had an insatiable demand) for two years, and then had taken to the sea, where they learned every aspect of the industry, including navigation and other arts of seamanship.[21] One vessel arrived with six hundred barrels of oil after thirteen months at sea; others took their spermaceti, whale oil, and whale bone directly to England, where it could be sold for ready cash instead of being bartered for other items of commercial value in the American colonies. Already there was talk of extending the chase to the South Seas and beyond.

HOBBIES, PASTIMES, AND GAMES FOR BOYS

All forms of gambling were popular throughout the colonies. The pervasiveness and general social acceptance of lotteries led one Quaker to offer an amendment when his sect finally got around to censuring the pastime; he wanted to exempt such lotteries as were held legally.[22] Cards and dice were also popular sources of amusement, providing an additional opportunity for social interaction, after a fashion.

Children of both genders were likely to overhear and, far less infrequently, be allowed to participate in the political discussions of their elders, which became increasingly common and belligerent as the Revolution approached. It is easy to imagine their playful reenactments of their fathers' tales of service in the French and Indian Wars, with sticks standing in for flintlocks and swords, and snowballs for bullets and shells, and with yells as fearsome as a frontier savage of any race could muster. As Revolutionary fervor in Boston reached fever pitch, young boys, evidently influenced by their fathers' debates, took to taunting the British regulars who were garrisoned in that city, even going so far as to pelt them with snowballs. On March 5, 1770, one such youth went too far and got too close in his mimicry. A British sentry struck the boy with his rifle butt, an act that seems far uglier today than it would have in that era of engrained obedience to authority and widespread use of physical correction. Nevertheless, it precipitated the Boston Massacre, as an aroused mob joined in the taunting until the entire British guard was turned out to protect the soldier. The game turned deadly as the crowd became more vocal and its demonstrations more physical; in the confusion some of the soldiers fired into the hostile mob in response to what they thought was an order to do so. Four more years would lapse before the battles of Lexington and Concord signaled the beginning of continuous warfare in the Revolutionary War and many youths soon found themselves bearing arms in deadly earnest. By 1781, every able-bodied freeman in Virginia between the ages of sixteen and fifty was enrolled in the state militia.[23] This made at least some military training part of every young man's experience.

FORMAL EDUCATION

Although schoolwork tended to center on rote memorization, it could be effective in providing children with the social and business skills (arithmetic, spelling, and penmanship) they would need as adults. As governor of Virginia, Thomas Jefferson would dream of universal education for everyone, including girls and slaves, but the colonies had not yet achieved that stage. Most people were lucky if they received the national average of three years of formal education.

Advanced formal education was an option for a privileged few white males from affluent families, some few of whom crossed the sea to study at the famed boarding schools and colleges of England. Even those who studied at one of the nine American colleges, however, were exposed to Latin and Greek, which paid enormous dividends to the cause of American liberty by elevating the intellectual tone of the debates over independence and the form of the new national government. This study of dead languages provided these relatively few individuals with classical arguments concerning the nature and limitations of democracy and the state, arguments that they would distill in such political laboratories as their local legislatures and the Continental Congress.

For a less sanguine appraisal of the benefits of exposure to the classics, however, one has only to read Philip Freneau's "Expedition of Timothy Taurus." A Princeton graduate of the class of 1771, Freneau had already established himself as a poet of serious ambition when he wrote a poem commemorating a situation he well understood, a college undergraduate's short vacation from his classes. He was not just pandering to the anti-intellectualism of the broadest popular audience of his day when he dismissed the study of Latin, Chaldaic, Greek, and Hebrew in what might have been a memorable couplet had its scansion been more regular:

> Too much of our time is employed on such trash
> When we ought to be taught to accumulate cash.

Many undergraduates of his time experienced the same linguistic frustrations; it did seem to the less successful among them that they could grow rich faster by the using the axe or spade, or mending a shoe.

A college degree did open up additional opportunities even during the Revolution, however. In another poem, "The Silent Academy," Freneau listed both the college curriculum of the era and the careers that graduates could pursue. The courses of study, translated here into their twenty-first-century titles, included Latin, Greek, rhetoric, composition, literature, classics, geometry, poetry, logic, accounting, art, and law. Despite these emphases, all the students went into unrelated fields, beginning with the most humorous:

> Some are in chains of wedlock bound,
> And some are hanged and some are drowned.

Others took governmental, academic, or religious posts, practiced law or medicine, joined the Continental Army, farmed, fished, or joined the merchant marine, and some became slaves (probably not literally, since college admissions and the expenses incurred usually precluded those who were not white, wealthy, or well connected with the ruling elite from attending college, much less graduating). A college degree was no guarantee of future success, as Freneau notes:

> Some court the great, and some the muse,
> And some subsist by mending shoes.

Since Freneau also made a slighting reference to cobblers in "Expedition of Timothy Taurus," suggesting ironically that knowledge of shoe repair was a better asset on the market than knowledge of the classical languages, it would appear that that trade was not held in very high esteem at this point in our country's history. A cursory glance at any soldier's journal or memoir of the war reveals how necessary cobblers really were, however, and the painfully obvious consequences when they were not available.

COURTSHIP AND MARRIAGE

Courtship on the frontier sometimes included "bundling," a chance for a young couple to get to know each other in an environment that otherwise lacked the opportunities for dating that would become popular in later centuries. A young man and woman of marriageable age would be permitted to lie in bed together, separated by a board. At irregular intervals, one or more parents would check to ensure that the board was still in place and that the interview was proceeding with the decorum and dignity proper for such a serious undertaking in a Christian home of the era. The practice was so widespread that Royall Tyler could refer to it on the New York City stage in 1787. In *The Contrast*, a country bumpkin yearning for homespun delights ends his list with "bundling with Maryanne."

Even in towns, however, a young man who called on the family of a girl whom he admired might be brought around to a proposal of marriage fairly quickly. In the South, William Bartram was privileged to witness the wedding celebrations of two young Indians because the bride was the sister-in-law of the trader upon whom he called. After an evening of dancing, music, and feasting, the couple retired to a pavilion formed of green boughs, their secret nuptial chamber; no one else approached it that night or the next day.[24] Among the Muscogulges, he learned of a marriage ceremony in which a suitor, after gaining the consent of the bride's relations, drove a reed into the ground near her house. If she accepted his proposal, the bride stuck her own reed next to his; finally, they exchanged these reeds and retained them like certificates of their marriage.[25] Marriage vows among this tribe were renewed each year, but couples rarely separated once they had been blessed with children.

The children of affluent urban couples and wealthy planters were often given formal dance lessons until they were considered accomplished and old enough to join the adults in ballrooms. They had far greater exposure to potential mates than did less fortunate youth. Even young George Washington's ability to impress on the dance floor turned nearly as many heads in his direction as his striking demeanor and national prominence would much later in his career.

The war could have an impact on even the most important of private and personal moments of courtship and marriage. In a 1775 poem, Philip Freneau told of a young swain's kisses as he bid his girl goodbye, promising to return in a month ("Mars and Hymen"). Alas, in this poem the suitor was killed on the Canadian expedition. Such poignant scenes were played out on both sides of the Atlantic for the entire six years of the war. Sometimes, however, love could triumph even as the armies prepared for battle. On one occasion in 1777 the Continental Army was throwing up barricades and other obstructions to deny the Delaware River to the British. A young man, too vocal in his objections at being separated from his fiancée by the barriers, which were between them, was arrested by American officers and taken to Washington himself. Unimpressed, the youth argued that Washington was too old to remember what it was like to join a future bride. Washington reportedly burst out laughing and set the man free.[26]

CHILDREN IN BONDAGE

For the southern plantation slave, youth frequently meant toil alongside a parent in the fields. A select few might be pressed into domestic service, but the wide range of temperaments and personalities found among the slaveholders, as among humans everywhere, could make the house servant's personal service, exacted under the very eyes of their chief oppressors, even more horrendous. Especially pernicious was the fact that American colonial slavery discriminated on the basis of race; except for a very few exceedingly fortunate individuals who could somehow find a way to purchase their own freedom, African slaves and their progeny were condemned to perpetual bondage. Deprived of other outlets for their creativity, individuality, and love, and unable to provide them physical comforts, many slave parents lavished affection on their children. The slave market could bring a quick end to such devotion, however. Even mothers could be separated from their children on the auction block.

Even in the North the inequalities and injustices inherent in the slave system must have grated unceasingly on the minds and spirits of the oppressed. Even in its most benign forms, like that described by the French immigrant Crèvecoeur in his attempt to present everything in America in its best possible light, the twenty-first-century mind recoils at the tale of the honest slave Tom, who—as his weary master comes home to a cheerful wife greeting him with a restorative mug of cider—must again brave the winter storm to rescue the children from their school.[27] Similarly, it is the careful Negro Jack who muscles a huge piece of firewood into the house for the back of the stove, expertly directing the heat into the family room instead of up the chimney. Although Crèvecoeur seems to include the slaves within the "industrious family, all gathered together under one roof and eating the same wholesome supper," his prior remark that they sit contentedly making their brooms and ladles with nothing on their minds diminishes their humanity. His contrast of the family's down and feather beds with the "bed of slavery and sorrow" one found in Europe among people of the family's class seems an extraordinary instance of farsightedness. The author's foreign nature is never more evident than when he asserts that the Almighty has no crime for which to punish the innocent family even with ominous dreams;[28] he overlooks such things as slavery and original sin. He states that there are no real poor in this happy country; however, it seems probable that the universally happy country he contemplates has not yet been found on earth.

Even in the rosiest picture of slavery that survives, there is an unconscious indictment of the institution. Crèvecoeur's statement that "just as our blacks divide with us the toils of our farms, they partake also of the mirth and good cheer of the season."[29] "Our blacks" might have had more mirth in all seasons had they been able to share in the profits of the farm as well as its toils and cheer. His introductory letter conveys the hopes of the American Farmer's wife that strangers would notice "how fat and well clad their negroes were," an insensitive remark that implicitly compares them with farm animals.[30] The condescension with which Crèvecoeur describes occasionally indulging the slaves by letting them borrow their master's horses and sleigh reaches a nadir when he states that sometimes they look as happy and merry as if they were free men. Their happiness always increased his own, provided, he argues, that it did not cross into licentiousness.[31] He evidently wanted his slaves to be happy, but not too happy.

At its worst, slavery permitted severe whippings on any premise whatsoever; the most recalcitrant might be tortured unmercifully as a warning to others. In several states there were no legal limits to the corporal
punishments that slave owners could inflict on their property. Enslaved
youths of both genders might be forced into an involuntary servitude of
an entirely different order, sometimes being coupled together or sold separately without regard for emotional ties. Sometimes plantation owners
mated with their own slaves for the purpose of increasing their property
by producing a new generation of slaves.[32]

Small wonder, then, that popular culture as well as the legal documents
of the era frequently presented slavery as the end result of any political
tyranny. The institution was so widely viewed as abominable that one of
the propagandists' most successful tricks was to create a false dichotomy.
The colonists were frequently asked to chose between a liberty for which
they must risk everything or a slavery that could begin with something
seemingly so simple as Parliament's right to tax the colonies to fund their
defense. Even the most deeply engrained apologists for the institution
acknowledged its horrific nature, arguing that the risks of war were pref-
erable to that degraded condition. Even the newest arrivals from central
Germany, not yet in command of English, realized the shame of slavery.
An entry from a private journal in 1777 comments on the uncooked food,
bad clothing of rough cloth, and beatings with clubs or even iron rods to
which slaves were exposed.[33]

A shortage of soldiers led both sides to recruit slaves into their armies,
and at various times each tried to bring slaves into the war by that most
extraordinary of promises, freedom in exchange for enlistment. In November 1775, Governor Dunmore of Virginia offered freedom to any slave who
joined the British Army. It is not hard to see how cost-effective this measure was, especially compared with paying German princes and shipping
mercenaries across the Atlantic. On February 14, 1778, Parliament extended this opportunity by passing the Slave Enlistment law, in hopes of
forming two battalions of able-bodied male black, mulatto, or Indian
slaves. Not only were all slaves who enlisted to be immediately freed, but
their former owners were to be compensated up to 120 British pounds,
depending on what an individual slave's value had been. The army's real
attitude toward the slaves is probably more evident in the orders issued
as the British left Rhode Island in 1778—the soldiers were ordered to bring
in all the Negroes they could find, as teamsters.[34] In spirit and language,
the order sounded much like an earlier order for the army to bring in all
the cattle they could find. On August 4, 1778, the same diarist noted that
all Negroes had been collected and sent in.[35]

The bold measure of offering freedom for military service was at first
thought impossible for the fledgling American government because delegates from the slave-rich southern states had to agree before the Conti-

nental Congress could act. There was not only a substantial loss of property when each slave turned soldier but also white fear of armed slave rebellion, especially in states in which slaves were the highest percentage of the general population. Hence, the plantation owner George Washington tried to keep even free blacks from joining the Continental Army in 1775; by December of that year he had changed his mind.

The northern states tended to offer the most liberal terms for slaves and free black men who joined the national army or their colonial militias. In June 1777, slaveholders who enlisted their men received a bounty of 180 dollars and half the soldier's pay, with the slave gaining the other half and freedom after three years' service.[36] The further south one went, the less favorable were the terms; Virginia required three years' service before granting freedom, and Georgia and South Carolina never allowed slave enlistment no matter how urgent their military needs. Still, the chance of freedom, or even any immediate change in their material condition, was enough to encourage many slaves to escape the plantation and attempt to attach themselves to the closest armies. Enough of them joined the Continental Army to make it the most racially integrated of any American army before the Second World War. Black soldiers served the cause of freedom with honor, and many paid for it with their blood.

PRACTICAL EDUCATIONS

Careers in Revolutionary America were typically divided along gender lines; consequently, boys and girls received different training. Since the majority of the population was rural, boys were generally expected to assist their fathers on the family farms, as John Woolman did until he was twenty-one. This could be rough service, especially in the frontier areas, where new land sometimes had to be cleared before the plowing could begin. As Crèvecoeur noted, the farmers had but five months of foresight, knowledge, and activity in which to provide a large family with clothes, fuel, and food for the entire year.[37] Girls would be trained for lives that to a modern observer would seem like endless domestic drudgery. An offhand remark by the uncle of one colonial girl suggests how girls were viewed at the time—he saw her as a "fine girl of about five years old who, if she lives and the smallpox doesn't disfigure her, will be a beauty."[38] He regretted that her family lacked the money to give her a good education.

Many colonial lives were circumscribed by their families' lack of funds, which sprang in part from the fact that the colonies were still sparsely populated and undeveloped commercially and industrially. Help was on the way, however. The extremely rapid growth of the coastal colonies was quickly changing the lives of the youth who inhabited them. In his *Notes on the State of Virginia*, Thomas Jefferson calculated that the colony grew from about two hundred thousand inhabitants in 1764 to three hundred thousand in 1774, and 567,614 in 1782, almost half of them slaves. Greater population densities meant greater economies of scale, more schools, and more demand for locally manufactured goods. Although some aspects of the old British class system still damped the prospects of many intelligent and ambitious men and women, excitement was in the air as the colonies in general, like the impatient youth they nurtured, slowly realized their strength. As a minister in Crèvecoeur's *Letters* argues, scientists and other learned men should come to America to observe "the humble rudiments and embryos of societies spreading everywhere" instead of trying to understand such things by studying the useless aqueducts and ancient battlements of Europe.[39] Benjamin Franklin's rise to prominence was only the best-known American success story of his time; everywhere, Crèvecoeur argued, the sober, honest, and industrious immigrants were flourishing on American soil. Later he simplified even this formula—all a poor man needed to rise to some degree of consequence was the gradual operation of sobriety, honesty, and industry.[40] He recalled a Frenchman who arrived literally naked on the shore, having swum to freedom from an English man-of-war. He was able to find clothes, friends, and a wife, eventually leaving a good farm to each of his sons.[41]

Among the privileged classes, moreover, the outlook was never so bleak as for their poorer neighbors. It was the Age of Enlightenment, after all, when men and women in certain quarters began to challenge traditional religious authorities and rely on their own intellects and upon rational inquiry to determine scientific reasons why things happened. This led them to experiment to determine the true nature of natural phenomena. While not all could be as astute as Benjamin Franklin, whose observations improved the world's knowledge about lightning, the Gulf Stream, and hurricane storm cells, they could applaud his efforts and accept such a scientific approach. In the political sphere, this general attitude led some Americans to question the justness of the ancestral rights of kings and the necessity of paying allegiance to such secular authorities. It also changed the world of youth; in earlier eras, divines had sometimes frowned on children who engaged in secular pursuits like sports and games. The time had come for some parents to question such censure, and books began to appear on a wide variety of subjects that had no connection to organized religion or the spiritual side of human nature. Fortunately for the historian interested in the daily life of the era, such books offered precise descriptions of how to sing, dance, and play games. A number of diaries and memoirs providing intimate portraits of childhood and family life during the Revolution have also been preserved.

The book of most lasting importance by an American of the eighteenth century appeared just as the political scene was beginning to simmer; Benjamin Franklin wrote the first part of his *Autobiography* in 1770. Although an invaluable resource as an account of his own youth, its primary interest for the present chapter lies less in its discussions of swimming, kite flying, and penny whistles than in the fact that everyone was reading it, studying their own children for signs of potential Franklins, and indulging and recording childish whims as they never had before. Life in the American colonies was undergoing dynamic changes quite apart from the question of political independence. It is possible to view the Revolutionary War as a symptom and not a cause of the social upheavals attendant upon this new secular and scientific view of the world.

THE EXCITEMENT OF REVOLUTIONARY TIMES

Even before the Revolutionary War, Boston was a stimulating place to be. The port was very actively engaged in commercial traffic; at times the wharves swam with drayage and the odd assortment of seafaring men who served on the vessels. Initially, the British Army had a rather low profile in the city. Sometimes a small contingent of soldiers could be seen drilling on the Boston Commons, an enormous green park, sometimes augmented by units of the local militia. Their muskets could occasionally be heard as they practiced on sundry targets that floated by the wharf, but they did not create much fuss except on January 18, the queen's birthday; June 4, the king's birthday; and October 21, the anniversary of the king's coronation (then called his accession). These dates were constant throughout the Revolutionary period, as the reign of George III lasted from 1760 to 1811. At specified times on such occasions the troops would fire volleys, and if a Royal Navy warship was in port, it would also fire a salute in celebration. Most of the colonists looked forward to raising their glasses in toasts to His Majesty's health. On Sundays, the numerous bells of the city's churches would peal out their greetings. Otherwise, the loudest regular noise came from the town crier, the official voice of colonial or city government.

For the boys and girls of Boston, the early 1770s were an especially exciting time because of the clamor raised in the streets by torchlit mobs of their protesting elders. Patriot propagandists like Sam Adams, formerly dismissed in some corners as a pompous blowhard and failed businessman, were developing a following for their indictments of parliamentary and even royal policy and were organizing secret groups to effect their political ends. Tavern arguments were spilling over into street scenes and brawls, and many adults were openly defiant of the British soldiers sent to preserve order in the colony. There was no telling where it all might lead; people had already been killed in the streets in one famous incident, and soon some of the most famous and richest Boston men would plan a nighttime raid to dump a cargo of tea into harbor before it could be sold in defiance of their boycott. As tensions mounted, a few citizens began trying to get the poorly paid soldiers to sell their weapons. The penalties

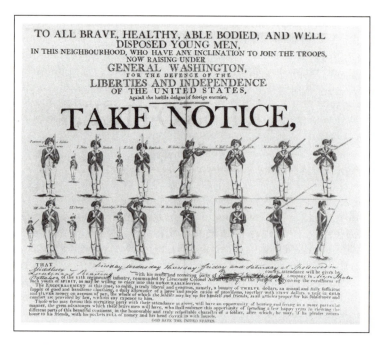

The illustrations on this recruiting poster for the
Continental Army in 1775 suggest a well-trained and well-
supplied professionalism that was years away. Courtesy of
the Library of Congress.

could be severe for any soldier who succumbed to this temptation; fifty
lashes were administered on the back of one such unfortunate.[42] On at
least one occasion, a would-be civilian arms dealer was tarred and feath-
ered by the soldiers for attempting to subvert them.

On the anniversaries of the Boston Massacre, annual commemorative
orations brought together the most vocal radicals and their opponents. On
the fifth anniversary of the event, March 5, 1775, Boston's Old South
Church was filled with such leading Patriot propagandists as Dr. Joseph
Warren, John Hancock, and Sam Adams. Among the crowd were British
officers intent on disrupting the proceedings by hissing their disapproval
and perhaps by using more direct means. The evening ended rather comi-
cally, however, when the officers' cries of "Oh, fie!" were mistaken by the
surly crowd for a warning of fire. Pandemonium ensued as everyone en-
deavored to leave the building at the same instant.[43]

Elsewhere in the colonies the controversy had generally not yet become
so heated, and the war of words more rarely carried over into action. A
few tax collectors had been driven out of other places and sometimes

brutalized in the process. On June 9, 1772, the captain of the *Gaspee*, a Royal Navy revenue schooner, had been deliberately shot, and the vessel burned, near Providence, Rhode Island. The real place to be, however, was Boston, a hotbed of seditious activity.

Parliament also recognized the Boston problem, and it reacted to the Tea Party of December 16, 1773, like a punishing parent. The resulting legislation was collectively referred to as the Coercive Acts in England but as the Intolerable Acts in the colonies. First, the city's economic life was cut off by the Boston Port Act, which effectively shut down trade by imposing a naval blockade until the damaged tea was paid for. Then its privileges of self-government were taken away by the Massachusetts Government Act, which granted more powers to the royal governor, and by the Administration of Justice Act, which promised royal officers a change of venue to a less radical colony or even England if they were brought to court for any legal reason. The Quartering Act restricted the colonists' living space by requiring them to house the four new regiments of troops arriving with the new governor, a military man. This was roughly analogous to having a sibling move into what had previously been a child's private room. The Quebec Act extended French control over the northern Ohio Valley, for which land speculators had been salivating since before the French and Indian War—a restriction of movement such as makes teenagers bristle today. Lest these seem like inept comparisons, it should be remembered that the analogy of Britain as the mother country frequently crept into the political discussions of the American Revolutionary era. The Loyalists frequently asserted that the colonies should feel as obligated to Britain as they did to their biological mothers.

Soon the new regiments of redcoats were clambering down the gangplanks and marching into the streets of Boston, where they could commandeer any public building for their barracks or force private homeowners to put them up. Their every move was carefully watched by the Patriots, who began arriving in the areas around Boston in sufficient numbers to openly oppose the army's forays into the countryside.

At first New England responded to the Boston Port Act by hauling produce overland into the city. After chasing the British back to Boston from Concord, they surrounded the city and proved their willingness to fight at the Battle of Bunker Hill on June 17, 1775. The British possessed the ground at the end of the battle, but their victory was hard won and accomplished little, since the colonials still encircled them. Many of the British soldiers who had made what had been intended as a punitive attack on Bunker Hill were brought back bleeding into Boston.

Now openly at war, the militia effectively closed access to the city by land. Almost no one who left the city was permitted to return, and prudent families who had children old enough to live without them sometimes sent them to relatives in the countryside. Thus, John Greenwood's formal schooling came to an abrupt end when he was sent to live with relatives at the age of thirteen. Striking out on his own to return to his parents but denied access to Boston, he enlisted as a fifer with the militia. He would not see his parents for nearly three years, by which time there had been numerous riots in Boston against the tyranny of the Continental Congress for its desperate levying of a variety of taxes and fines in order to finance the war.[44]

Few men stayed in the Continental Army for the money, especially when it became evident that Congress rarely had funds to feed or clothe them, much less pay them. A few were what later generations would term "adrenalin junkies," content to take risks for the pleasure of action and of beating the odds. Most joined out of patriotic fervor and stayed because they felt it their duty to be with their fellow soldiers. (Late in the war, however, with the entire outcome of the conflict in the balance, entire units of first the Pennsylvania and then the Delaware militias, both of which had been grafted onto the Continental Army, mutinied for back pay.) Most soldiers on both sides of the conflict saw more of the American colonies than would have been normal in peacetime, but for some the exhilaration of travel could end in one of the pestilential prison ships in New York Harbor, or in a mine converted to a prison, actually little more than a dungeon.

Even for those who survived the experience, service in the field in either army was far from pleasant. Soldiers on both sides were disciplined with corporal punishments that varied according to the severity of the crime and the policies of their respective armies. Transgressors among the Hessians were typically forced to run a gauntlet through two parallel lines of soldiers, each of whom was to deliver a blow to the miscreant as he passed. The court-martial determined the number of men in each line and the number of times the offender had to run through it. For stealing English linen from a merchant, two privates were ordered to run a gauntlet of two hundred men sixteen times each. For disrespect to an officer another man had to run twelve times past three hundred soldiers. Similar punishments were meted out for indebtedness, fighting, attempted desertion, or even complaining about one's pay.

In the British Army, flogging was the most common method of handling miscreants, and five hundred lashes could be handed out for the serious crime of attempting to sell one's weapons to the Boston insurgents.[45] A soldier could be hung for disobeying and attacking his captain;[46] standing orders directed sentries to shoot those who tried to desert. As the war progressed, soldiers on both sides risked their lives running past sentry posts to escape the service.

On both sides, toasts were drunk in celebration of the country's independence or to the king's health. At noon on the king's birthday in 1777,

As this mid-nineteenth-century engraving suggests, conditions on the notorious *Jersey* and other British prison ships were cramped and dispiriting. Courtesy of the Library of Congress.

every British ship and fortress around New York City fired all its cannon; one who heard them guessed there may have been three or four thousand cannon shots.[47] Beginning in 1777, thirteen-volley cannonades commemorating the Declaration of Independence were fired within hearing of the British troops in New York exactly a month later.[48] Such festivities underscore the patriotic motives that encouraged men to join one army or the other. The Hessian mercenaries had less reason to celebrate, and individual soldiers stood to profit little even if they served well in dangerous circumstances. Their captains fared far better; each received a premium from the English for each of their men killed. Three men wounded were reckoned as one man killed.[49]

In the Royal Navy, a captain could hang sailors who resisted him.[50] The fleet's constant need for recruits could make staying in New York City hazardous for even the staunchest Loyalists. On January 22 and May 4, 1781, men were rounded up off the streets and pressed into His Majesty's service as sailors, about three hundred on the second occasion.[51] The British even tried to recruit from among prisoners of war; at least two groups of such former prisoners in this way found an opportunity to escape with the vessels to which they had been assigned.[52]

Usually, however, army life had to settle into predictable patterns of maintenance and drill, and soldiers struggled to meet their everyday needs even during bombardments. This juxtaposition of the extraordinary and the mundane sometimes lent itself to macabre events, as when a soldier of the British Forty-fifth Light Infantry lost a leg to a cannonball while sitting in a hut busily mending his shoes.[53]

Service in the colonial army provided many young men with skills, resources, and connections they would never have had without the disruption in the nation's political life. Cobblers and carpenters could become sergeants and majors, and the experience and confidence that came from commanding men under fire helped many of them along the trail to professional success. Victory in the war suggested that no political office in the land was beyond the grasp of anyone with the ambition, talent, and connections to achieve it, and many veterans went on to fill innumerable public offices at all levels of government. The emphasis placed on American self-sufficiency by the boycotts of British goods gave greater impetus to entrepreneurial manufacturing than was lost through the deliberate destruction of factories and mills and scattering of trained workmen in the war. The United States emerged from the seven-year struggle with a national debt of only forty-five million dollars and a population of three million restless inhabitants just beginning to realize that there were no real impediments separating them from personal success.[54] Boys and girls who grew to maturity during these years learned to shoulder their share of their families', communities', and their nation's burdens.

Part II

Popular Culture of the Revolutionary War Era

3

Advertising

As late as 1763, the most financially successful planters, traders, and merchants everywhere were still so enamored of British aristocracy that they purchased whatever they could that would demonstrate their class identity. As such effective propagandists as James Otis, Samuel Adams, and eventually Thomas Paine slowly began getting people to question the value of this English connection, a rapidly growing group of highly politicized colonial consumers increasingly relied on American goods and boycotted British products as a patriotic gesture. A lack of sophisticated marketing knowledge and limited advertising venues contributed immeasurably to the success of these boycotts. Advertisements at this point in the country's mercantile development still appealed to the customer's intellect instead of his emotions, a fact that left most people more vulnerable to the radical's more emotional appeals for direct political action than would usually be the case in subsequent American history.

PRIMITIVE MARKETING IDEAS

Merchants in Revolutionary America who wished to gain public notice of their wares had very few options in terms of the media available to convey their message. Word-of-mouth advertising was the standard means by which a shopkeeper could attract potential clients from his most immediate vicinity. Customers who liked the quality of a particular good or service provided by a business would, ideally, inform their friends and neighbors where they had acquired it. The new customers who came searching after the same deal might be enticed to purchase something else while they were in the store and to tell still other people about the business. Modern marketers might classify what happened next as "point of sale" advertising and study the impact that such things as product placement, consumer behaviorism, and salesmanship have on sales, but at that point in the nation's commercial development the decisions made by local retailers were largely intuitive. The chief difficulties for most retail businesses were finding sufficient manufactured goods to meet consumer demand, and finding customers with sufficient cash to complete the transaction. The colonial tradition of bartering agricultural produce and sometimes labor in order to obtain whatever the consumer/producer needed carried over into the Revolutionary marketplace, where perpetual shortages of hard currency collided with the shortage in manufactured goods. The result was an increased willingness by both buyer and seller to negotiate the selling price of many items.

The practice of window dressing (placing the best or newest wares prominently in the store window and using manikins and other attractive or controversial display techniques to attract passers-by) was neither as widespread nor as studiously applied as it would be in later centuries. The sales potential of foot traffic had been recognized, however, and many merchants adopted the colorful practice of placing wooden signs above the entrance to their establishments. An artistically carved and painted signboard could be suspended from an iron rod over the front door to indicate clearly even to illiterate patrons the goods and services offered by the business. A business name or sign that was colorful or humorous enough had the added benefit of sticking in the customer's memory. The signs were so popular that people often agreed to meet "at the sign of the Fleece" instead of just "at the Fleece." This phenomenon might be viewed as the start of brand loyalty; many customers would prefer to remain with providers with whom they were familiar rather than patronize other competitors in the same business whose products might have been just as good. The colorful tavern name and imaginatively crafted sign were often the first steps involved in building such loyalty.

As popular sentiment for an independent America spread throughout the colonies, an increasing number of businesses changed their names and their signboards to convey the owners' and clienteles' shifting loyalties. Almost all references to British royalty were quickly dropped from store names as the Patriots gained dominance in an area, and many latched onto the names of the heroes of the colonial army once the outcome of the war was no longer in doubt. For their own protection, taverns with names like the King's Men or the Crown would change them to something more neutral, like the Pelican or the Publican, and eventually to the George Washington. A few Hessian prisoners of war still in American custody were startled to find a George Washington Tavern, complete with a signboard representing the famous man, only five miles from Philadelphia less than a month after the Treaty of Paris returned peace to the troubled land.

From the early 1760s and then throughout the history of the conflict, such taverns played a very important role. The various grievances against the British establishment, which at the time were only by a few individuals, were given their first public airing in such venues. Taverns served as convenient settings for the small groups of concerned citizens who had begun asking themselves what they could do about the unfavorable conditions imposed on the colonies, and eventually they provided convenient meeting rooms for larger groups of local activists on both sides. Even members of the Continental Congresses often met in taverns as they worked out their official responses to Parliament's tyranny. Taverns sustained numerous officers of both armies as they made their way to the various theatres of war, and they sheltered innumerable rank-and-file soldiers as they traveled to join their armies or sometimes staggered on the long trek homeward with disabling wounds or discharges at the conclusion of their specified terms of service. On December 4, 1783, when George Washington bade farewell to the principal officers of his army, it was a sign of the times that such an important emotional as well as historical moment occurred at Francis's Tavern in New York City.

ADVERTISING IN PRINT MEDIA

For commercial advertising purposes, conditions were generally not favorable for reaching a customer base beyond the traffic that passed by an establishment. Not only did the colonies generally lack the abundant quantities of goods that would make extended formal advertising profitable, but there were very few media available to carry their messages. Broadsides, sheets of printed paper often about the size of the modern newspaper page, were tacked up in prominent places for public perusal; they could be used to announce new products or for such political ends as recruiting for the British Army. Recruiting posters for the Continental Army also appeared after it was formed in 1775. Advertisements for runaway apprentices, slaves, and indentured servants were also common, as were ads for commercial products. Such advertising could be especially powerful because official documents, including copies of the Declaration of Independence, were sometimes printed and posted in such a manner. Placement of a commercial ad in a place where people were used to finding their news could enhance its chances of at least being perused. Similarly good locations could be found wherever people were forced to wait, such as the wharfs from which regularly scheduled packets were dispatched, and in alehouses near stagecoach stops. Alternatively, they could be printed in sufficient numbers to blanket an area, a strategy of saturation that might alienate a few people but had the definite advantage of making almost everyone aware of the announcement.

Besides broadsides, newspapers, and pamphlets were the only print media capable of dispersing topical information throughout the colonies when the Revolutionary War began. Although newspapers typically totaled only four to eight pages in length, they filled a far greater percentage of their available space with advertising than their modern counterparts do. They were usually not distributed outside of the major urban areas unless a reader happened to be on a post rider's route or did not mind waiting for delivery by a coastal packet. In either case, newspapers were unlikely to be of use in attracting new customers to a sale of limited duration; even news of the Declaration of Independence in Philadelphia did not reach the streets of Boston until eight days later. Since large cities were neither very numerous nor very densely populated in the colonies, most newspapers reached only a small portion of what would become an extensive potential customer base over the next two centuries. In the Revolutionary era there were clear limits on how much traffic even the best-designed advertisement could engender, because such difficulties kept potential customers from exposure to it.

The laborious task of hand-carving or engraving pictures and the difficulties attendant upon striking off multiple clean copies of an illustration on an eighteenth-century printing press made newspaper ads largely dependent upon variations in font and type size, creative use of white space, and descriptive language than would later be the case. Many printers lacked a broad variety of fonts, so the ads tended toward uniformity in appearance. Notwithstanding the relatively bland appearance of the usual advertisements, the importance of colonial newspapers as vehicles for expanding popular support was recognized by propagandists on both sides of the conflict. The Continental Congress sometimes released minutes of its meetings in what amounted to press releases; hence, the British officers in New York could read of congressional recruitment promises in the Newport, Rhode Island, *Mercury*.[1] In September 1776, Congress promised a twenty-dollar bounty for each new soldier who enlisted, and one hundred acres of land if he served to the end of the war or was discharged or killed. Of course, such promises were dependent upon the ultimate success of the American army, an outcome that seemed very unlikely at the time.

Colonial and Revolutionary newspapers also differed from their descendents in that many operated as virtual monopolies in their areas. Without a rival paper, there was very little incentive for a publisher to improve the visual appearance of his paper, maintain a high quality of writing, or hire a reporter who could investigate local news stories. A few owners seemed to think of their papers purely as revenue-producing businesses and evidently put as little effort and money into them as was possible.

Many seem to have thought of their newspapers almost like magazines, filling them with whatever interesting material they could borrow from the colonial papers in distant cities or with excerpts from books on ancient history or world celebrities. This had its good sides—the public was kept more aware of what was happening to their peers in other colonies than would otherwise have been the case, and much of the material required reading at an advanced level. The downside was that the paper could be painfully silent on even the most astonishing, potentially world-changing events in what should have been their journalistic backyards while rushing into print with excerpts from Dr. Smollet's travels through France and Italy, the latest news from Russia, or transcripts of the lengthy orations delivered perhaps a hundred years before on historical (sometimes ancient) events. Still, this was better than viewing a city's newspaper as primarily and sometimes almost exclusively as an advertising opportunity. This practice seems especially abhorrent when, as often occurred with *Rivington's New York Gazette,* the editor would place advertisements for his own products on page 1, column 1—a prominence suggesting that the Maredant's Antiscoreutic Drops or Dr. Keyser's Pills really did represent medical breakthroughs.

Rivington's newspaper was itself frequently no bargain. Instead of headlines that reflected the content of an article, he would print the news under the heading of the ship upon which it arrived. The following heading appeared in the November 16, 1775, issue:

> On Friday last arrived the *Mercury* Pacquet, Captain Dillion, in 60 days from Falmouth, and brought the following Intelligence: London, August 3.

The article announced that the land and property of the insurgents was to be confiscated by the crown, news of such consequence to his readership that a more scrupulous editor/owner might have considered letting it crowd the advertisement for Antiscoreutic Drops off page 1. The more typical Rivington heading listed only the place and date where the article originated, a convention still practiced by modern journalism except that the dateline information typically follows an interesting headline that provides at least some advance notice of the article's content, and a byline that identifies its author.

Sporting events were generally not thought newsworthy, and no mention was usually made of them outside of paid announcements aimed at encouraging horse owners to enter their mounts in an upcoming race, which might be two months off. Other sports were entirely ignored unless a travel narrator or correspondent happened to include some mention of them. Hence, readers of Rivington's November 11, 1773, issue could learn of wrestling matches in Otaheita (now known as Tahiti). The correspondent was not impressed, dismissing the combat as an awkward grabbing without the least dexterity or skill until one wrestler could throw the other down. Swimming came off better; the same writer marveled at the Tahitian's ability to swim amid high waves and even engage in body surfing. If any swimming was attempted anywhere else in the world or even on a second occasion in Tahiti, the readers of the *New York Gazette* or any other colonial paper were unlikely to learn of it.

Since centuries would lapse before marketing became a separate business discipline, the advertisements in colonial newspapers generally tended merely to inform the reader of the availability of an item instead of proactively attempting to broaden its appeal or create brand loyalty for a product, as opposed to the business itself. Few attempts were made at product differentiation, and no context was provided to help the reader know if the advertiser was offering bargain prices. Most businesses did not deal in overt self-promotion on the basis of the unique aspects of their establishments. With so few other options available, the question of where to place an advertisement typically had only one answer, unless there happened to be two rival newspapers in a city. There were no celebrity endorsements or pictures of toothsome youth of either gender to add sex appeal to the message. A lack of standards regulated by the government or widely accepted by the various industries made comparison shopping impossible unless the consumer chose to visit the various establishments in person. As will be become evident in the chapter on travel that follows, this was typically not a viable option.

While the colonial towns were frequently so small that businesses did not need to advertise to make their immediate customer base aware of them, this was decidedly not the case when a ship came to a port city in which it wanted to sell its cargo. Short of examining the actual manifests of the vessels or customs records for their clearance and tariff declarations, the historian's best introduction to the scope of colonial commerce comes from the advertisements such ships' captains-turned-merchants placed in the local newspapers. Even the radical *Massachusetts Spy* benefited from this opportunity.

Another important feature that distinguishes the typical Revolutionary-era newspaper advertisement from its descendents is the lack of an address in the form of a unique number assigned to each building on a street. Even advertisements in the *Philadelphia Evening Post,* which served the largest city in colonial America, tended to provide only the street on which the business was located and its general direction from a nearby landmark. Hence even potential advertisers and subscribers to the newspaper were directed to "Front Street, near the London Coffee House." Similarly, a publisher was described as being "next to St. Paul's church on Third-street in Philadelphia." The negative impression sometimes resulting from an unfashionable address could be multiplied because of this system:

Charles Oliver Bruss, Goldsmith and Jeweler, at the sign of the Tea-pot, Tankard and Ear-ring, has removed his Shop from Rotten-Row, opposite to the Fly-Market, and but two doors down from the Main Street.

This item in the July 1, 1768, *New York Gazette and Weekly Mercury* did not provide the new address, but it is a relief to see in the same man's advertisement in the July 6, 1778, issue of the same paper on July 6, 1778, his address became "At the sign of the Teapot and Tankard, No. 196, Queen-street, at the corner of Golden Hill." The later ad, more than six inches long, included two inches of icons representing a coat of arms and assorted items of jewelry. In most smaller towns, the proprietor's or seller's name alone was considered an adequate means of bringing buyer and seller together, suggesting that the advertisers had no illusions about their advertisements' ability to attract potential customers from any great distance.

Because print media (newspapers, broadsides, pamphlets and almanacs) were the sole means of reaching a broad, widely dispersed audience, and for keeping informed about political and economic developments, the heated response to the Stamp Act in 1765 can easily be appreciated. Imagine the added expense if every single copy of a newspaper or flyer printed in the United States today had to have a revenue stamp.

The overall quality of the newspapers also varied widely. The typical *Georgia Gazette*, published only on Thursdays, carried an excerpt from a pamphlet or public letter on its front page, followed by three pages of advertisements. On Thursday, November 10, 1763, even the first page was devoted to a comprehensive list of the books for sale at the printing office. The *Gazette* usually picked up a few news items by appropriating them from other newspapers, such as news from Boston and New York over a month old. Because the French and Indian War was still being waged, the issue included a letter from Fort Detroit—two months old. Americans have traditionally been considered conservative and isolationist except during their many wars, when painful geography lessons are driven home by reports of casualties or astonishing victories or defeats. As the articles of the *Gazette* indicate, battlefield news from the French and Indian War kept at least some of the Georgians apprised of developments in the northern colonies. The same thing happened during the Stamp Act crisis; the *Gazette* published the news that New Jersey lawyers had resolved to stop practicing rather than use the stamps. The November 14, 1765, edition thought this "a noble resolution, worthy of universal imitation."

The four words "product, price, placement, and promotion," which have become the mantra of modern marketing classes, represent concepts that were alien to eighteenth-century advertisers. Period newspapers

provided potential customers with common nouns signifying the availability of a given commodity at a store or ship's berth, but proper nouns,
which might have been used to suggest the superiority of one brand over
another, were used only for patent medicines. Today, price is clearly intended as one of the principal attractions of virtually every retail advertisement in a newspaper. Mid-eighteenth-century newspaper advertisers
almost never listed their prices, probably because they feared an experience like that of a Providence, Rhode Island, shoemaker whose innovative advertisement in the *Providence Gazette* of May 10, 1764, was highly
unusual in five surprising ways. First of all, it featured a graphic representation of a boot at a time when almost no other ads, and certainly no
features or breaking news stories, were accompanied by pictures. Secondly, the icon of the boot was tied in with the identity of the specific re-
tailer; potential customers were instructed to shop "At the Sign of the
Boot," in the north end of Providence. A third distinction was the ad's
mention of the specific style and perhaps even brand of the product—
these were Lynn shoes, and (the fourth distinction) "very neat" ones at
that. Because ads were sold by how much space they used, adjectives were
rare—and this one even had an adverb. Most striking of all, however, was
the ad's audacity in printing the price of the shoes: six shillings eight
pence. Customers who patronized the store because of the ad should have
heaped praise on the merchant for making their shopping so much easier.
It is unlikely, however, that many of them did, since on the same page,
just inches from this groundbreaking, truly revolutionary advertisement,
is a ship's ad offering Lynn shoes at its berth for only six shillings.

The psychology behind advertisers' reluctance to give prices stretched
far beyond the risk that someone else would publish an even lower price.
In the northern colonies founded for religious purposes, there had long
been an imbedded antipathy toward money, because it was so earth-
bound, even crass. Although there were very few Catholics north of New
York City, most people were aware of the seven deadly sins; the injunc-
tions against greed and usury called money the root of all evil. Although
the increasing popularity of deist and similar beliefs, and a broadly based
faith in rationality in all things, were breaking down some of the old fears
about the potential evils of money, enough of the old sentiments persisted
that most colonists were reticent when it came to focusing on money in
public. The fear that America might easily become a plutocracy, where
money was king, was already being discussed in some quarters. Further-
more, in the 1760s most colonists were still so enamored of everything
British that they valued noble birth and ancestral rights more than anything so déclassé as recently acquired wealth or public interest in the price
of an item.

There was also a long tradition of bartering in the colonies, and any
bargainer would naturally hesitate before naming his opening offer. This

habit sprang from the severe poverty most settlers experienced in their first years in a new area; British control of the colonial money supply kept the practice necessary long after most people recognized the benefits of dealing in currency. Some people willingly accepted suspect bills because of the frustrating absence of solid-currency alternatives. Advertisers who wished to purchase something instead of selling it frequently enhanced their pitch by adding that they would pay ready money instead of attempting to barter.

In August 1775, the Continental Congress voted to print paper money, to the value of two million Spanish dollars, to finance the war.[2] In accordance with the usual psychology of money, when two types of currency are simultaneously circulated, people tend to hoard the more valuable (in this case, gold and silver) and spend the lesser. Accordingly, the national currency soon chased gold and silver from circulation.

The war only made confusion about the money even worse, and the value of the Continental dollar fluctuated in accordance with the Continental Army's success in the field. It seemed to reach its nadir after the fall of Charleston in 1781, when sixty Continental dollars were worth only one of specie.[3] Even worse times were ahead. After the Pennsylvania mutiny, American paper fell to nearly one hundred to one and threatened to lose its entire value.[4] After it fell to a thousand to one, Congress was forced to completely annul its paper currency.[5]

With very few exceptions, promotion in the modern marketing sense was also not practical. The closest an eighteenth-century business generally came to offering a unique opportunity for customers to purchase something at an unusual price for a limited time came when a ship pulled into port and tried to sell its cargo by placing an advertisement in the local paper. Thus it could be argued that our shoe salesman in Providence who offered Lynn shoes for eight pence more than his competitor's price was not beaten because of his innovative advertising techniques but because a ship's captain chanced upon a formula that incorporated a better overall marketing strategy. Potential customers were implicitly encouraged to seek out the captain before his ship sailed. Perhaps he also received a little assistance from the newspaper editor, who may have shown him the competitor's advertised price.

MARKETING PATENT MEDICINES

Advertising has been considered somewhat disreputable throughout much of American history, because of its early association with patent medicines. In an age before the federal government began to regulate the production of drugs to ensure their safety as well as effectiveness, it was easy to claim to have applied for a patent on whatever elixir one cared to dream up. An impressive label, a memorable name, a dark glass bottle to deepen the mystery surrounding its contents, a bitter taste to convince the patient of its potency, and an exaggerated claim of curing a common illness or condition were all the stock-in-trade of an industry where the production cost could be pennies (or pence) and the return could be dollars (or shillings) per bottle. If one raised the alcohol content sufficiently, many patients would feel somewhat better (or at least different) until the effects of the dosage wore off.

In some ways, the most prominent of the medicinal concoctions of the Revolutionary era was Maredant's Antiscoreutic Drops, if only because it was sold by James Rivington, the owner of the *New York Gazette*. Such proprietary connections entitled the drug to page 1, column 1 treatment, as in the November 16, 1775, issue. It did not take long for the testimonials to start rolling in; these were prominently printed in the paper. Rivington also sold a second drug, Dr. Keyser's Pills, which "infallibly cure a disease not to be mentioned in a newspaper" and rheumatism. It seems a pity to the modern reader that Rivington got greedy and mentioned rheumatism. Without it, he had the perfect alibi if anyone complained about the medication—the victim's illness, if uncured, was obviously not the one to which Rivington was referring in the advertisement.

Hugh Gaine, printer of the *New York Gazette and Weekly Mercury*, also tried to profit from patent medicines. His ad in the July 3, 1769, issue demonstrates how a catchy name and an unsubstantiated claim that the product had been invented by a doctor could be used to enhance the appeal of a medicine. It also shows how patent medicines came by that name: "Dr. Ryan's incomparable Worm-destroying Sugar Plums; Levine's celebrated Eye-Water, Greenough's Tincture for the Teeth and Gums, by the King's Royal Letters Patent, Dr. Hill's Balsam of Honey, and Joyce's great American Balsam, sold by Hugh Gaine." The right political connections were more crucial in obtaining such a patent than successful laboratory tests or clinical trials.

PERSONAL SERVICES ADS

A survey of the advertisements of virtually any newspaper from this era quickly produces an appeal for a wet nurse, a lactating woman who could provide milk for an infant whose mother had died or otherwise become unable or unwilling to produce breast milk. Generally such appeals maintained the advertiser's privacy by asking interested parties to contact the printer at his newspaper office, but occasionally the need was so urgent that advertisers would provide their own names. By 1778, a few wet nurses had begun advertising their services, sometimes stressing their health, references, willingness to join a household, and ample supply of milk.

A remarkable advertisement placed in the October 28, 1775, *Pennsylvania Evening Post* offered the services of a tutor whose knowledge evidently rivaled that of the fabled Merlin, of Round Table fame:

An English, grammatic, and mathematical *school*. John Hefferman, after a tender of grateful acknowledgments, and fresh assurances of unremitting diligence, begs leave to acquaint the worthy and respectable, his friends and the public, that he has removed his school to that noted room over Mrs. Richardson's, near St. Paul's, in Third-street, lately occupied by Mr. Cannon, now of the college.—Where he continues to render perfectly familiar, inculcate and teach grammatic English, reading, writing, puerile declamation, arithmetic and accounts; the rudiments of Latin grammar, and a few of its subsequent classics; the elements of geometry, trigonometry and fluxions; the practical branches of mensuration, gauging, navigation and surveying; with the modern institutes of fortification, gunnery, astronomy and dialing.—And where the candid and judicious may depend on the constant exertion of every sensible effort to forward children, and fit youth for business with all possible expedition and certainty.

Said Hefferman's evening school, from six to half after eight, commences on Monday the 16th instant; when a few of the emulous sons of early industry may take the occasional opportunity of renewing their studies, refreshing their memories, or repairing the regretted loss of elapsed time; to the salutary end of not only *keeping out of harm's way*, as is the phrase, but, perhaps, of also founding some honorable promotion or eligible department in active life, or the bare improvement of a single winter, well spent, in tuitive lucubrations. Philadelphia, October 14, 1775.

Although one probably could not imagine a more erudite advertisement, the second paragraph suggests the opportunity of what twenty-first-century universities refer to as adult and continuing education. In fact, advertisements in this and other newspapers offered evening classes in everything from dancing to French. As for basic education, an advertisement for a grammar and general school in the *New York Gazette* ended by announcing that an evening school would also be opened if a sufficient number of scholars speedily applied (November 11, 1773). Such instruction was evidently not connected to any college degree program, but in the eighteenth-century American colonies high school diplomas or college degrees were not as important as demonstrable competence in a particular trade.

Sometimes a single advertisement can reveal a tremendous amount about labor relations in that distant time. This one appeared in the *Evening Post* on November 11, 1775:

Just arrived from London, in the ship Hawke, Jacob Getsheus, master, and now lying off Market-Street wharf, a few *likely healthy servants,* amongst whom are farmers, shoemakers, tailors, silversmiths, a jeweler, curriers, a plasterer, clothier, butcher, hatter, cabinet-maker, clerks, and two young women, whose time shall be disposed by Stephen and Joseph Shewell, William Craig, or the master on board.

That the time of these servants could be purchased from the ship's master suggests that they may have bartered a few years' servitude for the trip across the Atlantic, a rather common arrangement. The trades were probably listed in the order of their appeal to the widest number of potential purchasers, since the majority of the colonists still worked on farms and, as virtually every journal kept by a common Continental soldier during the war indicates, the nation faced a chronic shortage of good footwear. A currier prepares tanned hides for a shoemaker or other uses. It is interesting that so many diverse trades were represented, an indication that skilled English tradesmen were becoming aware of the good prospects for relative prosperity available on American shores. That the women are listed by gender instead of by their technical skills or crafts reflects a popular bias of the age, its neglect of practical training and sometimes even basic education for girls.

Personal ads based upon the subscriber's desire for a relationship ("Rapidly aging college professor seeks avid reader for discussion of old times and perhaps more," for example) were a later invention. About the closest thing in the Revolutionary era was this advertisement in the *New York Gazette and Weekly Mercury* on July 4, 1774:

Whereas some ill-minded persons in and about this city have propagated a false and scandalous story, that my son, now teacher of a public school in the Outworks of this city, was fathered by Joseph Bill, who was executed in the city of Albany about two years ago for counterfeiting money. To take away any ill impressions people may imbibe prejudicial to my son's reputation, I do in this public manner declare that the said Bill was never my husband, I never knew him, or had any concerns with him; and I think that I, who am his mother, know best who his father was. Deborah Connally.

ADVERTISING AND THE SLAVE TRADE

In the advertisements of the Revolutionary era, slaves were sometimes treated as just another commodity in a list of goods. Most southern readers were not shocked at finding human beings for sale, but such advertisements help the modern reader realize that slaves were viewed as property. By 1769, about half of all the advertisements in the *Georgia Gazette* focused on some aspect of slavery. Most commonly, they announced runaways by name, distinguishing tribal scars, age, height, and clothing. The area was still so sparsely populated that advertisements provided only the name of the person whom interested persons should contact; no address was necessary.

A second category of slavery advertisements announced not that a slave had escaped but that a suspected runaway had been captured. Such "taken up" ads typically included the age, gender, and place of apprehension. Despite the banality of their format, a few of the ads hint at the human misery behind them. On June 10, 1769, the following ad appeared in the *Gazette*:

> Taken up the 20th of January last, on the Indian Country Path, in a boat 20 miles from Augusta, and delivered to the Subscriber, *a negroe fellow,* and *a wench,* with *a child* about two months old. The fellow is about five feet ten inches high, pretty lofty, says his name is Sampson, and his wife's name Molly, but speaks such bad English as scarcely to be understood, says his master lives near the salt water, is a small man, and his name Jacab Middow, and has a wife and three children. The fellow had on a gown with a cap to it made out of a duffel blanket, and the wench an old ragged negroe cloth jacket and coat. The owner may have them by applying at Augusta to *Edward Barnard.*

The language used in this ad was typical; its spelling and capitalization have been preserved from the original. The desperation that would lead a father to risk his wife and infant son on a flight through Indian country can only be imagined.

A third category of ads tried to interest readers in slaves for sale. They were most commonly attached to the estate of their deceased master, although an occasional ad announced slaves seized for the master's unpaid debts or, almost as rarely, newly arrived in a new shipment from Africa or the West Indies.

Overseers, especially sober, industrious, honest, and knowledgeable men who could read and write were evidently in great demand (and perhaps in short supply). Most editions of the *Gazette* had at least one advertisement for such men. The fact that slaves were constantly fleeing the plantations while others were constantly being taken up suggests that the effective management of a slave-labor team was a nearly impossible task even when the state supported all the means of terror and coercion that the angry, narrow-minded, and occasionally vicious slave drivers could muster.

Some plantation owners allowed their slaves to visit the neighboring plantations if, for example, a family had been broken up by an auction. Even more frequently, individual slaves took it upon themselves to attempt such visits despite the threats of the owner or his overseer. The results could sometimes prove exasperating for the plantation owner as well as the slaves, as the following ad from the *Gazette* of September 22, 1763, indicates:

Whereas the subscriber's plantation, lately Chief Justice Grover's, now named Hermitage, is grievously and unsufferably annoyed and disturbed by negroes, who come there by land and water in the night-time, and not only rob, steal and carry off hogs, poultry, sheep, corn and his potatoes, but create very great disorders amongst his slaves by debauching his slave wenches, who have husbands, the property of the subscriber; and some are so audacious as to debauch his very house wenches: These therefore are to give notice to all proprietors of slaves, that, after the 16th Sept. 1763, the subscriber is determined to treat all negroes that shall be found within his fences, after sunset, and before sunrise, as thieves, robbers, and invaders of his property, by shooting them, and for that intent he has hired a white man properly armed for that purpose. *Patrick Mackay*

The same advertisement appeared in the November 10, 1763, issue, so it would appear that Mr. Mackay's potatoes were still being stolen two and a half months later. This ad suggests the awkwardness and inconsistency inherent in the slave proprietor's attitudes toward his property. While willing to describe his unwanted interlopers in human terms (as thieves, robbers, and invaders), he was especially troubled by the sensuality of his house slaves, whom he preferred to think of as sexless, and hence nonhuman.

The most startling aspect of the more typical slavery advertisements in southern newspapers is not just their number but the prominence that slaves are given in ads for which other "goods" are also offered. The fact that slaves are almost always mentioned first shows how important they were to the colony's economy. Their priority of place in the ads suggests their value to the target audience, the colony's most affluent men and women. These ideal customers might be counted on to purchase some of the other wares if they could be convinced to attend the auction. In the northern colonies, announcements for the sale of a mixed consignment that included slaves typically placed such human chattel in the middle or at the end of the list.

In the northern colonies, many Quakers refused to accept the mundane banality of the evil behind such ads, which tended to ignore or trivialize the human misery involved, and continued to lobby for the abolition of slavery whenever they could. In the South, slaves were of such vital economic importance that the institution could not be so publicly attacked with impunity.

ADVERTISING IN THE MARKETPLACE OF IDEAS

Since copyright laws were either ineffective or favored the publisher's rights over the author's, publishers throughout the American colonies were free to print anything of potential interest to their readers. Since many papers operated under the censorship of the local representatives

Propagandists on both sides were quick to use the broadside
as a means of creating support for their political positions.
This is Paul Revere's incendiary poster of the Boston Massacre
of March 5, 1770. Courtesy of the Library of Congress.

of royal authority, committees of correspondence were formed in Massachusetts to cultivate sentiments for independence in the other colonies. Sometimes local authorities were cited to put a regional spin on the political developments, as when the *Georgia Gazette* published excerpts from a pamphlet by a writer identified only as "A Freeholder in South Carolina." This writer, in several issues in the summer of 1769, examined the colonies' dependence on Parliament and its right to tax them. Since the British Army maintained strict control over New York City from September 1776 to the end of the war, that colonial city, which had the most news-papers, eventually contained few without an announced Loyalist bias. Conversely, it would have been extremely foolish for a Boston editor to adopt a Loyalist slant in his columns even before the British Army was forced from the city on March 17, 1776. The publisher of the leading Tory newspaper in New York City was forced to leave the business when the British lost the war.

Aside from newspaper items, ideas could be advertised in broadsides. The most famous and probably the most effective of these propagandized the events of March 5, 1770, as the horrid "Boston Massacre." Its exquisite graphics, which included an engraving by Paul Revere based on a draw-ing by another man, were remarkably more detailed than those of the news-papers or other broadsides of the era. Five coffins, each bearing a skull and crossbones as well as the initials of one of the six men mortally wounded that night, were placed in the last of the five columns of an incendiary *Boston Gazette* account of the incident. The entire text was enclosed in a black border, and strong black lines separated the columns within the text.

It is the wonderfully charged Revere engraving that truly distinguishes this broadsheet, however. As it appeared at a time when pictorial repre-sentations of current events were entirely lacking in the weekly colonial papers, its impact on its immediate audience must have been striking. That it recognizably rendered the outlines of Boston buildings and labeled one as Butcher's Hall would have provided an additional shock of familiar-ity, but it is the figures in the foreground that command the most atten-tion. The extraordinary portrayal of the life's blood spurting out of the side of the foremost victim might have unsettled even the strongest colonial mind, unaccustomed as it was to graphic displays of such wounds. To the right are highly disciplined, uniformed British regulars, shown in the in-stant after firing into the crowd; not only does the black-powder smoke still coil above their heads, but they have not yet lowered their single-shot weapons. An officer stands behind their line, his upraised sword giving the impression that he had ordered them to fire.

On the receiving end of the volley, five men have already either fallen prostrate upon the ground or have been caught in the supporting arms of their neighbors. The limited space available forced the two sides so closely together that the discharge seems to have come at point-blank range. Most of the victims were portrayed in several layers of elegant coats, fashionable shoes, and breeches, such fashionable attire that a pre-Revolutionary reader would have no trouble identifying the victims as men of significant affluence, influence, and property. Three additional details suggest that they had not suspected or deserved the fate that had so suddenly befallen them. A woman can be seen in the very center of the crowd; she is easily identifiable by the shawl she tightly clasps around her shoulders, and by her feminine head wrap. Since members of her gender were usually strictly noncombatants in the civilized battles of the era, her presence in harm's way implicitly indicts the unchivalrous behavior of the soldiers. Some of the men who make up the crowd are not even looking in the direction of the soldiers, which suggests that there had been no provocation or any direct threat to the soldiers at the moment of attack. The chief indictment, however, comes from the wholly unexpected presence of a small dog in the extreme foreground of the illustration, his nose touching the center of the drawing and perfectly aligned with the center of a steeple that similarly divides the picture. The docile and even submissive attitude of this animal suggests that the volley had penetrated a rather perfect calm, which would further underscore the innocence of the crowd. He might also be interpreted as a symbol of the people's fidelity, a trust violently betrayed by the shooting.

The article accompanying the engraving describes each wound in gut-wrenching detail, which changes in language and much more graphic portrayals of violence in the popular culture of the twentieth and early twenty-first centuries have rendered almost ludicrous. The altercation began when two men passed a narrow alley where

> a soldier [was] brandishing a broad sword of an uncommon size against the walls out of which he struck fire plentifully. A person of mean countenance armed with a large cudgel bore him company. Edward Archbald admonished Mr. Merchant to take care of the sword, on which the soldier turned round and struck Archbald on the arm, then pushed at Merchant and pierced thro' his cloaths inside the arm close to the armpit and grazed the skin. Merchant then struck the soldier with a short stick he had, and the other person ran to the barrack and bro't with him two soldiers, one armed with a pair of tongs the other with a shovel; he with the tongs pursued Archbald back thro' the alley, collar'd and laid him over the head with the tongs. The noise bro't people together, and John Hicks, a young lad, coming up, knock'd the soldier down, but let him get up again; and more lads gathering, drove them back to the barrack, where the boys stood some time as it were to keep them in.

A cudgel is a short heavy club, frequently used on sporting occasions as a means of enhancing the spectator appeal of what would otherwise be a boxing match (this was an age when bulls were still baited by dogs, and bears could be similarly tortured if taken alive). The fact that a mean rascal armed with such a weapon could so easily be compelled to run to the barracks for help, that a soldier with such an enormous sword could have his blow returned by a short stick, and that soldiers would take up a chase not with bayonet and charged musket but with tongs and a shovel approach a hilarity not surpassed except by "laid him over the head with the tongs." The final irony, that even this enraged warrior could be knocked down by a mere boy, is a touch worthy of Mark Twain.

By this time a dozen soldiers had arrived, still intending to murder people "root and branch." The townspeople were, of course, opposed to this action and hurled snowballs to hinder its execution. The officer ordered the soldiers to fire, and at that point the humor ends in a bloodbath. Each wound is described in excruciating detail; here a ball carried off a portion of man's skull, and there another horribly gored a lung and liver.

Sermons, especially those preaching on the last words of a condemned criminal, were occasionally published as broadsides. Ministers were held in such generally high regard by New Englanders that as a class they came closest to having what twentieth-century marketers would term the power of celebrity endorsement. At a crucial period in colonial history, many of them chose to number themselves among the most vocal opponents of British oppression. Seldom before in America had advocacy for a particular political cause received such an important venue as the pulpits, which still regulated the social life of many towns and villages. The British officers who occupied Boston during the siege were well aware of which side most ministers were taking in the conflict, and they desecrated or destroyed two of the city's more famous churches in retaliation. The spacious Old South Church, in which many prewar meetings had to some extent led to the present crisis, was commandeered for use as a stable and exercise facility for the dragoons' horses, and an ornate pew and other carvings were converted to a pigsty. Still, it fared better than the North Church, which was torn down and consumed as fuel. To the British soldiers, such vengeance may have seemed just retribution against an enemy whose unlawful force against its own army, sent from their homes across the ocean for the colonists' protection, had resulted in the wounding and death of so many of their comrades in arms. As an advertisement of the benefits of remaining a British colony, however, it sent emphatically the wrong message. Religious sentiment remained strong in New England for at least the next two hundred years, and the soldiers' desecration of the churches probably helped convince many formerly neutral people of the righteousness of the Patriot cause.

A good example of an execution broadside is that containing the last words of the pedophile Robert Young; it was printed and sold at the Worcester printing office in 1779. Well-executed engravings for broadsides were a little more common by then than they had been when Revere's engraving permanently preserved the Boston Massacre in the American mind. Such pictures were more common for broadsides than newspapers, because the former did not have strict deadlines. The illustration of the execution reveals much about capital punishment as it was practiced in the colonies. In the foreground on the left side of the scene the body of the condemned man is shown suspended from a beam; next to him a ladder has evidently not yet come to rest after being twisted from under his feet. This method of hanging was more gruesome than the scaffold-

and-trapdoor method because the latter could usually break the criminal's neck, whereas if the ladder was used there was no escaping the slower death from strangulation. Next to the gallows the criminal's casket awaits his body on a two-wheeled cart drawn by an ass; the animal is headed toward the woods that dominate the right side of the scene as if ready to carry the hanged man's body away from the company of men. A rather large crowd has come to witness the spectacle, but their poorly rendered expressions reveal no more emotion than one would expect from a herd of cows. Between the coffin and the wagon an official of some sort, mounted on a horse, has raised his sword; his prominence suggests that the hanging had been conducted by the authority of the state.

A preamble to the text relates that Young was hanged on November 11, 1779, for the rape of Jane Green, age eleven, on September 3 of that year. However painful the few minutes of suffocation that ended the criminal's life may have been, at least the short time between the crime and the execution spared him the years of confinement and false hopes that would plague the men and women condemned by the American judicial system in the twentieth century despite the Constitution's eventual promise of a speedy trial. The argument of his confession was that women had found him irresistible; having become fond of alcohol, he had soon used his winning ways to seduce one after another, usually taking their money to support his life of drunken excess. The regret he expresses for the specific crime that had brought his final punishment is unconvincing; he stated that he had barely used the child. He seems to show little remorse for all the havoc he had created in so many lives throughout his twenty-nine years of self-absorbed life.

If advertising is not simply as the means by which commercial goods or services are offered for sale, it can be argued that the work of the letter-writing committees effectively created a new medium for advertising their ideology. Thus, a series of letters by John Dickinson calling for united resistance against the British was widely circulated among the newspapers of the Atlantic seaboard after their first appearance in the *Philadelphia Chronicle* in 1768. Letter-writing campaigns were remarkably successful in keeping remote colonies informed about the resistance (or subversive, depending upon one's orientation) activities in the earliest stages of the propaganda war. Later they were sometimes used effectively to deter colonial officials, as when a suspected stamp master received a succession of anonymous letters conveying vague threats unless he publicly stated he did not hold that office. Inspired by actions taken in other colonies, South Carolinians were ready when George Saxby, Esq., arrived in Charleston on November 7, 1765; he immediately resigned his commission. His reception must have been similar to that accorded the new stamp master of Savannah. Upon learning that a Mr. Angus had taken up that office, a local Sons of Liberty group met at Machenry's Tavern to consult on the proper measures at "this very alarming and critical juncture." According to the *Georgia Gazette*, they unanimously agreed to wait upon the new stamp master as soon as he arrived. As he was a stranger and unacquainted with the sentiments of the people, he was "desired to resign an office so universally disagreeable to his Majesty's American subjects."

In 1775, Isaiah Thomas began publishing the *Massachusetts Spy* with its qualifying alternative title of *American Oracle of Liberty*. It lived up to its title by devoting its three pages to news from the Continental Congress, including its important economic measures; to speeches favorable to the colonial cause in Parliament; and to lists of such things as the British ships stationed in America, along with their firepower. Few businessmen would be foolish enough to advertise in such a radical paper when the war was only just beginning. Publicly advocating the independence of the country, though discussed everywhere, could still be punished as treason, so the few ads in the early issues were mostly limited to announcements of strayed, stolen, or found livestock.

Since most industries were relatively underdeveloped and money was scarce, self-reliance was often necessary during the first century and a half of the American colonial experience. As a measure of domestic economy, a majority of Americans tried first to grow or make what they needed and only reluctantly bartered their produce or parted with their precious hard cash to procure everything else. A variety of marketing strategies developed to lure customers within range of the merchants who depended upon their ready money. Businessmen and governmental officials were the first to make use of the few advertising opportunities that were available and, in what became a true marketplace of ideas, propagandists on both sides began to avail themselves of many of the same venues used by regular advertisers to get their messages out to the American people.

*The Revolutionary
War Era*

4

Architecture and Design

The most startling thing about the architecture of the American Revolution is that virtually every type of structure constructed since the arrival of the *Mayflower* pilgrims continued in service at some place in the colonies. Moreover, there was no great clamor for urban renewal as would arise in later centuries; structures tended to remain standing until destroyed by fire or other disaster or until they were demolished by their owners to make room for more modern structures. While these tendencies resulted in a wider variety of housing than would later be the case, a countercurrent had arisen as a consequence of the aesthetics acquired by university students through their studies of classical literature and Greek and Roman art. The newest styles of architecture tended to stress planning and balance; such cities as Baltimore, Maryland, and Williamsburg, Virginia, reflected more urban planning than could be found in older cities.

The city fathers of Williamsburg anticipated many late-twentieth-century civic movements in mandating the size of the town's lots, regulating the types of structures that individuals were allowed to erect, and dictating how far they had to be recessed from the streets.[1] New immigrants from Europe and the British and Hessian soldiers ferried across the Atlantic to fight in first the French and Indian War and then in the Revolution were often surprised to find thriving cities, some larger than many of those they had left behind, instead of native forest extending uninterrupted across the continent. As if to signify the colonists' connectedness with the British monarchy, many of the larger public structures erected after the ascension of George III were constructed in a new style collectively known as Georgian; after the Revolution began, larger federal-style and eventually neoclassical buildings were planned whenever individuals or communities had sufficient wealth for such growth despite the economic chaos brought on by the war.

Surviving prints of the streets and waterfronts of New York City, Philadelphia, and Boston during the Revolution reveal remarkably solid structures standing shoulder to shoulder; these row houses sometimes towered three stories above the sidewalks. Philadelphia had already achieved an extensive system of paved streets, which were routinely swept, lit, and patrolled at night thanks to the civic-mindedness of men like Benjamin Franklin. Likewise, many southern plantation masters poured the fruits of the labors of multiple generations into their mansions and estates. Charleston, South Carolina, featured some of the most elaborate and best-appointed homes and one of the richest high-cultural environments on this side of the Atlantic.

Because its virgin forests seemed to promise inexhaustible supplies of timber, most of British America's earliest European structures had been built of wood. On the frontier, settlers still constructed log cabins, but as they became more prosperous and better building materials became available, they sometimes added rooms to their basic four-sided log structures. An increasing population density soon created a demand for finished lumber, and frame houses gradually joined or replaced their more rustic cousins. Nowhere was this more apparent than on the island of Nantucket in Massachusetts, which by 1774 had about 530 houses, framed on the mainland and assembled and plastered locally. Handsomely painted and boarded exteriors called attention to the fact that some of the inhabitants were worth over twenty thousand pounds sterling, wealth they had accumulated from whaling on the open seas. Although built on sandbanks, many of the houses sported cellars of stone.[2]

By the start of the Revolution, some portions of the American colonies had experienced European habitation for over 150 years, and the landscape had been changed repeatedly because of the continual building necessary to meet the housing demands of immigration and natural increase. Wooden structures were very slowly giving way to more expensive buildings of brick and stone, a change in taste sparked in part by perennial and predictable conflagrations that decimated the wooden structures in even the largest cities. Volunteer fire companies had been organized in most urban areas, but their technology did not extend beyond the application of human muscle to apply water from buckets to the base of the flames. Architects and historians as well as the original inhabitants of most surviving eighteenth-century buildings are indebted to Benjamin Franklin's invention of the lightning rod, without which many of the oldest structures would have perished by fire over the centuries. A few less fortunate structures were ruined by cannon fire by one army or another or by naval bombardment. Most of the surviving older structures were eventually demolished in many cities to make room for newer, taller, and more costly buildings.

The near collapse of America's finances during the Revolutionary War slowed the pace of new housing starts and other construction projects even more than did the loss of manpower to the armies. As funding became available, however, Revolutionary leaders who had been steeped in classical literature in their college years and had acquired exposure to the architecture of the great European capitals unveiled their designs for an architecture worthy of the aspirations of the new country. The new nationalism seemed to demand flamboyant advertisement of America's connection with the highest ideals of antiquity. Most of the magnificent governmental buildings erected in the new national period, especially those of Washington, D.C., reflected the new country's allegiance to republican ideals. The important institutions were given buildings inspired by the classical Greek and Roman designs of antiquity. This retrospective revival had the added benefit of reinforcing the educated elite's pride by connecting the colonies with an aesthetic tradition that had anticipated that of the proud but now supplanted British establishment by two thousand years.

WHERE HISTORY HAPPENED

It is important to distinguish between buildings already standing in which some of the most important historical events of the Revolutionary era transpired, those constructed at this time in the nation's history, and those erected in the aftermath of the great events. A study of the first group can reveal much about the immediate surroundings that housed, facilitated, and perhaps even inspired the events of the Revolution, while studying the buildings in the second and third categories can reveal much about the aspirations of the men who made the Revolution happen.

The single most important historical building still surviving from the American Revolution is the State House in Philadelphia, now known as Independence Hall. This is where the Second Continental Congress discussed its options for dealing with the British Parliament and eventually concluded that independence was the best answer. The actual proclamation was read, debated, altered, and ultimately signed here; George Washington was named commander in chief of the Continental Army in the same room. Construction on Independence Hall, destined to become one of the largest buildings in America, began in 1732 and continued until 1747. Today the building has been carefully preserved as a national historical monument; the Liberty Bell hung in the building's bell tower until it was moved to a nearby shrine in 2003. Because the building's symmetry extends to its windows and doors—the same number of openings appear on each side, as though the architect were consciously aiming to

Unlike the small, twisting streets by which some European cities expanded over the course of centuries, many American cities benefited from city planning that permitted broad avenues. Here a contemporary etching shows British troops entering New York City in 1776. Courtesy of the Library of Congress.

achieve numerical balance—it is a good building with which to begin studying the typical aspects of what became known as Georgian architecture. Of course, architects typically draw on the best features of styles they are trying to supplant even as they attempt to create new statements; it has been pointed out that the bell tower combines Baroque and Wrenian elements.[3] However, its large size (it has an impressive square footage relative to other buildings in Philadelphia at the time), expansive yet horizontal symmetry, and formal entrance place it near the start of the Georgian period. Because of the monumental events that it sheltered, the building's lines influenced much of the architecture over the next forty years.

Crèvecoeur's *American Farmer* quoted a newly arrived Scotsman to the effect that Philadelphia was already finer than Greenock and Glasgow;[4] the new State House was not the only structure to merit this praise. Contemporary drawings reveal row upon row of multiple-level dwellings, wall to wall in street after street. In his autobiography, Benjamin Franklin relates how he was instrumental in the fund-raising efforts that added several important public buildings to the Philadelphia cityscape, including a meeting house that eventually held the beginnings of the University of Pennsylvania, and a new hospital. Other important Philadelphia buildings include the City Tavern, which from approximately 1773 to 1790 served as Philadelphia's unofficial social center. It sometimes provided a more relaxed and convivial atmosphere in which congressional delegates could work out compromises on the pressing issues of the day.

The streets of Boston (note the background in Paul Revere's famous engraving of the Boston Massacre) and New York (as in prints of the British Army marching in to take over the city, or the American army's repatriation of the same streets in 1783) were similar to those of Philadelphia in that their row houses suggested the general prosperity of its citizenry. The overall effect of their tall buildings must have been rather claustrophobic to soldiers and travelers who happened upon these cities from relatively undeveloped towns or rural communities on either side of the Atlantic.

Any ranking of the importance of the buildings in which the Revolution was staged is open to debate, but among the most hallowed must be the rough-hewed cabins so hastily thrown up by the American soldiers to house themselves at Valley Forge in the winter of 1777–78. One of the soldiers remembered their dimensions as fourteen by sixteen feet; these huts were constructed in the last half of December from the trees chopped down on the spot, and each housed twelve men.[5] In these blockhouses starvation, disease, exposure, and desertion combined to reduce the Continental Army by one-fourth of its original ten thousand men. Those who survived reported seeing blood in the snow that marked the tracks of ill-clad soldiers through the camp. These men were the victors of the important battles of Trenton and Princeton, bright if limited successes after a series of major defeats. Thomas Paine wrote the first of his *Crisis* pamphlets in the field at Valley Forge, and a Prussian general, the Baron von Steuben, who had attached himself to Washington's staff, here began instilling the discipline that enabled the American soldiers to face the British regulars on an even basis at several subsequent battles.

Like most of the battlefields of the Revolutionary War, the early actions at Lexington and Concord were small enough affairs to be centered on specific points in the landscape. At Lexington Green on April 14, 1774, the British ran into a unit of the local militia and inflicted the first casualties of the Revolutionary War. Ralph Waldo Emerson later did much to preserve Concord's North Bridge in the public memory by commemorating in one of his most popular poems "the shot heard around the world." Its simple architecture belies its stature as the most famous bridge in America during at least the first century and a half of the new nation's history. The overwhelming numbers that the local militia were able to throw into the defense of the bridge against the small company of British soldiers who sought to keep them across the river by destroying it started the overextended regulars on their precipitous flight back to Boston. Today the bridge stands in utter tranquility, surrounded by green pastures and so picturesquely framing the Concord River that it might have been preserved for its beauty even without its historical significance.

It was the heated responses of the Boston radicals that galvanized the colonies' defiance of Parliament, and, fortunately, many of the historic sites in that city have been preserved. The Old North Church in Boston lent its pews to angry debate by rebellious agitators as they drummed up support for resistance to British taxation. Then known as Christ Church, in Salem Street, it is today the oldest church building in Boston, having been built by the Episcopalians in 1723.[6] It was from its tower that lantern beams informed Paul Revere's associates to procure a horse for his famous ride to alert the countryside that the British would be advancing overland to Lexington and Concord. The tower was blown down in an 1805 windstorm but was rebuilt.[7] Such churches frequently doubled as meeting houses throughout the northern colonies, as they were often the only structures large enough to house public assemblies.

A slightly later building, the old Town Hall on Boston's King (now State) Street, also witnessed its share of history. Known today as the Old State House, it was erected in 1748 in the same place and for the same function as two earlier buildings that had burned down.[8] At the time it was the seat of the colonial court, and it was here that John Adams defended the soldiers who fired on a threatening mob during what the Boston propagandists had been quick to name the Boston Massacre. Close by these colonial courts were the Boston Jail, on the south side of Queen (now Court) Street, which once unjustly held accused witches and, later, the notorious William Kidd, an infamous pirate.[9] Yet another outstanding example of Georgian architecture is King's Chapel, a stone building that replaced its wooden predecessor in 1749.[10]

Any discussion of Revolutionary architecture must eventually turn from the sacred to the profane. In 1778, the high ground commanding two critical turns of the vital Hudson River were extensively fortified by the American army; it was crucial to denying access of that strategic corridor to the Royal Navy. The fort at West Point had been so well situated that its supremacy was never challenged by direct enemy assault; it has been in real jeopardy only once in its history. One of the ironies of American history is that the fort was nearly lost due to the treachery of a general who up to that point had been famous as one of the ablest and most trustworthy warriors in the entire American army. In 1780, Major General Benedict Arnold, the hero of Saratoga but a British spy since 1779, attempted to surrender the garrison to the British in exchange for twenty thousand British pounds and a British Army officer's commission.

ARCHITECTURAL DEVELOPMENTS IN THE ERA'S NEW BUILDINGS

Most farmers, Crèvecoeur noted, were more concerned with the situation, size, convenience, and good finishing of their barns than with their houses. He argued that barns were the true indicators of a farmer's prosperity, and he took a farmer's pride in noting that his own barn measured sixty by thirty-five feet while the middle-sized barns were fifty by thirty. One assumes the house would be next in the farmer's heart, but Crèvecoeur argues that a skillful farmer's next concerns are his hog pen, his hen house, his shop and then his corn cribs.[11] As further proof of his priorities, it should be noted that he placed his lightning rod not on his house but on a staff situated between his house and his barn so that it protected both.

A traveler from prosperous Philadelphia could not help but look down on the rudimentary buildings he found in less developed areas. Thus the American soldier Benjamin Mifflin wrote slightingly of the sixty rough wooden houses he found in Charlestown, Pennsylvania, only six of them brick. His list of what the town lacked—a church, courthouse, and jail— reveals much about what he considered the most basic architecture of civilization at the time.[12] He never failed to mention the presence of precisely these three buildings in the other, more prosperous towns he encountered.

At the other extreme were the six thousand buildings already packed into New York City by 1777, some of them six stories high. Built of brick and tile, they sometimes housed forty or fifty people and were covered with wooden shingles painted in a variety of colors. To a German mercenary they seemed splendidly furnished, with expensive mirrors and beautiful portraits.[13] Philadelphia boasted 4,740 brick buildings and fifty thousand inhabitants by 1778; a Hessian invader corroborated the claim in Benjamin Franklin's autobiography that all its streets were paved, swept twice weekly, lit at night, and patrolled by a watch. They were also shaded in summer by an abundance of leafy trees.[14]

A popular building style of the period reminded people of a salt box because of its rectangular lines and sloping roof. Such a building temporarily housed the speaker of Philip Freneau's poem on "The Expedition of Timothy Taurus"; in it he described the inn as no more than a box that might be called a shed. In keeping with the entrepreneurial spirit of the age, the innkeepers in that poem had thrown up a tavern along the way taken by travelers visiting the waterfalls of what later became Paterson, New Jersey. In such inns the customers sometimes represented a living cross section of colonial Americans; Freneau used their diversity to poke fun at Quakers, Jews, pretentiously rich merchants who suffered at being away from their wealth, and proselytizers who bored even their co-religionists.

HOMES OF THE FOUNDING FATHERS

Ostentatious private architecture may have reached its extravagant height in the southern mansion, as the carefully preserved estates of George Washington (Mount Vernon) and Thomas Jefferson (Monticello) attest. Jefferson designed, built, and continually rebuilt his Virginia estate over the course of four decades beginning in 1784; and its domes and Doric columns did much to inspire similar neoclassical architecture in the new federal capital, which was also a postwar development. Monticello is a model of personal efficiency, in that whereas several rooms were devoted to his main interests, the circular interior design of mansion meant that he was never more than a few rooms away from any of them. Its many windows permitted far more light and air to enter than was normal in colonial houses while at the same time offering a variety of enchanting perspectives of his extensive grounds and gardens. It seems the perfect outward expression of Jefferson's vision of the gentleman farmer, a class of independent stewards of the land with whom he hoped the future of the country could safely be entrusted.

Mount Vernon, for its part, is of interest to students of the American Revolution in that it had been in the Washington family for more than a century before the battles of Lexington and Concord. George Washington quadrupled its surrounding acreage and eventually added an additional story, a large dining hall, two extensive wings, and a distinctive cupola— a small, glass-enclosed octagonal lookout perched atop the roof for viewing the countryside in relative comfort in all seasons. The fact that Washington personally designed many of the distinctive features of the mansion underscores the fact that the ideal Revolutionary-era gentleman was something of a Renaissance man, capable of understanding many diverse arts and sciences and applying them to enhance his daily life.

COLONIAL PARKS AND GARDENS

Most grand houses of the time had spacious grounds and elegant gardens, laid out with English formality. The Boston Common, originally forty-five acres purchased by the town in 1634, was a public expression of this deeply held preference.[15] British soldiers drilled here until forced to withdraw from Boston, but before and after their encroachments the Common grazed horses and cattle, and in addition it served many of the same recreational activities that are still seen there.

The private gardens of the Revolutionary generation tended to be based on the English model of spacious lawns and elaborately landscaped and manicured gardens. The more affluent of the southern gentry could stroll in parklike surroundings on their private estates. Many of the buildings of Williamsburg have been preserved or restored to their appearance during the town's service as the colony's capital, from 1699 to 1780. Its planners, however, have gone beyond that to create a prototypical living-history museum. The extensive yards and gardens of the private homes preserved in Colonial Williamsburg reflect that the town had an abundance of wealthy citizens, but it is the colorful personalities, period costumes, and crafts that attract the modern visitor. Of special note are the Governor's Palace and the capitol building. Anyone beginning a study of Revolutionary America should spend at least as much time here as in Boston and Philadelphia. Many questions about colonial construction methods can be answered by closely watching the Williamsburg craftsmen.

FACTORIES AND INDUSTRIES

Despite British proscriptions against colonial manufacturing, there were already breweries and iron works in the Pennsylvania countryside in 1762, when Benjamin Mifflin saw them.[16] Baltimore had but 150 houses in 1762, but they were mostly brick, and another thirty were being constructed that summer. Already three merchant mills were being built within two miles of the town.[17] Near Fredericksburg, Virginia, two iron mills combined to produce up to eight hundred tons of iron sheets or rods each year.[18]

British accounts of the destruction they caused as they marched southward from Canada late in the war are remarkable for the numerous mills destroyed in an attempt to prevent their use by the enemy. Enough buildings were burned on the march to suggest that a regular housing boom was already transforming the region from the pristine wilderness it had so recently been.

If the buildings that survive in Colonial Williamsburg are an accurate indication of the typical plantation system, the southern economy was based on self-sufficient manors in which almost all the means necessary for the production, packaging, and shipment of agricultural products were integrated. The largest of such establishments would naturally benefit from economies of scale that would permit the specialization of labor conducive to the development of superior craftsmanship. Smaller plantations were at a competitive disadvantage in these systems because their workers were forced to divide their time among a wider variety of tasks.

SURVIVING PRIVATE HOMES

Some fortunes had been made in America, and some of the later immigrants brought their European wealth and aesthetic preferences to the design of their homes and businesses. The southern buildings of the Revolutionary era that have been preserved are typically of a high classical style. Pillars and porticos began gracing the homes of the tidewater gentry

Fire was a constant hazard in cities without running water where the predominant building material was wood and meals were cooked over open hearths. Pictured here is a conflagration in New York on September 19, 1776. Courtesy of the Library of Congress.

who could afford them; they were emblematic of established wealth, social ambition, their owners' exposure to classical architecture as a side benefit of a classical education, and the necessity for high, open structures to furnish their own shade and channel whatever breeze might happen their way. Large ballrooms facilitated private dances and other entertainments at the same time that they intimidated the servants and less successful neighbors, conveying a sense of the vast difference in social class that separated them from the obviously special and privileged people who lived in such homes. At the other end of the spectrum were the slaves, whose labor contributed enormously to the economic viability of the plantations but they usually were relegated to small cabins that often had dirt floors.

Just as their colonial assemblies searched the antiquities for alternative forms of government, their architects borrowed heavily on neoclassical precedents to instill a proper sense of grandeur in the loftiest government buildings. Eventually, Washington, D.C., would sport enough of the enormous structures to rival many of the far older European capitals in magnificence.

All architectural structures on both sides of the Atlantic still lacked the indoor plumbing that we take so much for granted in America today. Outhouses, frequently light enough to be dragged over a fresh hole as the old one filled, were an indispensable feature on even the most elegant plantations. At night, chamber pots would catch waste until they could be emptied in daylight, a task frequently delegated to servants or slaves in houses wealthy enough to afford them. Most elaborate bedrooms had pitchers of water and shallow basins in which to wash one's hands and face.

REGIONAL AND TRIBAL VARIATIONS IN INDIAN HOUSING

References are often made to the American Indians as if they were an homogenous people, but they never saw themselves as such until long after the eighteenth century. Prior to the twentieth century, their self-identification rarely stretched beyond the tribe, and wide chasms separated the cultures of the different Indian nations. Nowhere was this more evident than in their architecture. By the late eighteenth century, many eastern tribes had well-established communities with wooden buildings. The *typee*, consisting of buffalo hides stretched across wooden poles, served only the nomadic plains Indians farther to the west. In his travels throughout the southern colonies, William Bartram found the Alachua tribe living in houses. Each of the thirty buildings in their capital city of Cuscowilla was about thirty feet long and twelve feet wide, and featured a kitchen, a common hall, and a bedroom, all with twelve-foot ceilings. Another building of approximately the same size served each house as a storage facility for potatoes and corn; it usually included a second-story loft where the master of the house could rest from the heat or entertain visitors. Both buildings were roofed with cypress bark. Each house had a small garden, but most of the food came from the community's plantation, which was worked in common.[19]

Some of the Indians Bartram encountered on his journey through the southern colonies were settled farmers with individually held fields of beans and corn around their houses.[20] Entering the Cherokee village of Cowe, he found a hundred one-story, three-room cabins made of logs with interlocking notches at their ends and walls plastered with clay and dry grass. The roofs were covered with chestnut bark or broad shingles.[21] At the village center was a council house with a large rotunda. As it had been erected on an ancient artificial mound some twenty feet higher than the surrounding ground, the top of the roof towered some sixty feet overhead. Bartram described the building's posts, walls, pillars, rafters, and cross beams at considerable length. Inside a sequence of steps led down to the musician's places, next to the small fire in the center of the building. Dances and other public festivals were held in the council house almost every night of the year. Another southern tribe, the Muscogulges, commonly built four long oblong buildings into a square enclosing a quarter of an acre.[22] When a couple were wedded according to the customs of their tribe, the entire town labored to create a house for them in a single day.[23]

John Woolman found the Indians living in about forty houses in western Pennsylvania. On average the houses were about thirty feet long and eighteen feet wide, built of split planks, each with one end set in the ground and the other pinned to a plate. Their rafters rested on the plate, and bark covered the roof.[24] That two men as different as Woolman and Bartram would discuss the architectural designs of the houses they encountered demonstrates that familiarity with the construction process was part of the popular culture of the American Revolutionary era. Crèvecoeur may have been close to the truth when he imagined a high level of competence in the carpenters throughout colonial America; he claimed that the meanest of American log houses was dry and comfortable.[25] In a single day about forty people in one instance helped a new immigrant clear about two acres of woods and erect a rude house from twenty-four large logs in Pennsylvania, although a carpenter was hired to roof and floor the building.[26] Community house and barn-raisings and the necessity of maintaining one's own home gave the eighteenth-century American a more thorough understanding of carpentry than their twenty-first century descendents would typically possess.

HOME FURNISHINGS

Just prior to the American Revolution, a family's wealth determined how it furnished its home. The poorest colonists or the most recent pioneers on the underdeveloped frontiers considered themselves fortunate to have roofs over their heads. They slept directly on the floor, sometimes with only a few blankets as padding or covers. Straw or cornhusks could be carried in for additional warmth, and such materials could be sewn into a primitive mattress, as time and cloth permitted. Eventually bird feathers, especially goose down, could be used in the same way.

Bedsprings were not yet available, so the mattress might be raised off the floor, supported by ropes strung across a bed frame and tightened or replaced as needed. The bed might be freestanding or consist of a single leg from which two boards extended at right angles from each other. They each served as a side of the bed, with walls of the house serving as the third and fourth sides. Increasing affluence brought a wider choice of beds, with some of them attaining a four-poster, carved, and engraved elegance that still impresses. Most Americans by 1776 began their days by awaking in beds, but in the less affluent homes the number of people in the household, the individual's place in the birth order, and age could determine how close one slept to the fireplace and how much privacy one was accorded. The fires generally died down during the night, so the luxury of a multitude of blankets was appreciated in the northern colonies. In the South, long white muslin curtains sometimes enveloped the beds, ensuring a modicum of protection against the pestilent mosquitoes of some areas.[27] As a family's prosperity increased, so did the refinement of its home's interior. During the war years, families sometimes hid their silver and precious china to prevent looting, robbery, and private censure for affluence during a time of national crisis.

5

Fashion

As in virtually every major war in American history, popular culture in the Revolutionary era became much more highly politicized than it had been in peacetime. Even one's choice in clothing could have political ramifications, as no one knew better than that master of public appearance Benjamin Franklin. Arriving in Paris in 1776 to develop American interests in France, he donned a decidedly unfashionable beaver hat in a calculated attempt to demonstrate visibly the difference between American and British interests. His unique clothing helped pique French interest; this self-made statesman, already a scientist of international reputation, presented himself as representative of the new America in ways that had nothing to do with his diplomatic credentials. The relatively simple brown suit he sometimes wore to the most fashionable Parisian soirees must have struck his hosts as the height of Quaker simplicity. Since his mission was to borrow money on behalf of the Continental Congress, to talk the representatives of France's own hereditary monarchy into supporting the overthrow of another king, he devised his plain outfit to suggest solid rural virtues. Like the biblical Esther, who was chosen to be queen from among all other women because she dared to appear before the king in durable goods instead of flimsy fabrics, Franklin's success was at least partially a result of his clothes sense.

That Franklin's choices in clothing while he was in France were neither accidental nor the result of an ignorance of Parisian elegance becomes evident as one examines his services as a quasi-ambassador to Britain earlier in his career. As the official representative of several American colonies, he sometimes chose relatively austere outfits from among his several suits of more cosmopolitan clothing, always with an eye toward influencing whatever was the main purpose of his private as well as official visits.

Summoned before a British Privy Council committee in 1774 for what he thought would be an investigation of a royal governor whom he hoped to have removed from office, Franklin chose his clothes carefully to present just the right look. A century and a half before the appearance of *Dress for Success,* and in keeping with his usual practice of letting other people feel that his ideas were their own, Franklin chose a nondescript, somewhat humble suit that visually projected his approach to achieving his personal as well as political aims. So unassuming an appearance—an image of forthright rural virtue undiluted by big-city elegance and sophistication—would help dispel any apprehensions that his personal motives and ambitions were motivating his attacks.

Unfortunately, on that occasion Franklin suddenly found himself in the entirely unexpected position of being asked to answer specific charges of malfeasance of his own as postmaster and to explain the colonial resistance to Parliament's will, for which he was personally blamed. He listened to the solicitor general's insults without interrupting but left the meeting under a cloud of official opprobrium and was soon stripped of his office of postmaster. Having been professionally called to task, publicly humiliated, and addressed in a manner that punctured any illusion that he, although an important man in the colonies, was considered to be on anything like the same level as British peers, Franklin realized the immense distance between England and the colonies, and their seemingly irreconcilable differences. His clothing on that day had, as things turned out, sent precisely the wrong message; it would have been better to show how worldly, prosperous, fashionable, and above all, gentlemanly the colonies had become.

In yet a third area did Franklin make an important fashion statement—he invented designer glasses. More accurately, he invented bifocal lenses, which enabled farsighted people to read through the bottom of their glasses but to shift to the upper half of their lenses to see clearly at a distance. Complete lenses were ground to correct the patients' farsightedness, and then another set was ground to enable them to read. Each of the four lenses was then divided, and half of each nearsighted lens was fitted in an eyeglass frame along with half of a farsighted lens. The line separating the two halves of each lens in a pair of eyeglasses probably struck a first-time observer as a visible crack, but the innovation seemed a godsend to people whose eyesight had faded as they aged. Prior to Franklin's innovation, people who needed bifocals had to chose between reading or seeing the things around them.

IMPORTED FASHIONS

Fashion in America reached new heights prior to the Revolutionary period, when headdresses were added to formal ensembles. Powdered wigs were popular for both men and women. Women's hair owed much of its towering height and volume to a wire frame covered with wool padding, which was then fitted with a wig, powdered, and covered with lace. This "beehive" wig took its name from the conical beehives then widely used for apiaries; only the wealthiest and most class-conscious Americans could afford them. It was also common for prosperous men and their wives to wear ornamental ruffles around their wrists when trying to be fashionable; sometimes ruffles also adorned men's shirtfronts, appearing over the top of their vests.

On formal occasions before the war the richest women wore gowns of silk imported from Europe; the lower half of such dresses was frequently

The abundance of buttons on the men's attire and the elevated wiggery on the very fashionable women represent just two of the ways that fashion could be used to broadcast one's social status. The occasion was the tarring and feathering of Boston tax collector John Malcom on January 25, 1774. Courtesy of the Library of Congress.

suspended from the body by stays and other contrivances. The highest fashion of the age might have been inspired by the life cycle of a butter-fly—or more precisely, the moment when a butterfly emerged. The conical wig extending from a woman's head could give the impression that she was just quitting the cocoon, and the colorful dyes that brought life to the silk of her outer garments could refract and reflect light like the dust on a butterfly's wings. This effect would have been furthered by devices be-neath her dress.

When it came to undergarments, Peter Hulick, a stay maker in New York City, got a head up on his competition by offering his devices via home delivery: "Ladies at any distance may be supplied by sending the length before, and the width round the top and waist."[1] This helped alle-viate whatever concerns his customers may have had about preserving their modesty, but it probably left some women wondering if their cloth-ing was uncomfortable because of improper fit or if it was supposed to hurt. Upon consultation with trusted friends at the ball, they would learn that their complaint was endemic.

A "farthingale," a contrivance consisting of three or four slats of wood, cured, carved, or bent in the form of a half-circle, could be strapped onto one's waist on each side to add width to the hips of a garment. This pro-duced the happy effect of exposing more of the gown's luster or skillful embroidery to view. The upper half of the garment could reveal a some-what bare but powdered bodice (typically more open in the highest so-cial circles than they had been earlier), or even more minutely fashioned embroidery, or colorful silk. Corsets were also skillfully employed to keep up appearances. The mere sight of such beautiful fabrics must have ex-cited flights of fancy in the breasts of any young men who chanced to view them. As they lived in a mercantile age, the wealth required for an entire collection of such gowns would have been a further enticement for any young man who looked to advance in his station in life, as most did. The farthingale could typically more than double a lady's width while flatten-ing and smoothing her natural curvature, resulting in an almost two-dimensional effect. A man had to tread carefully around such protuberances; thus no woman could fail to attract notice, if only as a navigational hazard.

At least three ball gowns from the Revolutionary era have been pre-served by the Smithsonian Museum of American History. The first, a blue one-piece affair, is made of silk and features woven pink, yellow, white, and green pastel flowers. The other two belonged to a minister's wife in New York City, but all three are similar in their slight enhancements of the hips and the raising of the ruffled silk outer layer on the sides or in the back, as though a curtain were being lowered or raised on a theatri-cal stage. Women with ample busts, splendid shoulders, and narrow waists would probably have found these fashions especially flattering. As displayed in the Smithsonian, their lower edges nearly skim the floor, hiding the body from the waist down.

Modesty was the touchstone by which many women chose their everyday clothing in the era, so the layered look was definitely in. Comfort was also essential, but it was not the decisive factor for wealthy women whose work would be done by other hands. Women of all classes put on or removed shawls to regulate their upper-body temperature and used aprons of coarser fabrics to keep their better clothing unsoiled. Undergarments, except those adapted for use with the most fashionable gowns, tended to flatten the bust and broaden the hips. Whalebone had become valuable to the fashion industry; stays fashioned from it could provide strong but lightweight horizontal support for a corset. One of the many downsides of the multiple layers of clothing most women donned during this era was that if it caught fire, perhaps through momentary contact with the flames, sparks, or embers of the open hearth, it could blaze out of control before the problem was even detected by the wearer.

The growing affluence among the mercantile classes before the war made portraiture among them increasingly common. Both the formal portraits and the caricatures of men of substance that found their way into print tended to feature embroidered lace cuffs and shirtfronts. Buttons are everywhere in evidence in these paintings; sometimes they form opposing lines down the front of an ensemble, like opposing lines of infantry; one or more buttons can also be seen serving sentry duty on each sleeve. One early portrait shows no fewer than thirty buttons. Waistcoats were generally worn under the coat—to provide, one suspects, a surface upon which more buttons could be fastened. Often constructed of velvet or satin, the brilliance of these waistcoats must have contributed to an overall effect like that of a male songbird (male robins and many finches, for example, typically have relatively drab feathers elsewhere but brighter breasts). Shoes generally sported buckles in this era, and the richest men saw to it that their shoe buckles were crafted of silver, as were their many buttons. The silver buckles on young ladies' shoes often sported a fake jewel or two, although the long dresses then popular meant that other people rarely saw them in formal situations.

Shortages in manufactured clothing occurred before the war, exacerbated by boycotts and blockades, but they were nothing compared with the wartime shortages. The average wealthy American was more poorly dressed at the end of the war than at its start. In particular, the footwear manufactured in the colonies and pressed into use by the Continental Army was not equal to prolonged marching in all weather. As an economy measure, many soldiers undertook their own shoe as well as clothing repair, with predictably unhappy results. Almost all the journals kept by

American soldiers in the early years of the war mention bloody footprints in the snow.

Prior to the politically mandated boycotts and nonimportation agreements aimed at demonstrating the economic importance of the colonies, most people of wealth and property took pains to publicize their prosperity at every opportunity, especially in their clothing. Among the affluent, exceptions to this general rule were most evident in Philadelphia, where the Quakers always avoided ostentation in their clothing and hairstyles. Among many other religious sects as well, humility remained a cardinal virtue.

WINTER WEAR

An advertisement in *Rivington's Royal New York Gazette* on November 10, 1778, provides some hints about what the fashion-conscious woman might have worn that winter. A furrier (a maker of clothes out of animal hides and furs) advertised his new muffs and tippets, the most elegant of which were of ermine sewn in the newest style, with cloth linings. A muff is a cylinder of animal fur into which one's hands can be slid to keep them warm; they were especially useful when the wearer was likely to remain stationary and not use her hands, such as in an extended ride in an open coach or sleigh. A tippet, also typically made of fur, could be draped over the shoulders like a stole and swung around the front of one's coat for extra warmth or to cover the décolletage of low-cut gowns that gained popularity throughout the era (a function performed in other seasons by a "modesty cloth"). For those thin enough to wear stripes or who wanted to keep up with the fashions without bankruptcy, the same furrier offered ground-squirrel muffs and tippets. The very best export-quality black martin might offer a middle ground between the two.

Working men and women tended to wear leather or cloth hats and as many layers of clothing as necessary to avoid freezing to death as they went about their chores in all weather. Winter was the one season when the usual distinctions in the clothing of various classes had practical consequences. Richer men and women could afford clothing that was warmer as well as more stylish. In an era of natural fibers and fabrics, wool was king; it retained warmth even when wet. For this and other reasons, sheep were a far more precious commodity on colonial farms than they would be in later centuries. For the urban and rural poor who lacked multiple sets of clothing, it was probably better to swelter and itch in woolen garments in the summer than to freeze in lesser fabrics once the snows came.

MILITARY UNIFORMS

By far the most distinctive clothing in America at the time belonged to the infantry of the British Army. Most wore resplendent red uniforms (for which British soldiers had long been known as "redcoats") with black leather accessories, intended to send a bloodcurdling message to any opponent so bold as to take the field against them. Officers, traditionally drawn from the fashion-conscious gentry ranks, were given some latitude

George Washington was very affluent in 1772 when he posed for Charles Willson Peale as the colonel of his old Virginia regiment of the French and Indian War. For his contemporaries, the uniform's multiple layers of fine fabrics, ornamental buttons, and frilled cuff would immediately signal his wealth and prominence. Courtesy of the Library of Congress.

in dress as they progressed up the ranks (sometimes by purchase of advanced commissions). Their clothing choices sometimes had the unforeseen effect of attracting the attention of American marksmen; European soldiers, in contrast, generally were taught not to single out the enemy's officers. (This made tactical sense in any case, as notoriously inaccurate muskets were most effective in close-range volleys aimed at lines or clusters of the enemy. It was usually more important to maintain the discipline in the ranks, so as to achieve faster reloading and simultaneous controlled fire, than to attempt to hit targets as small as single individuals.)

Certain elements of the British Army wore colors besides scarlet. Artillery uniforms were blue, some musicians wore white, and drummers and fifers wore yellow. Cavalry uniforms combined red, green, and white elements.[2] The uniforms of the Continental Army's opponents were made even more diverse by those of the German mercenaries. Some arrived in the uniforms of their separate German states; hence on August 15, 1781, a battalion from Hesse Hanau arrived in New York City in green uniforms with red cuffs and collars, white belts, and laced boots. On the same day, troops from Anhalt Zerbst appeared in white uniforms faced with red, accented by felt caps, boots, and red cloaks. The whole ensemble was unified by red and yellow worsted sashes worn over their belts.[3]

General Washington, in command of the Continental troops that besieged Boston in 1775 and anxious to project an air of authority appropriate to his position, could be seen in a blue coat with buff-colored facings, an epaulette on each shoulder, a buff underdress, and a black cockade in his hat. On that occasion he was within cannon shot of Boston.[4] (Most cannons of the era could not have hit so small a target at any distance, even had the British been aware of his identity and exact location.) In 1780, Washington recommended that officers wear black and white cockades in their hats as a symbol of unity with the French officers, who wore white cockades.[5]

As militia units had served beside the regular British Army since the French and Indian War, a few of the American soldiers entered the Revolutionary War as well equipped as their opponents. At the start of open hostilities, many Patriot militias had uniforms designating their regimental affiliation. One militiaman, John Greenwood, found himself behind enemy lines on a scouting mission in the Canadian woods in a blue and buff coat trimmed with silver lace, clothing he thought uncomfortably conspicuous.[6] As the war went on, however, uniforms wore out, and boots especially took a beating. The clothing shortage was exacerbated by the fact that the colonial army was typically forced to stay in the field, while its opponents were sequestered in towns and cities. In addition to its normal wear, the rebels' clothing suffered irreversible losses whenever their supply wagons carrying uniforms were taken and burned. Many socks and other clothes suffered burn holes when strung up wet around campfires to dry out.

The relative ease with which the British Army could be supplied was reflected in the crispness and regularity of its uniforms, which were replaced every year, whereas most accounts of the rebel forces after 1775 dwell on their haggard appearance. As Burgoyne's army passed by its conquerors in the forests of upstate New York, one of the British soldiers remarked that these were the new men of the new continent—in fighting trim notwithstanding their tailoring.

Indigo, recently introduced as an agricultural crop, yielded a dark blue dye, which was adopted for the official Continental Army's uniforms in the fall of 1779, but new uniforms were rare. Late in the war, the women of Philadelphia contributed to the war effort by personally manufacturing 2,177 shirts and collecting $300,766 in paper currency in donations for the army.[7] The women received praise from Washington himself for their work. Generally, however, the soldiers fought in their own clothing or, far less frequently, that furnished by their state militias. A British Army officer on Long Island in 1776 noted that clothing was the greatest need of the enemy; in fact, he expected the Continental Army to disperse before Christmas because of the cold weather it would face. Many of the rebel slain as the British Army mauled the Continentals defending New York City had had neither shoes nor stockings, and several had worn only linen drawers and a hunting shirt, without proper shirts or waistcoats.[8] It was easy for British officers, country gentlemen with professionally tailored uniforms, to mistake the enemy's tattered dress as emblematic of their lack of fighting spirit. Such wishful thinking led to the useless capture of Philadelphia and to the destruction of the Burgoyne's army at Saratoga in 1777. The former was the largest American city and the seat of the pesky Continental Congress; the British failed to recognize that the decentralized nature of American politics lent their capitol no particular significance in itself. To General Burgoyne it seemed impossible that the countryside could pour out antagonists in such numbers as he met at Saratoga. As they marched out in defeat in October 1777, Burgoyne's infantrymen were surprised by the haphazard, even haggard, attire of the victors.

The French army under the Count de Rochambeau arrived in 1781 in coats of white broadcloth trimmed in green, white shirts and trousers, and two-cornered hats (rather like those made famous by Napoleon twenty-five years later) instead of the American tricornered hat.[9] It is an indication of how effectively they were kept supplied, and of how quickly the fighting ended after they joined the conflict, that the French uniforms stayed in fairly pristine condition at Yorktown, though the French served in the trenches during the siege.

Only after the surrender of Cornwallis in 1781 was the entire American army equipped with new uniforms, brought by the French or taken from British storehouses.[10] Until then, keeping one's clothes in fighting trim had been an unceasing struggle. The journal of one American soldier recorded how he had his shoes taped in Dartmouth for two shillings and mended in Providence seven days later for another ten shillings.[11] Even as late as December 1783, Jeremiah Greenman, now an officer, found that the some of the garrison at Saratoga lacked shoes and stockings despite the severity of the weather.[12]

WORK CLOTHES AND BREECHES

America was so new that most people worked with their hands in one way or another. Aprons were worn by both genders—cloth aprons to protect the fine fabrics of a housekeeper's gown, and heavy leather aprons served blacksmiths, printers, and other craftsmen.

Zippers were not yet available in Revolutionary America, so a man's legs were usually covered by breeches. These resembled trousers, with the important difference that a man first stepped through a waist band and then into his pant legs. The front of the breeches included a flap that extended from the crotch to the waistband, where it would be secured by up to half a dozen buttons. The principle is that of the back flap of a pair of modern "long johns," except that the flap was on the front of colonial breeches. Men of the upper classes tended to prefer breeches that stopped at midcalf or above, accentuating the musculature of the leg and showing off elegant silk stockings. The modern viewer is likely to mistake the short eighteenth-century breeches for juvenile wear or hand-me-downs, as if the founding fathers completely lacked fashion sense or were so poor that they wore trousers long outgrown. Nothing could be farther from the truth.

HOMESPUN

Travelers from Europe in the American colonies before the Revolutionary War frequently commented on the stylishness of the women in cities like Boston, New York, and Charlestown. These women not only had access to European clothiers but could avail themselves of the leading commercial seamstresses. South Carolina produced the finest fabric in the colonies, harvesting its own silk from silkworms that infested the local mulberry trees. Flax was also produced in that colony.

Immediately after the French and Indian War, a general progression of fabrics would have been observable as a traveler ventured west to the far side of the Appalachian Mountains. If inhabitants of cities on the Atlantic coast tended to model their clothing on that of their European peers, frontiersmen supplemented whatever remained of their coastal wardrobes with leather breeches and occasionally deerskin moccasins. At least one countercurrent made a few American materials fashionable in Europe; the international fur trade provided ready markets for most American hides and furs. Beaver hats fashioned from the pelts of the American animals

A few of the satirical cartoonists of Britain had a field day with the American obsession with boycotting tea. In this 1775 drawing, the women of Edenton, North Carolina, appear willing to abandon themselves to every possible sin except the drinking of the infernal beverage. Courtesy of the Library of Congress.

also eventually became popular in Europe, although those on the frontier differed greatly from the beaver hats of London and Paris. By the start of open hostilities in 1775, the clothing worn by most Americans was homespun, which even many colonists who could afford manufactured clothing had adopted to support the prewar boycotts of British imports. These boycotts were first advocated by the rebel propagandists and sanctioned by the local governments, but by 1774 the First Continental Congress had formed an association to enforce its nonimportation agreements.

As the war progressed, blockades by the Royal Navy made acquiring imported fashions even more problematic.

All clothing had to eventually be hand-washed, though personal hygiene was not generally as regular in the eighteenth century as it would later be. Baths were rare; the average man or woman of the age thought water a potentially debilitating substance. Even drinking water was generally suspect; people of all classes generally preferred malted, brewed, distilled, or fermented beverages whenever available at a reasonable price. Anecdotal evidence bears out their fear of as yet unknown waterborne pathogens. Typhus, spread by lice and other small parasites, and various forms of dysentery, spread by what twenty-first-century Americans would consider deplorable standards of cleanliness, contributed to an average life expectancy of less than forty years.

The period clothing and fabrics so carefully preserved over the centuries give a sense of refined elegance that really did not exist for most levels of society. A variety of perfumes and "sachets," little pouches of fragrant flowers or powders, helped mask the scents of most laborers in pre-industrial societies, many of whom worked in close contact with horses and other draft animals. Most people had only a few, perhaps two, changes of clothes, because fabrics were either expensively imported or had to be laboriously made from raw materials. Garments were mended until they could be altered no more; even castoff clothing was sometimes tightly rolled into strips that could be sewn together to form circular rugs. An alternative method of recycling involved rag pickers, men and women who scoured the countryside gathering cloth. Printers were the main industrial consumers of old clothes; recycled cloth could be shredded, bleached white, and used for making paper.

Clothing purchased for slaves who served as field hands tended to be extremely utilitarian. Otherwise, it was created by the same laborious processes used for homespun for any other wearer. House servants might be given finer raiment as an expression of their owners' affluence; such ostentatious display was a way for some American gentry to show they belonged to the elite class.

Prior to the Revolutionary War, a traveler could fathom much about the people he encountered on the basis of their clothing alone. During the war, however, boycotts, blockades, embargoes, and the nearly total collapse of the colonial currency took their toll. By the end of the war, the clothing worn by Americans of all classes had become more closely uniform in material, styling, and craftsmanship than it had ever been or ever would be again.

6

Food

A properly seasoned and knowledgeable frontiersman on the run in the Revolutionary-era northern forests could, if properly motivated, put all thought of food behind him for days on end. John Slover, in 1781, having escaped certain death by just hours by staying awake until the Indians who guarded him fell asleep and working free from the ropes that bound him, finally found seven raspberries to eat four days later. He later remembered weakness but very little hunger. On the fifth day, he caught and consumed two small crawfish, and on the sixth day he made it to an outpost on the Ohio River.[1]

Only over the incautious, the inexpert pioneer whose rambles took him too far afield, the snowbound farmer who failed properly to estimate or provide for his family's needs, the shipwrecked sailor, the ill-provisioned soldiers in the ill-advised attempt to invade Canada, the prisoners of war, or the soldiers of the Continental Army at its Valley Forge winter quarters in 1778, would the specter of starvation hover. The only four survivors of the American frigate *Randolph* lived for four days on rainwater until they were saved from the open sea by the vessel that had sank theirs.[2] Only in the slave quarters of the worst-managed southern plantations or northern farms, or among villages of Indians driven from their traditional hunting grounds was hunger a routine visitor in Revolutionary America.

A typical slave's diet could include cornpone (cornbread baked on a griddle or in hot ashes), grits (boiled cornmeal), and other inexpensive fare that would in time be developed into regional specialties. (Tobacco remained an important cash crop in the South, and the time, energy, and acreage devoted to its cultivation diminished the resources available for subsistence agriculture.) At the other extreme, Thomas Jefferson's well-documented fondness for ice cream and his experiments raising a wide variety of fruits and vegetables, along with the widespread practice of animal husbandry throughout the colonies, suggest a greater variety on the colonial American table than could be found in other parts of the world at the time. Even the simple but wholesome diets of the common man were superior to those of his landless peers in Great Britain. The commodities of tea and tobacco each played an important role in America's war for independence.

By 1776, the extent of the commercial livestock wealth of America was astonishing. On fewer than 160 square miles, the four thousand human inhabitants on the tiny island of Martha's Vineyard, eight miles offshore, supported two thousand cattle and twenty thousand sheep, along with numerous horses and goats.[3] Notwithstanding the widespread success of animal husbandry and other branches of agriculture, however, human nutrition was still largely a mystery in 1776. Without a clear understanding of how the human body digested its food and very little knowledge of the importance of vitamins and minerals, there was little hope that even the best-intentioned wife on the best-provisioned colonial farm could offer what later generations would consider a balanced diet throughout the year.

Many food-related antiques have been preserved from Revolutionary times, ranging from the elegant tableware once used in the richest homes to the spits, andirons, and boiling pots widely used in colonial kitchens. In the wealthiest homes, the silverware was likely to be made from the element that gave it its name. The metal represented a serious financial investment, especially if it was elaborately crafted by skilled silversmiths like Paul Revere. The silver portions of the tableware, including chalices, serving bowls, and candlesticks, were among the first things snatched up by householders fleeing an angry mob or an enemy army. Wealthy people sometimes preserved their finely wrought settings by burying them until the war ended.

Since pre-Revolutionary Americans of the well-established seaboard cities were extremely conscious of their class and place in society, the elegance of their domestic accoutrements was a clear claim to innate nobility in a time and place where notions of hereditary nobility were being broken down by almost universal landownership, general prosperity, and political equality. The necessity of entertaining business associates as well as important travelers was an opportunity to lavish more funds on an elegant table and the most sumptuous dishes than would have been judicious in an earlier generation. Less affluent homes made do with pewter bowls and plates, perhaps because the color of that alloy of tin with copper, antimony, or lead suggested the silver used in the better homes— an affectation that could lead to lead poisoning. The most self-sufficient farmers in frontier areas might carve their place settings out of wood.

Virtually very able person in America spent far more time procuring or preparing food for the family table than would Americans of subsequent centuries, either directly (by cooking, agriculture, hunting, or fishing) or indirectly (by earning the money or creating goods or services to trade for foodstuffs). Few people were so wealthy that they did not have to work for their sustenance, and the temper of the times discouraged indolent lifestyles even for the extremely rich. Households of substance could hire skilled labor to prepare their meals. At the other extreme were the soldiers in the Continental army. Food preparation typically required an open, wood-fueled flame, which turned kitchens into hothouses and fire hazards. Meats and vegetables, where time and affluence permitted, could be stewed together in large iron cooking pots suspended over the fire, but even this method required a skilled hand to keep the contents from burning on the bottom and remaining raw on top. Copper and brass strainers and stirrers offered faster and more uniform cooking as well as the opportunity to brighten a kitchen and celebrate the importance of culinary arts when they were suspended over the hearth or hung on a wall. The affluence of the family dictated the type of wood used in the dinner table's construction as well as its design, and whether the sauces and main dishes were served in imported Delft or Chinese pottery or in lesser vessels.

WILD GAME

One of the cruel surprises awaiting the British Army during the Revolution was the superior marksmanship of the colonial riflemen. Because of the inaccuracy of muskets, British infantry tactics were based on lining up as many soldiers as were available and having them simultaneously fire on order at close range; a bayonet charge after the first or second volley would carry through the enemy's lines, routing them. Colonial arms had typically evolved along different lines, enabling individual hunters to bag game with a single shot at a distance. The time it took to reload such long-barreled weapons was not as important as making the first shot count; some frontiersmen became so proficient that bigger game animals became scarce in their wake.

Sometimes wild game was so abundant that exceptional marksmanship was not required to bring them down, however. Crèvecoeur's American Farmer wrote of flocks of passenger pigeons so numerous that their flights blocked out the sun. Twice a year they migrated past his Pennsylvania farm and, lured by decoys, were trapped in nets. The Farmer's personal record was fourteen dozen birds at one time, and other people trapped or shot much larger quantities. Although their flesh was excellent, the ease of their capture so flooded the market that a single penny might purchase all the pigeons a man could carry.[4] Their sociability was the bird's ultimate undoing, and by 1900 it would be hunted into extinction.

There were probably no American mammals, birds, reptiles, amphibians or fish that did not at some point find their way onto the spits or into the cooking pots of the colonists, and some such experiments were found to be so successful that their unusual meats came to be considered regional delicacies. In *A Concise Account of North America*, Robert Rogers stated that the flesh of the beaver's tail was tastier and more wholesome than any other meat, poultry, or fish.[5] The same writer noted that panther flesh was white like veal.[6]

In 1778 in Philadelphia, though the city was occupied by the British, it was still possible to buy bear and turtle meat. To a Hessian palate, the former was lean and dry, while the latter tasted like chicken, only better. Sea turtles each weighing up to six hundred pounds were imported from the West Indies.[7] Another German soldier noted the abundance of rattlesnakes in the American forests and the eagerness of the English colonists to consume their meat as a delicacy superior in flavor to the best eel. Even General Burgoyne served a soup made from it.[8] In the northern forests, deer and an occasional moose could be surprised and ambushed by an advancing army.[9]

ARMY RATIONS

Eighteenth-century armies considered flour and salted meat, the most common rations, essential war material. Hence, when the British marched to Concord to seize the supplies stockpiled for militia use, they destroyed two cannon, five hundred pounds of cannonballs, and sixty barrels of flour.[10] In the early years of the war the Continental Army consisted of volunteers who willingly took up arms for short periods and of state militia units that had, by rushing to help free Boston from its blockade, more or less placed themselves under congressional authority. The army's greatest weakness was its lack of professional military experience, exacerbated by the short enlistment terms for which most men joined. This weakness was also a source of strength, however. When the main focus of the war shifted from Boston to New York, Congress called upon the states surrounding New York to increase their militias, while most men who had joined the southern militias were still free to follow their ordinary occupations. This meant that the Patriots were not under the financial burden of supporting large armies in fields remote from contact with the enemy, whereas the British were burdened with the logistical nightmare of supplying their marching armies with rations from across the Atlantic that could be supplemented only by local foraging. The vulnerability of their foraging parties, their supply trains while on the march, and cargo ships (which increasingly fell prey to American privateers) exposed the British to many embarrassments. The problem of supply forced General Burgoyne to divert eight hundred men from his army during its march south through New York to their destruction in Vermont in 1777.

As the colonial blockade began squeezing Boston in 1775, the British force there found itself without fresh rations. Sorties were planned to gather cattle from the farms across the river and return to Boston before the militia could respond; Lives were lost on both sides on such livestock raids.[11] Many civilians in the city found themselves reduced to eating horseflesh.[12] Rations, even when plentiful, typically consisted of salted pork or beef and rice or flour, which individual soldiers were frequently required to cook for themselves over the open fires of their camps. This would be supplemented by fresh meat and, less frequently, vegetables, when they could be procured. If posted in the same spot long enough, a few soldiers might plant their own gardens, as did a British garrison in Rhode Island. They could also procure whatever they might loot from gardens they passed on the road; the losses incurred have never been documented but given the nutritional deficiencies of the usual rations in both armies, they must have been substantial. In sharp contrast to the privations endured by the Continental and eventually the southern British Army, the French Army was so well supplied that its troops marched through a succession of orchards on the hottest Virginia days without taking a single peach or other fruit from a tree unless bidden to do so.[13]

The journal of a lieutenant in the British force that began its march south from Canada in 1780 reveals much about the official attitude toward civilian property. Some soldiers and royalists were already occupying the cabin of an old settler and his wife when a canoeist stopped by for refreshment. The newcomer was immediately seized and a deer carcass taken from his canoe and served in the army mess as a ration of fresh meat.[14] On the march into New York, that British army proceeded to burn every house and barn it encountered after first seizing whatever grain it needed for immediate use. Later, a raiding party of a hundred soldiers and their Indian allies destroyed houses and a mill near Ticonderoga, and another detachment was ordered to burn the settlement of Otter Creek.[15]

These adventures were conducted with the aid of the Indians, whose murderous raids in retribution for having themselves been driven from the land were a constant danger to the settlers; it is no wonder that the very hills seemed to breed Continental opposition to Burgoyne's march. It could be argued that the British burned only the homes of known rebels in retaliation for similar attacks by Patriot forces on the homes of loyalists, but this rationalization taken to the extreme would have led to the destruction of every building in America. Similar forays were conducted by entire British corps operating out of New York City in 1777.[16] While the raids brought many cattle and sheep back to camp, they did little to engender support among the inhabitants of New Jersey. On the British march to Philadelphia in 1777 many cattle and tons of grain were taken from the rebels, a label the foragers injudiciously applied to all who lived in the surrounding countryside.

At the beginning of the war, soldiers who enlisted in the Continental Army were expected to bring their own food, which typically consisted of hardtack biscuits, hard cheese, and beef jerky. The army did a relatively good job of supplying them as long as it operated in the Patriot-friendly fields of New England. However, the strain of providing for ten thousand men in the dead of winter broke the system down. The army ran out of rations at Valley Forge in 1778, and some soldiers actually starved to death before the supply problem was solved. The foraging that might have supplemented their rations was severely limited as the colonials, operating in their own countryside, were under strict orders not to alienate the local populace. Since most Americans lived on farms in the period, it must have been especially maddening for the average soldier, sometimes given nothing to eat for up to four days at a time, to reflect on the prior fall's harvest. They must have known that the larders in the surrounding country were full of all the rich varieties of food that could be found in America.

When Jeremiah Greenman joined Benedict Arnold's expedition to secure Canada in 1775, he probably did not foresee the year of hardship and disappointment that awaited him. The expedition found the going much tougher than its planners had imagined, and its men began killing and eating their dogs only a month and a half into the journey.[17] Dog meat, a squirrel's head, and a few candle wicks boiled as a soup provided the next day's supper. Fortunately, the main body finally found the herdsmen tending cattle that their advance party had purchased, and they eagerly bought flour cakes and potatoes from such Indians as they infrequently encountered. Their destination was Quebec, and it was no accident that the first of them to die from hostile fire was buying sheep and flour at the time.

Occasionally, in any campaign, an individual soldier temporarily separated from his unit or returning home on parole or after fulfilling his enlistment might be welcomed into the homes he encountered, especially if the inhabitants had relatives of their own in the Continental Army or an active militia unit. John Greenwood was given a dinner of milk and mush as well as a blanket by the fire in a farmer's home on one such occasion.[18]

Gradually, the success of official foraging parties and personnel changes, most notably the appointment of General Nathanael Greene and other competent men to head the quartermaster corps, alleviated the hunger that had stalked the American army. Occasional American victories in the field and the British Army's less-than-enlightened foraging policies gradually garnered enough support for the Patriot cause that the Continental Army never again faced such pervasive starvation as in the first three months of 1778. Still, it must not be assumed that regular army rations throughout the war ever reached the gourmet level. On their retreat from Canada in 1776, soldiers of four New England regiments were given a pint of flour and a quarter-pound of pork.[19] Each of them cooked his own food over the campfire at noon each day.

When General Greene, reassigned to the southern theatre of the war, was forced to retreat almost continually from the better supplied and more numerous army under General Cornwallis in 1781, his army was rumored to have little more to eat than rice, frogs from ponds or ditches, and sometimes peaches and berries.[20]

Militia members assembled for a punitive raid against the Indians of western Pennsylvania were told to furnish themselves with a horse, a gun, and a month's provisions before their rendezvous forty miles from Fort Pitt on May 20, 1781.[21] Some of the men brought only enough food for five days and thus had to leave the ill-fated expedition before its destruction. Those who persisted soon found themselves in a rout; in the long days of active pursuit or torturous captivity that followed, hunger was the least of their problems.

Although water was generally plentiful in colonial America, drinking water that was known to be safe was much more rarer. Occasionally good sources of fresh water provided opportunities for the soldiers to slake their thirsts, but they preferred grog when it was available. The meager financial resources often gave the Continental Congress the difficult choice of buying weapons and ammunition, paying the soldiers' wages, or procuring food. Whereas the British Army was usually kept well provisioned by sea and could pay in gold, silver, or British pounds for the food requisitioned from private farmers, the Continental Army frequently had to pay with paper money that was essentially just a promise to pay later. Sometimes the soldiers could force the local farmers to accept Continental currency in exchange for their fodder, but it could be extremely difficult to feed thousands of soldiers in the field on a system of foraging and forced requisition.

Things became more difficult for both armies as the British Army shifted its focus to the South. The tidal basins of the coastal states were relatively unproductive or devoted to traditional cash crops like tobacco and indigo. Men, horses, and mules wilted under the strain of forced marches in the hot sun. The situation was exacerbated when, late in the war, both armies pursued a scorched-earth policy and emphasized tactical speed. The food situation turned deadly among the British at Yorktown. Preparing to endure a sustained siege by combined French and American forces, they forced the former slaves who had flocked to their banners to leave their camp. Many of these noncombatants were killed as they rushed across the open ground between the two armies.

Ultimately, though British raids solved tactical problems and local needs, the fecundity of the soil and the ingenuity, industriousness, and scope of American agriculture overwhelmed the British military imagination. Frustrated at their inability to subdue the Colonial army, British commanders began a desultory campaign of wanton destruction of property in the states nearest New York City, burning the cities of Fairfield and Norwalk to the ground. Benedict Arnold, now serving as a British officer in the South, offered to spare Richmond if the city would peaceably surrender its tobacco. When Richmond refused to capitulate on his terms, he burned both the city and its tobacco.[22] Reports of the destruction or capture of entire warehouses filled with food or of hundreds of hogsheads of tobacco must have delighted the British military establishment in England, but these losses represented a small fraction of the agricultural resources the colonies were already generating. Ultimately, their extensive fields and plantations secured the independence of the new country.

REGIONAL VARIATIONS

Outside of the army, and away from the battlefields of the southern tidewaters, the culinary situation was not so desperate. As Crèvecoeur noted, the inhabitants living near the coast tended to feast on fish rather than on flesh, an observation that especially applies to the New England states.[23] Most of the middle colonies had been developed by independent freeholders who prospered without strict governance or religious oppression; tobacco furnished the farmers of Maryland and Virginia with an important cash crop, even as their gentler climate afforded a more varied table than could normally be found along the northern coast. South Carolina planters enjoyed the citrus fruits, rice, and meats grown on their own farms as well as all the tropical fruits and foods that Caribbean traders could bring into Charleston.

In his *Letters from an American Farmer,* Crèvecoeur lauds the sport of bee hunting; he includes precise instructions for following wild bees from back from melted-wax and honey bait back to the hive.[24] Devoting a week to the pursuit after the spring planting, he found up to eleven wild swarms a year. He claims that the western Pennsylvanian ground was so productive that he was not only able to feed his family but to extend hospitality to any number of strangers. Even modern readers are intrigued with his inventories of dried pumpkins, pumpkin pies, pumpkin beer, apples (and apple beer and cider), herds of cattle, sheep, and hogs, and fields of grain. Even his few slaves eat well; he pictures them contentedly gathered round the kitchen stove in the family's home and evidently sharing in the same fodder as the farmer. Some of the northern Indian tribes knew how to tap maple trees in February and March for their sugar, and by 1765 a commercial production of the commodity had begun in the colony of New York.

A vegetable dish called succotash consisted of boiled corn and beans; in some colonies these ingredients would be boiled with bear meat, when available. In 1796, Joel Barlow produced a poem celebrating hasty pudding, including the recipe for its creation: sifted corn flour is stirred into boiling water until it rises and thickens to a paste. The chef continues stirring until all lumps are blended, and the dish is to be served with cold milk while still warm. Sometimes New Englanders would add pumpkin to their pudding, and another popular variation added wheat flour to the hasty pudding recipe, which could then be baked for Johnnycake, or hoecake.[25] Although "Hasty Pudding" was not published until 1796, the blandness of such dishes, which were popular even before the American Revolution, might give the wrong impression about the colonial diet. An abundance of seafood along the coast, plentiful game inland, and widely successful agriculture meant that the colonial diet before the war was richer and more varied as that of the common man in England at the start of the war.

Although not published until long after the Revolutionary War, the first cookbook concerned with uniquely American recipes attests to this variety; in addition to the conventional meats still available in the twenty-first century market—beef, pork, mutton and chicken—the book guided readers through the preparation of game animals such as hares, wild ducks, partridges, geese, turkeys, and even turtles. The list of available vegetables includes potatoes, pumpkins, onions, beets, parsnips, carrots, garlic, asparagus, parsley, radishes, artichokes, horse radish, cucumbers, lettuce, cabbage, cauliflower, nine types of beans, seven types of peas, and seven herbs and spices.[26] The fruits include melons, muskmelons, pears, apples, currants, grapes, mulberries, gooseberries, peaches, apricots, cherries, lemons, plums, raspberries, and blackberries.[27] The author advocated planting an apple tree and grafting a dozen other kinds of fruit trees onto its limbs to supply a family with the variety of an entire orchard.[28] Citrus fruits like pomegranates and oranges were available in South Carolina but tended to spoil before reaching markets any farther north.[29]

Even the sandy island of Nantucket in Massachusetts sported cherry and peach trees.[30] The surrounding ocean furnished the citizens of Nantucket with more than the wealth gained by hunting whales around the world. The tables on the island were often graced with streaked bass, sea bass, black fish, bluefish, cod, mackerel, herring, smelt, perch, shadine, flounder, pike, eel, porpoises, shark, clams, or oysters.[31] Cattle, sheep, and turkeys were raised on the island, and braces of teal, brandts, and sea fowl offered further variety to the tables. Despite all that abundance and the fortunes some made from whaling, however, most Nantuckers died relatively poor because of the expense involved in transporting hay and other mainland crops to their island.[32]

Travelers in Revolutionary times could find themselves exposed to fruits, meats, and other dishes not found in their home colonies. Benjamin Mifflin remembered feasting on Indian Johnnycake and fresh sun perch, which he called "oldwives," at an inn in rural Pennsylvania.[33] A native of a region usually would not write with such obvious relish about foods that were in fact rather common fare.

After the war, a British officer sailed on a packet boat out of Falmouth, Massachusetts. Seeing the success a few Frenchmen were having in a nearby boat, he soon had soldiers baiting their own hooks and hauling up cod from a depth of about two hundred feet. Their rations were supplemented by the freshest fish that night, and the next day they enjoyed a chowder made of fresh fish, salt pork, and biscuit all boiled together.[34] The recipe was popular both before and during the war, when the proper ingredients could be found.

SOUTHERN BARBECUES

To the fields of corn, tomatoes, and potatoes, crops that the Indians had introduced to the Europeans, many colonists and Indian farmers added grains originally imported from Europe. The famous southern barbecue evidently had a long history even prior to the European settlement, as Bartram's travel narrative indicates. A trading caravan he accompanied to the village of the southern Georgia tribes of the Creek nation was regaled with venison stewed with bear's oil. Fresh corn cakes, milk, and hominy added variety, and they drank a mixture of honey, and water.[35] They were treated to barbecued beef when they arrived at the principal Indian town, and three barbecued or broiled bears a few days later.[36] Each successive village seemed bent on bettering the hospitality of the one before. The menu at the White King's farewell banquet would impress even the modern guest: bears' ribs, venison, fish of various varieties, roasted turkeys, corn cakes, and a jelly of China briar sweetened with honey. Hotcakes were made from corn flour cakes or fritters mixed with the jelly.[37] Visiting a white trader and his Indian wife, Bartram was treated to butter, cheese, coffee, and strawberries. Later he learned of the reverence an Indian held for corn as a gift that the Great Spirit had reserved as food for man only.[38] He does not consider how the frequent raids on the corn by deer, raccoons, and even bears could have been reconciled with this belief.

Among affluent southern planters, the simple elegance of roasted meats could be complemented by piquant sauces and superior French and domestic wines and brandies. Cattle, poultry, sheep, and swine could offer a great variety of meat, and experiments were being made with fruits and vegetables to provide those fortunate enough to partake in them with novel dining experiences.

ALCOHOLIC BEVERAGES AND OPIUM

The drinking of alcohol beverages was far more common and socially acceptable in the Revolutionary generation than it would become in subsequent American centuries; Crèvecoeur noted the northern man's love of the cheerful cup.[39] Beer and rum were important commercial products, so prevalent that the Tories slandered the First Continental Congress with the charge that its courage derived exclusively from alcohol. The most affluent colonists could drink Madeira and other expensive imported wines; others had the time to cultivate their own grapes and experiment with their own brews and fermentations. The deeply ingrained self-sufficiency of the average man or woman of that time made them far more competent home-brewers than the amateurs of the current century. Crèvecoeur's American Farmer added water to honey and allowed it to ferment, creating mead.[40] His wife added two gallons of brandy to each barrow of mead to ripen the concoction and make it less sweet, which would otherwise require much longer aging.

During the war, alcohol sometimes played a role in the nation's history. Many people in Boston encouraged soldiers to drink in hopes of inducing them to desert;[41] two British soldiers drank themselves to death on tainted New England rum in early 1775. A colonial army of 3,500 men was once saved from annihilation by a single cake and few glasses of wine. Following the debacle of American arms at New York City in 1776, the British generals occupied themselves with the hospitality offered by a Mrs. Robert Murray, and their dalliance of around two hours enabled the retreating colonials to find and safely march down a side road without opposition.[42]

Travelers on the highway were likely to drink punch or wine with their evening meals at a tavern. Benjamin Mifflin was disappointed if rum toddy was the only beverage an inn could offer. A better-stocked tavern could offer him a sillabub, a popular concoction of either wine or cider with milk.[43] Men everywhere were expected to drink the numerous toasts offered at social occasions. On May 23, 1782, First Lt. Jeremiah Greenman of the Continental Army recorded the thirteen toasts he drank at a dinner put on by the governor of Pennsylvania for the American officers then in the city. Six of the toasts were in honor of the various French royalty and their American alliance.[44] By July 4, 1783, the toasts offered at an officer's dinner in Saratoga varied in content but not in number. They tended toward abstract expressions of goodwill toward all men, especially women, and only once did they drink to the king and people of France.[45]

In South Carolina, two of the popular alcoholic drinks were sangria and sallabul. The former was made of wine, sugar, water, and nutmeg, while sallabul combined wine, sugar, and the freshest cow's milk.[46] Peacock Biggers Distillery was "up and running" in Charlestown, Pennsylvania, before the town even had a church, courthouse, or jail.[47] The average colonist probably agreed with the poet Philip Freneau, whose remarks on the uses of alcoholic spirits note its use in the purification of water.[48]

Following the surrender of Cornwallis in Virginia in 1781, civilians along the route of the captive British army's march sometimes advanced on the prisoners of war and tried to sell them a variety of spirits ranging from punch, cider, and rum to brandy, whiskey, and cognac.[49] They met with fair success until the soldiers ran out of money.

Opium was such a daily habit among the women of Nantucket in Revolutionary times "that they would be at a loss how to live without this indulgence"; Crèvecoeur thought them ready to forgo any necessity other than this luxury.[50] This was a century before the long-term dangers of the drug were realized. It was legal at the time; the Nantucket sheriff, the leading person on the island, was himself addicted to the three grains of opium he had after breakfast every day.[51]

FOOD PRESERVATION

The eighteenth-century diet was far more dependent upon the seasonal availability of fruits and vegetables than would later be the case. Fruits could be dried or canned, and apples and potatoes could sometimes be kept through an entire winter in a fruit cellar. If one or more hogs could be butchered in the fall, their ham could be cured by smoking. Dried beef can add much flavor to a stew and, if properly prepared and stored, remain edible as hardtack or jerky well into the coming year. Fresh fish might be available the year round, if one had the skill and time necessary to catch them, and salted or pickled fish could last as long as other meats. The American Farmer brought a hornet's nest into his parlor; they helped solve his summer fly problem by catching the other insects, even on the eyelids of Crèvecoeur's children.[52] He claims that his family got used to their buzzing.

From Massachusetts to Georgia, summer and fall offered the most variety and the freshest ingredients for the Revolutionary-era table. Not coincidentally, they were also the seasons of plenty among the Native American tribes throughout the region. From November to April or May, how well one ate largely depended upon foresight, culinary skill, and wealth, or that of one's officers or masters. In the eighteenth century, men of property were frequently responsible for providing food for their soldiers, sailors, slaves, indentured servants, or apprentices. Finding fresh ingredients was a never-ending problem for shoppers in an age that lacked electric refrigeration and depended upon horse-drawn vehicles or boats to bring meat and produce to market. Amelia Simmons, the author of the first uniquely American cookbook, devoted considerable space to distinguishing between fresh and stale ingredients. Her best advice was to choose still-living fish "brought flouncing into the market" and eels that can "jump in the pan."[53] The smart shopper sought bright eyes, red gills, and wet tails as signs of freshness in other cases. She warned against the fishmonger's practice of wetting fins and adding animal blood to the gills to fool his customers, practices with potentially deadly health as well as economic consequences.

Salt was often the only widely available means of food preservation, although more efficient homemakers created a variety of jams and jellies to keep fruits. Simple homemade breads could be compounded from wheat or corn and the yeast obtained as a byproduct of brewing beer. Smoking meats could prolong the shelf life of most flesh, and beef could be cut into strips and carefully dried in the sun to produce jerky.

SEA RATIONS AND PRISON FODDER

Sea voyages in the eighteenth century were likely to be long, tedious, and dangerous, and the one thing everyone who survived a transatlantic crossing agreed upon was how bad the food was. Rations of rum or grog might help down the moldy biscuits and hardtack that were standard fare. Even if passengers were fortunate enough to avoid illnesses spread by the close confines of the ships, they were subject to dietary woes that could undermine the fighting capacity of an army. The Count de Rochambeau, for example, estimated that two-thirds of the French sailors and soldiers sent under his command to aid the American cause were hospitalized for scurvy soon after their crossing to Newport, Rhode Island, in 1781.[54]

For the German mercenaries, many of whom, natives of landlocked principalities, had never been at sea before, the rations started bad and got progressively worse until they arrived on American shores. In 1777, one group of Hessians received twenty-eight grams of bread per day, a half-pound of salt beef or pork four days a week, a small allotment of rum, and peas, rice, and flour for the trip from Germany to England. Even on that small leg of their trip the ship's water contained small worms and was already stale.[55] The German soldiers drank a weekly cup of seawater as a purgative and chewed tobacco in hopes of warding off scurvy, a disease later known to be caused by vitamin deficiency.

If it was so immensely difficult to keep one's own soldiers healthy, well fed, and adequately clothed, conditions for their prisoners can be imagined. Jeremiah Greenman, twice a prisoner of the British during the war, saw men, newly released, die after gorging themselves on rich food after having being deprived of adequate nutrition for lengthy periods of time.[56] Following their surrender at Yorktown, Cornwallis's Hessians were marched north across Virginia. Some days they were forced to ford icy rivers and sleep in the open air, but once they were allowed to board with German families. When the prisoners ran out of money, they had to depend on their rations of water, coarse bread, and herring so rotten that it could not be eaten.

It would take a poet to describe the British prison ships in their full horror; unfortunately for himself, Philip Freneau gained the requisite experience. On May 25, 1780, he was on board the *Aurora* on its maiden voyage from Philadelphia when it was taken by the British frigate *Iris*. On June 1 he was transferred to the *Scorpion,* one of four derelict vessels anchored off New York to hold prisoners of war. Freneau's sensitive nature seems to have suffered as much from the condemning looks and harsh words he received from the Tory and Hessian guards as from their threats of physical violence. They frequently brandished their weapons and sometimes cudgeled his fellow prisoners, whom they allowed to burn in the direct sunlight on deck during the day but shackled in the sweltering, damp, pestilent holds in the night. The water was putrid, and the food consisted of moldy bread and rotten pork.

When a dozen other prisoners, including Freneau, became ill, they at first thought themselves fortunate to be transferred to the *Hunter,* a prison hospital ship, but it was as crowded, dirty, and unseaworthy as the other ship had been. At least here the rations improved to a pound of bread and a pound of fresh meat per day, although the later generally consisted of head or shank portions that could be used only for soup. Every other day a cask of spruce beer was also put at their disposal, but even this indulgence was pointless in the face of scurvy or typhus. Freneau thought the food looked like carrion torn from hungry crows, but showing the rotten bones, which he said a Christian would not feed to his dogs, to the captain only brought the rebuke that rebel dogs deserved no better.[57] Freneau was exchanged for a British soldier on July 12, 1780, and was restored to his countrymen.

TEA

Faced with effective American resistance to any taxes Parliament placed on the colonies, Lord North, who became prime minister of England in 1770, had all the taxes (on such things as glass, led, paper, and tea) established by the Townshend Acts repealed except for the tax on tea. It must have seemed a master stroke to the British policy maker, for it kept in place the right of Parliament to tax *something.* Tea was really a luxury, not a necessity, but it contributed to a distinctly British identity. It also served as a reminder of the advantages of remaining linked to the empire, as the commodity originated only in India and the Far East. The beverage was so widely used that even country laborers drank it with their bed-and-

The political crisis soon heated to a boil after the radical Bostonians dumped a ship's consignment of tea into Boston Harbor on December 16, 1773. Courtesy of the Library of Congress.

butter breakfasts in 1762.[58] Everyone would be contributing to the empire every time they drank the taxed substance. Moreover, the revenue would be relatively easy to collect, because in 1773 all official tea distribution had been awarded to a single concern, the East India Company, which as a near monopoly could sell the commodity at prices even the smugglers could not match. The British may have overestimated the popularity of the beverage, but it seems equally likely that they thought any boycotts and public demonstrations against tea were unlikely to boil over into open rebellion. On the other side, the Patriot propagandist Sam Adams also thought that the shiploads of British tea, if they were offloaded and offered as cheaply as planned, would present too great a temptation for the American people.

Only rarely in history does a food commodity take center stage in world events, but this time a standoff ensued. American merchants were unwilling to break the boycott on this, the last British good still taxed, and the royal governor was unwilling to let the luckless ships sail back to England. On December 16, 1773, a mob of protestors painted and dressed in imitation of Mohawk Indian clothing overran the ship and dumped the tea into Boston Harbor. The next morning a farsighted colonist gathered enough of the floating leaves to fill a bottle that, labeled to attest to its place in history, has been preserved in the hands of a private collector to this day.

George Washington continued to drink tea throughout the war, even taking a daily cup during the winter camping at Valley Forge;[59] many other patriotic Americans, however, refused to take a single drop until after the Revolution had been won. For some during the war the very act of drinking tea became an open avowal of Toryism.[60] In North Carolina, some people even tried boiling raspberry leaves instead of tea.[61] Cocoa, coffee, alcoholic beverages of assorted varieties and other drinks gained as the ban on tea decreased the demand for it.

PUBLIC FASTS

The Continental Congress designated July 20, 1775, as a public fast day to invoke divine favor, prevent further bloodshed, and remove afflictions. As a unifying gesture, the simple declaration had the advantages of bringing the national crisis to that most intimate of settings, the private dining room; of helping individuals feel as though by means of a small sacrifice they were part of the resistance movement; and of claiming the moral high ground by showing their subordination to God. On December 11, 1776, at arguably the darkest hour of the Revolution, Congress encouraged the individual states to appoint a day of solemn fasting and humiliation to implore God to forgive their sins and aid in their persecution of the just and necessary war.[62] It was an appeal to religion that the British were unwilling to make.

7

Leisure Activities

Although American life in later centuries was increasingly centered around leisure activities, the typical men and women of the generation that eventually became revered as the "founding fathers" had far less time for their hobbies than their twenty-first-century descendents would have. What little spare time they did enjoy tended to be spent in more productive pastimes than would be the case when television and movies consumed huge chunks of everyone's life, national organizations had codified the rules of a few privileged athletic endeavors, and mass media conveyed major sports news and highlights into the living room at the press of a button.

Before the Revolution, one's station in life tended to determine how one would spend one's leisure. For the cultured elite, the necessity of sharpening social skills to an acceptable level occupied many hours and eventually many years of one's life. There were dance steps for the entire family to learn if they were not to appear awkward and appallingly backward at their richer neighbor's ball, and sometimes hours spent daily on the violin or other musical instrument for entertainment, stress release, and practice before a concert or other performance.

The rising merchant class of the pre-Revolutionary American coastal cities tended to devote their lives to increasing their wealth through speculative ventures that included the importation and sale of manufactured goods from England and, frequently, contraband goods from other countries. What free time and energy they had left could be spent with their families or privately attempting to make up whatever educational deficiencies they felt most lacking in their backgrounds. Drinking and socializing at local taverns had the advantage of contact with business associates; some indulged in these activities chiefly as a way of relieving the stress of their commercial lives. Not all merchants and craftsmen were as diligent or temperate as Benjamin Franklin, but most understood the necessity of making the most of their opportunities in the still-fragile economy.

Leisure as twenty-first-century people understand the term was still far in the future as far as most colonists were concerned. The privileged British nobility, with hereditary estates and proprietary incomes, probably came closest to possessing the time, money, and eclecticism that led to respectable members of subsequent generations to care as passionately about what the colonists would consider frivolous pursuits as they did about their work lives. The industrial revolution was instrumental in this change, but most colonial enterprises were still dependent upon human or animal power and the skill of individual craftsmen. Once the colonists began entertaining arguments about independence, and the British tried a variety of mostly economic sanctions to quell their dissatisfaction, political arguments became a widespread avocation. Once the fighting began, most people turned to a variety of less conspicuous and less costly pursuits, but even religion tended to become politicized. Membership in the Church of England identified one as a Tory, whereas membership in many of the sects that had split from the official church tended to encourage independence in other areas of thought as well.

FREEMASONRY AND OTHER FRATERNAL ORGANIZATIONS

Benjamin Franklin created a few mutual-aid societies, which he called "juntos," among the Philadelphians of his acquaintance. The notion of a secret society that combined the attractions of an exclusive British gentleman's club with public service and self-improvement did not begin with him, however. Freemasonry had already established a strong foothold in America, and Franklin was instrumental in keeping a Freemasonry lodge going in his adopted city. The movement's popularity and national political power probably reached their zenith among such leaders of the Revolutionary generation as George Washington, many of his leading generals, and the men who controlled the American political scene for the fifty years following 1776. Even the self-educated Jeremiah Greenman, commissioned as an officer from the enlisted ranks, joined the Freemasons. The most celebrated colonial martyr of Bunker Hill, Major General Joseph Warren, was exhumed from Breed's Hill in 1776 and placed in a vault beneath a Boston church with full Masonic honors. There was enough interest in the organization that *Rivington's New York Gazette* (November 11, 1773) devoted considerable space to the history of Freemasonry in the time of King Henry VI. Many ambitious young men became Masons as a means of obtaining the business and social contacts that later generations could obtain at exclusive Ivy League colleges.

With the end of the war, many of the American officers felt it would be advantageous to continue the friendships and connections they had established during their service. The Society of Cincinnati took its name from an early Roman senator who set an example by his graceful return to civilian life after a war. George Washington, who had similarly given up the enormous power that had been handed to him by Congress, was elected to serve as its first president, and its first general meeting was held in 1784.

CURATIVE BATHS AND SPURIOUS MEDICATIONS

The spirit of their new Age of Enlightenment, with its easy faith in man's reason and his ability to solve any earthly problem, moved many men to trust in medicine for treatment of their bodily ills with the same faith that their ancestors had invested in their various religions. Unfortunately, medicine was still being practiced at such a primitive level that it often undermined their health as well as their faith.

James Rivington, owner and editor of the *New York Gazette,* not only used his paper to hawk medicinal concoctions but imported whatever instruments the latest medical quackery required. His October 4, 1777, advertisement for a new shipment of manufactured goods included "flesh brushes, designed to animate a dull circulation in the human system." Because there were no governmental regulations, medicines could be concocted from such dangerous substances as mercury or oil. Standard medical practice called for "correcting" the body's chemistry by administering purges to eliminate an excess of bile, or by draining off some of the patient's blood, which could be accomplished by judiciously applying of a knife to a patient's forearm or by placing medicinal leeches on an affected area. Because of the scarcity of medical professionals throughout the colonies, dentists and even barbers were often asked to bleed patients. The death of George Washington in 1799 could be attributed to an overuse of this method; Washington ordered one of his servants to attempt this cure and then a quick succession of doctors prescribed the same approach—bleeding.

By the Revolutionary era, myths arose surrounding the curative effects of bathing at natural spas or waterfalls, and important local industries sprang up to serve the influx of travelers. The water resources of Passaick Village, later Paterson, New Jersey, attracted not only a variety of manufacturing plants but also a horde of vacationers who sought relief from a variety of ailments by bathing in the waterfall, or who merely desired a change of scene. That many of these people availed themselves of the opportunity to bathe more or less unclothed in public led the poet Philip Freneau to comment that the hides of some of the bathers who so publicly revealed their charms were a disgrace to the waves.

In his "Expedition of Timothy Taurus," Freneau described an early forerunner of the colorful nineteenth-century patent medicine man. A Doctor Sangrado, his own health evidently so impaired that he had to waddle about, went among the Passaick Villagers

> . . . with potent and pill,
> And his price was the same, to recover or kill.

Typical of his practice was a prescription of calomel tea and twelve doses of bark as a purge for the son of his landlord, despite the fact that the youth showed no signs of illness that his skeptical parents could discern.

The practice of medicine was not to be taken up lightly, however; a few dedicated professionals struggled manfully against epidemics ranging from smallpox to yellow fever. Outbreaks of typhus, frequently called "putrid fever" at the time because of its symptoms, were common and deadly. The average American died before reaching forty years of age, even aside from the fatalities of the Revolutionary War. Military doctors had to perform all manner of amputations besides treating everything from heat prostration to snakebite, and all of it without knowledge of such modern medical resources as anesthesia, antiseptics, or antibiotics. Serious diseases such as autumnal fevers and "dysenteric complaints," terms used by an attending surgeon's mate at the time, killed a considerable number of the soldiers involved in the siege of Boston even as early as November 1775.[1] At a time when the chief means of preventing the spread of contagious diseases was to isolate the victims and, in the case of smallpox or measles, burn all their clothing after their recovery, for a doctor to care for the patients was deliberately to step into the path of the holocaust, being as vulnerable as everyone else. A vaccine for smallpox had been developed and was gradually gaining acceptance at this time, but thousands of people were still dying from this highly contagious disease as well as from other maladies for which the medicine of the day had no effective remedies.

At the time, serious medicine had to be learned through apprenticeships to other doctors, and the standards of certification were not as rigorous as they would later become. The most challenging medical board a doctor would have to face in America controlled the provincial hospitals. On one occasion, sixteen candidates who applied to practice medicine were given a rigorous examination by doctors who already worked at a provincial hospital, and only ten passed.

BALLS, DANCES, AND PARTIES

Wherever the British occupied a colonial city in sufficient numbers to discourage attack by the rebels, they quickly began trying to replicate the varied and interesting social environments of London. In the absence of professional actors, they organized their own amateur theatricals; even important generals such as John Burgoyne found time to write a play or two. Gala dinners were held on special occasions, and a suitable building was found to house what amounted to a gentleman's club. Even Gen. William Howe, in command of the British expedition, rarely missed social events, plays, or dances in the city.[2] Unlike their behavior in the countryside, where foraging parties sometimes conveniently labeled livestock as rebel property so as to treat it like contraband, the British paid their own way in the cities, and their pounds, shillings, and pence always held their value, unlike the unsupported American dollar of the time. Regardless of their political sympathies, many farmers found themselves shipping forage and other supplies by the wagonload to British-held Philadelphia. The good times persisted in that city, even though it was forcibly occupied by an enemy army from late in 1777 until June 1778.

As first Boston and then New York became the principal military centers of the British establishment; amateur theatricals flourished there, and the clever, handsome, and uniformed young British officers were a welcome presence in many Tory homes. Their pleasant interactions with each city's inhabitants were encouraged by the military hierarchy as a means of maintaining officer morale and of rewarding the remaining inhabitants for their continued loyalty to the crown. Such fraternization also had the theoretical advantages of helping them gauge the attitudes of the American people and of facilitating useful intelligence networks. Unfortunately for the British cause, it led their leaders to misinterpret the goodwill and active support of the people who surrounded them as representative of the attitudes of the American people as a whole, a miscalculation that contributed to their always imagining more active support for their cause than they actually found in the countryside. Their fraternization with civilians also helped the Patriots to spy on them.

In late September 1777, the American army had been unable to stop the British advance into Philadelphia, but the British Army had also been unsuccessful in luring it into a full-scale battle in defense of the city. The British occupation did not have the effect that a similar occupation of an enemy's capital would have had in Europe because the American states were so loosely confederated. Congress simply met elsewhere, first in Lancaster and then in York, and the British Army's cursory contact with the American military during the nine months of their occupation of Philadelphia consisted of easily repulsed feints.

Both armies remained in Pennsylvania until mid-June of 1778, when the surrender of Burgoyne at Saratoga in New York and the colonies' subsequent alliance with France raised the possibility that the British Army could be cut off by a French fleet and encircled by a superior combined French and American force, the same fortuitous combination that was to lead to the surrender of Gen. Charles Cornwallis in Virginia. Howe's army scampered back to the safety of New York City despite General Washington's attempt to end the war with a decisive attack on its extended elements. The fighting would continue for another three years before the colonial victory at Yorktown brought an end to it; Until that time most fads, fashions, and entertainment in the colonies would be severely hampered by a chronic shortage of funds and American sumptuary laws, which discouraged those who had cash from spending it on luxuries.

The American army and its supporters picked up the British tradition of marking public holidays with gun salutes, even lengthening the tribute to a volley for each of its thirteen states. Fireworks were well known and widely used to commemorate public events before the American Revolution. An especially elegant display was launched from the State House lawn in Philadelphia on May 13, 1782, to commemorate news of the birth of the dauphin, the heir apparent to the throne of France, even though the blessed event had actually occurred much earlier.[3] The pyrotechnic displays that have become nearly synonymous with Fourth of July celebrations actually predate the Declaration of Independence. They were already so popular that John Adams readily predicted that the tradition would continue throughout the life of the nation.

RIOTS, MOBS, AND THE BOSTON TEA PARTY

One of the leading fads of the Revolutionary era was the formation of groups to achieve short-term social goals. At one end of this spectrum were "committees of correspondence," which notified other colonies of British transgressions, their own rebellious schemes for fostering political unrest, and the sometimes effective results of their activities. At a time when most colonists viewed themselves as staunchly British, devoting any further loyalty to their particular colonies instead of to British America as a whole, these committees took upon themselves the difficult task of educating the public about the advantages of thinking of themselves as British Americans. Finding common cause with their fellow aristocrats, craftsmen, or merchants, colonists up and down the coast began to conceive the benefits of an exclusively colonial union.

Most of the eventual leaders of the Revolution were men of substantial property, for whom the specter of mob rule, with its spontaneous violence and wanton destruction of property, was the least desirable but most probably outcome of severing the ties with England's civil authority. Direct action could sometimes, unquestionably, yield good results, however; the mere threat of violence was enough to convince most tax collectors to resign their posts, for example, and the Boston Tea Party of December 16, 1773, demonstrated that, properly organized, a sizable number of men could operate within responsible boundaries and demonstrate seemingly irresistible political will. Even the Boston firebrand John Adams was careful to distinguish between a properly organized political gesture and the villainous actions of an unruly mob.

THE BOSTON TRAGEDIES AS "SPECTATOR SPORTS"

The advent of war was sudden at Concord, but virtually the whole of Boston turned out on rooftops and in steeples to view the subsequent British assaults on Bunker Hill. This new and quite diverting pastime probably reached its peak of popularity on the morning of March 5, 1776, when the British prepared to expel Washington's troops from Dorchester Heights, where they had thrown up trenches and emplaced cannon so as to command the city and port. In the words of one eyewitness, "The hills and elevations in this vicinity were covered with spectators to witness deeds of horror."[4] The crowds expected to witness nothing less than the carnage of another Bunker Hill. The time, energy and innovativeness that might have been absorbed in peacetime by fads, games, toys, hobbies, was instead diverted to preparations for the defense; two thousand bandages were prepared, as well as a great number of large barrels filled with stones and sand "to break the ranks and legs" of the assailants.[5]

GAMES AND PASTIMES

Even as the forces that propelled the colonists to take the drastic step of openly rebelling against the crown were approaching the breaking point—indeed, even as open warfare raged in the countryside—numerous colonists continued to focus their attention on the popular games that they had enjoyed during less troubling times. Card playing was so popular in the two armies that orders to curb gambling were occasionally issued. Several sets of improvised dominoes carved by prisoners of war have survived to the twenty-first century.

Card Games

The most popular card game among the leisured class was whist, which required four players, divided into two teams. The object was to take the most "tricks," which were captured by the player who had the highest card among each four. The highest bidder or the person who had won the previous trick led off each round with a strong card, and the others followed suit. The last card dealt determined which suit was trumps. Anyone who seriously wanted to master the rules of the game would probably have considered four shillings for a book like *Hoyle Improved; or the New Maxims for the Game of Whist* a good investment.

Rivaling whist in popularity was quadrille, which required a forty-card deck instead of the usual fifty two. It was commonly thought a game for women or girls, perhaps because modern descriptions of its rules suggest that it placed considerable emphasis upon the relationships among the cards.

Board Games

No less a personage than Benjamin Franklin wrote at least twice on the advantages of playing chess. It should come as no surprise that one of his regular chess-playing acquaintances decided to begin studying Italian at the same time as Franklin, for his enthusiasms were contagious. Because chess was cutting into his time for serious study on a variety of subjects, Franklin continued to play only on the condition that the loser of each game had to memorize a set of grammatical rules or translate a passage from Italian to English, or vice versa. Chess mattered so much to Franklin that he took up his pen in its defense in 1779, a year during which affairs of state would have entirely consumed the concentration of a less energetic man. Chess had fallen under the sumptuary laws encouraged by the Continental Congress and passed by several states as economy measures to meet the financial crisis. Probably prodded by the discrepancies between the official line, which he had helped devise, and his own behavior, Franklin took pains to point out the virtues inculcated by the game.

The popularity of dominoes throughout this period can at least partially be explained by the cheapness of the wood and other materials from which they could be fashioned. Although the game was clearly less strategic than chess, it offered a similar opportunity for friendly rivalry while also affording an evening's entertainment and a chance to converse with one's neighbors and friends.

Toys

A scarcity of manufactured toys forced colonial American children to rely upon their imagination and creativity to a great extent. The luckiest boys received highly crafted wooden toys from their parents and joined their elders or their own peers at dice, dominoes, checkers, and chess— at least in families that did not observe religious strictures against such idle pastimes. It did not take extraordinary skill to carve a top for the enjoyment of young boys. As long as the bottom end was much larger than the other and ended in a point, and the top end was sufficiently long to permit yarn to be wound around it, a skilled player could keep the top spinning. A variation was called "whipping the top"; the object was to keep the top spinning by striking it accurately with the tail of a whip.

A doll could be fashioned for a young girl out of whatever materials were available. Many girls received homemade cloth, corn-husk, or wooden dolls, but the wealthiest children had imported dolls. Enough girls had play houses by 1785 for the Society of Friends to list them in an advisory against foolish and wicked diversions.[6] In one important sense, however, dolls all served as emblems of their owners' birthright and biological identities. A few of the more lucky dolls passed through a succession of relationships with their owners, from surrogate security blanket to confidential friends, finally being preserved as mementos of all the happiness and wonder of young girlhood. Regardless of the materials with which they had been constructed, the luckiest dolls were showered with affection; many were so lovingly preserved that they have survived two centuries. Great care was sometimes taken with their adornment, and some of their dresses provide cultural historians with glimpses into the adult fashions of the era. Samples of their carefully preserved fabrics can sometimes reveal information about the materials then produced for human as well as doll clothing.

All children can imaginatively create their own toys; imaginations in these years had not yet been atrophied by mass-produced action figures or programmed electronic games. The hoop and stick was a popular pastime, providing opportunities for both physical activity and eye-hand coordination. A skilled player used a short stick to keep a hoop upright and correctly oriented as it gained momentum rolling down a gentle slope. Quoits, a forerunner of horseshoes, challenged participants to throw a ring made of twigs or rope over the top of a stick that had been driven into the ground. "Battledore and shuttlecock," a game named for its equipment, was also popular. It resembled a combination of tennis (in that the rackets were framed with heavy wood) and badminton (the players hit a light wood shuttlecock to which feathers had been tied). For an advertisement of an entire shipment of miscellaneous goods in the October 4, 1777, *New York Gazette*, James Rivington advertised battledores and shuttlecocks as "the wholesomest exercise during the winter season." Since use of the heavy rackets would have been calamitous in the crowded confines of most colonial homes, Rivington may have envisioned clearing snow to create playing fields. Children of both genders would occasionally take turns at jumping rope, with girls frequently becoming more adept than boys.

An early biographer of George Washington, Parson Weems, is generally thought to have fabricated or uncritically accepted an account of the future president's taking responsibility for destroying one of his father's cherry trees with a hatchet. What strikes the twenty-first-century reader as least appropriate, however, is the gift of a hatchet for a six-year-old boy. Even Weems inserted an exclamation point after the age at which Washington received the gift. Such gifts speak volumes about how children were perceived in the era, as does their portrayal in adult garb in many portraits.

In the urban areas, some shops sold toys. In a charming letter to a friend written over seventy years after the fact, Benjamin Franklin related his purchase of an overpriced whistle when he was seven years old. The lessons in consumer economics Franklin learned from the incident included the advantages of comparison shopping and of taking the time to consider opportunity costs. The anecdote also provides an instance in which a young child had a small amount of cash in hand, a member of a consumer base still miniscule and readily ignored until the twentieth century.

Many shipments of finished goods brought to the colonies by the transatlantic trade included toys of the latest manufacture, but these fell under the boycott of British goods. Otherwise, children of both genders in families of abundant means might have been able to find one of the wide variety of books of instructions or rules for many of their favorite pastimes.

Hobbies

Enough engraved powder horns, hand-crafted dominoes, and other work survives from the Revolutionary era to suggest that carving was a popular pastime. Novel materials were sometimes pressed into service when no others were available; several sets of dominoes carved from the cattle bones given in a prisoner of war camp still exist in private collections.

Among the most costly diversions available in the colonies was horseracing, which offered older, richer gentlemen farmers a chance to keep their competitive fires stoked long after they had outgrown more direct combat. The procurement, training, breeding, and general management of the sometimes magnificent horses required such attention that absorption in their care transcended the brief excitement they provided as they flew past on race days. Races also provided employment for a lucky few race-day officials and opportunities for gaming and other amusements for the masses.

Rural Sports

As they lived long before the invention of basketball, football, or baseball, and since much of their energy was expended in subsistence farming or housekeeping, rural youth of either gender had few opportunities for organized sports.

When entire families gathered to help a new frontier neighbor raise a house or barn, the event took on a festive atmosphere. The children tested their strength, speed, and stamina in unofficial wrestling matches or footraces. A few of very courageous, hardy, or simply foolhardy northern frontier youths might try their mettle in lacrosse with the Iroquois, when the prospect of trade brought Indian youth into a white settlement. Several contemporary books mentioned an activity called "baseball," but most refer to a Native American variation more closely akin to lacrosse. The British also introduced cricket and fox hunting. Fencing manuals also promised introductory lessons in that sport.

By the Revolutionary War, hunting rifles had been so perfected that they could be used in marksmanship contests. The rustic origins and traditions of the sport were still preserved in the prize offerings; in some contests, "turkey shoots," the winner won a live bird. Elsewhere a wily captive turkey cock would be positioned so that only his head would occasionally appear in view, as the mark at which the sharpshooters were to aim. This more literal form of turkey shooting added elements of timing and luck to the marksman's other concerns and reminded both contestants and spectators why hunting is called a "blood sport." During their occupation of Philadelphia, a few British officers diverted themselves with shooting trips to nearby areas.[7] In 1778, two doctors assigned to a military hospital wagered on which was the better shot. Both missed their intended target three times, but one of their errant shots killed a general's horse, for which they had to pay $150.[8]

Other blood sports included hunting, fishing, prizefighting, and cockfighting. Although a few states tried to eliminate the third and fourth items on this list, their regulations regarding the first two were mainly aimed at preserving the game so that the sport and the natural resource could be sustained. Winter activities included ice skating and snowball fights.

Hunting and fishing were seasonal diversions for many rural boys once their chores were done; the recent French and Indian Wars imbued the local woods everywhere with an aura of danger that was in normal times really only present on the frontier. Swimming in lakes and ponds offered quick relief from the summer heat and, occasionally, the ambiance and camaraderie that would be found in the saunas and pools of the better men's clubs in later generations. This diversion carried the terrible risk of drowning, however, since another 150 years would pass before formal swimming lessons and lifeguard training were widely available. Many were the days begun with the highest spirits that were doomed to end in an abyss of bottomless anguish as unforeseen depths, unexpected currents, physical exhaustion or inappropriate pranks took their toll.

Urban Sports

In the towns, wrestling matches and foot races could also be observed among youth, and sometimes grown men, when a holiday provided opportunities. Many men of fortune sought the fleeting fame that superb carriages or race horses could bring them, sometimes pitting their stock in informal competition against those of their peers. Gambling on the game of skittles or ninepins, a precursor to the modern sport of bowling, was so prevalent among the troops captured with Burgoyne that he issued an order forbidding it.[9] In April, 1782, a Continental officer remembered passing a Saturday morning playing wicket ball, which might have been similar to either modern cricket or croquet.[10]

It is doubtful, however, that many grown men had the time to play such games on a regular basis at this point in American history. There were no collegiate sports and no sports organized nationally at any level. Many aspects of colonial life were so poorly developed that much of the spare time of the increasingly skilled craftsmen was spent in devising better approaches to the problems of their trade, and many women found their days consumed by the endless cycle of tasks needed to maintain their families. Moments that could be spared for leisure activities were far less abundant than they would later become, and were probably treasured all the more for that reason.

EXTRAVAGANT EUROPEAN FASHIONS AND SILVER PLATE

Before the war, residents of Boston, Philadelphia, New York, and Charlestown dressed so fashionably that some newcomers thought their clothing surpassed that of European nobility. Advertisements in the major newspapers reveal an astonishing variety of fabrics and materials, even white ostrich feathers for ladies' riding hats.[11] As the rebels began clamoring for independence, however, Americans began resisting English tastes in clothes and donning cheaper fabrics of domestic manufacture, as both an economic and political response to the crisis.

As the security situation deteriorated, colonists wealthy enough to afford silver plate and place settings began hiding them. Despite these precautions, on March 22, 1780, the Hessians conducted a quick raid into New Jersey to loot and burn Hackensack. They stole numerous silver pocket watches and spoons, as well as much silver plate and fine linen and other clothing, but they had to discard much of the loot when the countryside rose against them the next day.[12] Conspicuous consumption, so necessary to the pre-Revolutionary gentry as the mark of the nobility, was a wartime hazard to be minimized.

8

Literature

With luck, a visitor to an American stationer or printer prior to the American Revolution would find a small assortment of books offered for sale. Such a customer would be unlikely to ask for the fiction section of this very limited bookstore unless he was a recent arrival from England, where such sentimental novels as Samuel Richardson's *Pamela* (1740) and *Clarissa* (1748) and Henry Fielding's picaresque *Tom Jones* (1749) were instrumental in creating an audience for such book-length fiction. The few shelves allotted to books in an American shop were unlikely to contain even these three titles, but if one of the novels was in stock, it could have been either ferried across the seas or printed in the colonies. In either case, it would have been expensive.

There were as yet no American novelists or even writers who were producing what they would proudly proclaim as "fiction." Creative writing was still not a profession from which an American could derive a living. Toward the end of his life, Philip Freneau, the best American poet of his generation, attacked in "To a New England Poet" (1823) the unfortunate fact that America had not yet gotten to the point where it could support its writers:

Though skilled in Latin and in Greek,
And earning fifty cents a week
Such knowledge, and the income, too,
Should teach you better what to do.

Some of the poignancy of the poem arises from the fact that its speaker might have been chastising the author. From a very young age Freneau had dedicated his life to poetry, but he found a readier market for his political satires than for less topical subjects. Financial frustrations had reduced him to teaching school as a recent college graduate for the paltry sum mentioned in his poem despite all his education and aesthetic knowledge. Although his material circumstances improved with the patronage attendant upon Thomas Jefferson's assumption of the presidency, fifty years of the general public's neglect of his verse forced him to admit that he would have been financially better off to have devoted himself to a different muse or to have sold out to British interests and plied his trade in a country with more appreciation for its authors and that paid them better.

Before the Revolution, the university-trained American colonists preferred neoclassical balance in most art forms, and this was especially true in the realm of poetry. Judging from their output, it would appear that most colonial poets felt that they had to challenge their European rivals by writing on the same themes in traditional forms. This put aspiring American writers at a tremendous disadvantage, and their work thus seems more derivative than the potential richness of the new American materials would seem to have promised. For most colonists, there were still far more immediate physical challenges to overcome before they had the leisure and inclination to attempt artistic expression in any but the folk arts. As lasting political independence was not assured until the British surrender at Yorktown in 1781, most Americans were unable to make use of opportunities for social and economic advancement thrust upon them. Only after the war could undisrupted merchant shipping return general prosperity to the Atlantic coast, and it was not until Alexander Hamilton's policies were adopted in the 1790s that the American government was able to restore value to the American dollar. Consequently, most American writers were slow in developing the talent and their reading public to realize fully the value of experimentation with new, uniquely American subjects and forms.

It would be difficult to choose a single piece of writing to represent the Revolutionary era. Thomas Paine's *The American Crisis* would not be a bad choice, although it might be considered too exclusively military in its appeal. While the first two paragraphs of the Declaration of Independence admirably sum up the noblest sentiments then current about the rights of man, the rest of the document is a self-serving and often distorting indictment of the excesses of the king. The best choice would probably be Benjamin Franklin's *Autobiography*, with its celebrations of the limitless potential of the individual American unfettered by class, religion, or political oppression. Usually, however, the privileged Americans, especially those who had spent their formative years in the cultural richness of European capitals, keenly felt the inadequacy of their training and the comparative paucity of material in their agrarian backwaters.

By the end of the American Revolution, the American reading public was eager for a new national literature that could help them find answers to the question posed by the French writer Crèvecoeur in his *Letters from an American Farmer* (1782): Who is this new man, this new American? It would take another seventy-five years and a civil war before a complete answer could be discovered, but already market forces were at work that would create a growing demand for American voices. These voices were most clearly heard in the numerous political pamphlets that were cheaply printed and widely disseminated during the twenty years after the French and Indian War and throughout the first half-century of the new republic.

The fledgling republic offered a host of new political offices and innumerable other opportunities for advancement, and many of the newly important men, responding to the same impulses that led such important citizens to preserve their images in formal portraiture, took steps to preserve their ideas. As a result of the democratic spirit engendered by the Revolution, they began keeping journals and eventually writing their autobiographies. The phenomenon was so pervasive that their output can be considered the first aesthetic fruits of independence. In discovering their rights under the new government, ordinary people also discovered their worth

THE IMPORTANCE OF BOOKS

The average educated members of the Revolutionary-era gentry, merchant, and professional craftsmen classes were more literate and more dependent upon their literacy to learn how to do things than their twenty-first-century descendents would be. Books were published on a wide variety of practical subjects. When Benjamin Franklin wanted to learn to swim, study French or mathematics, or develop a few primitive practical electrical experiments, he found a book on each subject. When Henry Knox wanted to learn how to become an artillery officer, he read a book, eventually becoming proficient enough to make major contributions to the American war effort. Books could provide an introduction to almost any trade, or at least enough direction to support innovative and self-sufficient colonial craftsmen. Sometimes a single volume promised instruction in curing practically all diseases afflicting farm animals. Because horses routinely served as both draft and transport animals and a few were groomed for the race course, more books were devoted to their care than to that of any other animal. William Burdon's guide to keeping a horse fit over great distances came out in at least four editions between 1734 and 1778. Prior to the war, if the necessary books were not available, a growing number of university graduates were becoming available to write them. The effect of the printed word becomes apparent in the rapid propagation of the lightning rod and the Franklin stove; they were widely published, and soon many homes throughout the colonies possessed the devices. Franklin also tried to perfect human nature by developing the system for self-improvement that makes his *Autobiography* the first in the uniquely American genre of secular self-help books.

Americans who lived in Boston, Philadelphia or Charleston frequently encountered literature in their local newspapers, which sometimes printed poems and essays gleaned from other newspapers or from books. Most such work was published anonymously, a tradition that had real value once the temper of the times forced circumspection even among writers and printers without political agendas. The magazine was coming onto its own in America; Franklin and other printers had created an audience for it with the miscellaneous articles that began appearing in their almanacs. The *Tatler* and the *Spectator* in England were already demonstrating what a highly literate journal could mean to England, but colonial entrepreneurs and editors produced only a few such magazines with very short life spans before the end of the Revolutionary War.

Aside from chance exposure to literature in newspapers and magazines, however, the average rural American had very little opportunity to read much beyond the family Bible, perhaps an almanac, and a few political pamphlets. Most educated men kept a few books. Some private libraries grew to be quite extensive; Thomas Jefferson's personal collection eventually served as the nucleus of the Library of Congress. Benjamin Franklin borrowed books from acquaintances until he became rich enough to afford his own, and his innovation of the lending library provided an opportunity to read in large cities. Most universities also had libraries, where exposure to the world's great thinkers helped add the polish that distinguished their graduates from other men.

AUTOBIOGRAPHIES

The American colonies had begun producing a few of their own great men, and the autobiographies of this select company attracted international interest. Franklin's *Autobiography* is arguably the outstanding literary achievement of the era. Its rags-to-riches tale is timeless in its appeal and decidedly American in its approach. Although such success stories subsequently became a genre in American letters, no one ever did it quite so well as Franklin. The prose of his autobiography would merit lasting attention even if he had not played such important roles in American history. To focus on just three, he turned a profit for the British government as postmaster general of the northern colonies. He also became the colonies' chief representative in Great Britain before they became independent, and he served as American ambassador to France with panache and ultimate success that probably no other American political leader could have matched. It has often been observed that his signature is the only one that appears on all the principal political documents that came out of the Revolution: the Declaration of Independence, the treaty with France that made American victory possible, the Treaty of Paris that ended the war, and the Constitution, which preserved its gains. The *Autobiography* does not even cover the last forty-five years of his life, including his efforts in the Continental Congresses and the new American government, but focuses on his early years of preparation.

Part of the charm of his text lies in its multiple layers; innumerable threads of narrative are tied together by the strength of his personality, his evident goodwill, and his eagerness to achieve a philosophical unity between his ends and his chosen means. The *Autobiography* includes a love story that had to overcome the complication that his eventual wife was already married; she could not obtain a divorce because no one knew where to find her wayward spouse.

No matter to what manner of business the young Franklin turned his hand, it was almost certain that it would make money. He was so successful as a printer that he was soon entrusted with printing the colony's money. He was excellent as a shopkeeper and extraordinary in his work for many benevolent civic improvements, most of which began as his own ideas. He provides invaluable advice on how to become a writer, demonstrating the excellence of his own method even as he explains his program for self-improvement in this craft. Franklin first became internationally famous as a scientist, and the autobiography reveals how he acquired his apparatus and devised some of his groundbreaking experiments with electricity. Best of all, however, is his program for self-improvement in general; he is humble enough (or affects to be) to believe that other people can follow his system. His self-promotion, aggressive mercantilism, and boosterism is tempered with self-effacing humor. Franklin's entire self-improvement model was predicated on exercising nearly complete self-control. The crowning conclusion to his list of thirteen virtues aimed at fostering his own humility, which, paradoxically, he intended to achieve by imitating Jesus and Socrates. His willingness to admit errors in his life and the steps he undertook to atone for them lends an extraordinary aura of honesty to the work.

A book with such earnest assertions lends itself to charges of smugness, and Franklin's autobiography has had its share of critics. The best negative (and humorous) response was penned by the twentieth-century writer D. H. Lawrence in his *Studies in Classic American Literature*. Caricaturing Dr. Franklin as an old gray nag who happily stands in a small fenced pasture of his own creation instead of recognizing and acting upon his stronger impulses, Lawrence reveals more about himself than about his predecessor. Franklin's *Autobiography* conveys the optimism of its age, its belief in the perfectibility of man and reliance on human reason. His main point, however, is that the life of a commoner can be at least as interesting as that of someone of noble or royal birth. Our views of eighteenth-century American life would have been vastly different if Franklin had not seized a rare interval of relative idleness to begin penning his memoirs in 1771.

Other remarkable achievements with autobiographical materials that appeared during the Revolutionary era include John Woolman's *Journals,* which appeared in 1774, and St. John de Crèvecoeur's *Letters from an American Farmer.* The former chronicles the painful process by which a dyed-in-the-wool Quaker attempts to reconcile his spiritual life with the inequities of the world and his own baser instincts. Like Franklin's *Autobiography,* Woolman's journal begins with the facts of his nativity; Woolman's account of his youth included dalliances with wanton company, although the temptations that the young Quaker resisted seem of less moment to modern readers than they did to him. In many respects, Woolman's childhood journey was the opposite of Franklin's. While Franklin put much stake in always appearing sober and industrious in order to preserve his business reputation and community standing despite occasional and private errors, Woolman secretly attended to his religious faith while publicly associating with youth who did not share it. Although Woolman was preserved from what he considered the serious sin of profanity or other scandalous conduct, he felt his indiscretions terribly. It was a dark moment when he killed a robin with a stone and, upon discovering her now doomed nestlings, proceeded to kill them to prevent their more prolonged suffering and inevitable death by starvation. About with a serious illness prompted his return to religion, amid promises to God never to sin again. His health restored, Woolman gradually slid back into his old ways, however, and it was not until he turned eighteen that he felt the true weight of his iniquity and truly reformed his behavior.

Typical of Woolman's soul-searching integrity as an adult are his self-doubts. As an example, although he felt called to travel to share his testaments to God, he considered the possibility that he was really motivated by personal vanity. He was also tortured by doubts as to whether his calling justified leaving his wife.

Similar doubts arose because of his opposition to slavery. Asked by his employer to write a bill of sale for a Negro woman, Woolman acquiesced from motives of loyalty. Troubled, he subsequently expressed his opposition to slavery and later refused to help a friend with a similar bill of sale. However, he realized that other men did not share this view. He was silenced by his sect's belief in the primacy of individual insight and by his sense of decorum—because his criticism would be directed at his hosts as he traveled among them. In 1754, at the age of thirty-four, Woolman published a pamphlet, "Considerations on the Keeping of Negroes," in hopes of winning other adherents to his views. The entire narrative of his

Journals reveals a unique blend of intelligence and sensitivity, and the process by which he came to oppose slavery publicly closely parallels the mental path traveled by Mark Twain's fictional Huckleberry Finn a hundred years later.

Woolman also wrote against abuse of the Indians, criticizing the traders who sold them rum despite being aware of its effects, and those who cheated and defrauded them in bargaining for their furs. He was most out of step with his time in criticizing land speculation, especially when the practice was predicated on defrauding the Indians who lived on it.

Crèvecoeur's *Letters from an American Farmer* is interesting for its insights into the daily life of a northern farm family, but equally valuable is its French author's appreciation of the aesthetics of the agrarian ideal. His letter on the frontier woman, however, is too maudlin for most modern tastes. Its narrator is a Tory who laments having joined with Indians to raid frontier houses. As propaganda, the letter seems directly aimed at its French readers, who still vacillated on the question of French alliance with America in its war for independence.

The *Letters* are the most consciously literary of any autobiographical text of the Revolutionary era. In the introductory letter, Crèvecoeur feigns a reluctance to write that only his minister can help him overcome, and then only with the understanding that his correspondent will make allowances for his lack of education. They end with the narrator's planning to take up life among the Indians, where he hopes his family will be spared the horrors of the Revolutionary War.

ECLECTIC TASTES OF THE READING PUBLIC

Many men who rose to positions of authority in the army during the war wanted to make good use of the opportunities of which they had so recently become aware. The most intelligent among them prepared themselves for success in government, industry, or at sea after the war ended. They tried by extensive reading to make up for their lack of preparation and polish that can come with a formal education. There were few guides available for navigating the veritable sea of books and, especially, pamphlets that, thanks to the Enlightenment's shift from religious to secular literature, began to appear.

The books mentioned in the journal of John Greenwood can be taken as typical of the path such men might choose. Greenwood came to the army with little formal education and was commissioned on the basis of his performance in the field as a private soldier. The religious history, tradition, and culture of New England was such that anyone born in Newport, Rhode Island, like Greenwood was likely to begin his adult reading with the Bible. After that, the eagerness with which he devoured George Whitefield's journal can readily be imagined. By virtue of his dynamic style of preaching, Whitefield had almost single-handedly created the Great Awakening, an evangelistic Christian movement that swept the country during the 1740s. His journal not only whetted young Greenwood's appetite for his own wartime travels but reinforced his religious values.

The literary works or historical studies that found their way into newspapers of the era were often of such remoteness that a modern reader wonders how an eighteenth-century editor could have found them. Sometimes worthy work of a decidedly literary bent would make its way into print, such as the excerpts from Dr. Smollet's *Travels through France and Italy*, which appeared in the *Georgia Gazette* on November 12, 1766. Since comedy appeals to the intellect, it should come as no surprise that an age proudly calling itself the Enlightenment would embrace various types of humor.

SATIRES GREAT AND SMALL

The satirical bent of the most popular British plays of the mid-eighteenth century had some influence on the popular response to the American Revolution. An anonymous letter to the *Providence Gazette* published on August 25, 1764, early revealed how deeply the Stamp Act alienated the colonists. The writer posed as a confused Englishman who, not realizing exactly what the language of the act meant, imagined it referred to the branding of colonial animals. Drifting off to sleep, he dreamed a parable in which all the livestock were rounded up and the asses were the first to be branded. They submitted, but the horses ran off, leaving the writer to surmise that only asses will stand still to be branded.

The satires that were popular in England at this time, most famously in the work of Jonathan Swift, spawned a whole tribe of American imitators. Most literate Americans were keenly aware of the British satirical tradition and quickly seized on that tool in the propaganda war that led to the Revolution. This is most easily seen in the dramas they eventually wrote, but their responses to the Stamp Act were even more immediate and biting. The vitriol aroused by this hated legislation helped prepare the Harvard Wits for their successful satires, an approach that increased in popularity after the Revolution.

One of the most interesting political poems of the era is John Trumbull's *M'Fingal*, a satire aimed at the Tories of Boston and their faith in British arms. The first two cantos appeared in 1775; the rest did not appear until 1782. Since authors lacked copyright protection, thirty different postwar pirated versions appeared, a large enough number to suggest that the work is as inspiring as a work of art as it was effective as propaganda.[1] M'Fingal is a Tory who plots his revenge after being forced to renounce his beliefs at a Liberty pole. Despite his blustering as loudly as Shakespeare's Falstaff, his schemes are doomed to failure. The modern reader is likely to be more aghast at the physical punishment inflicted on M'Fingal than appalled by his counter-revolutionary efforts.

POLITICAL PAMPHLETS

One important result of the French and Indian War was that the British colonists began to recognize that they had more in common with their neighboring colonies than with the mother country. For a dozen years before the start of the Revolutionary War, graduates of several American universities increasingly celebrated the potential of the new continent. Much of the best creative efforts of the colonial writers went into such propaganda, and their arguments gradually led to pamphlets arguing for greater independence from Great Britain. The propagandists' first task was to alert the colonists to the injustices they were suffering, and Samuel Adams and John Dickinson took the lead. Such pamphleteers for the Revolution easily found popular support for even their most radical suggestions because the political blunders of the colonial administration frequently had an adverse economic impact on entire colonies.

The anarchy that sometimes prevailed before the war frightened the founding fathers. They saw to it that even the Declaration of Independence has its conservative clause: "Prudence, indeed, will dictate that governments long established should not be changed for light and transient causes." Pamphleteers on both sides continued propagandizing throughout the Revolution, but eight years of war had a tendency to remove or sober even the most dangerous men.

The best of the patriot pamphleteers during the Revolution was Thomas Paine; his *Common Sense,* which sold 120,000 copies in the first three months of 1776, was instrumental in garnering widespread popular support for independence. His essential argument was that England was too small to rule an entire continent and so American independence was inevitable. Freedom would come cheaper earlier than later, and 1776 would be the perfect time. Paine wrote the early numbers of *The Crisis,* his second series of pamphlets, as a common soldier in Washington's army during its bleakest winter. Appropriately, he used a drumhead as a desk. His most brilliant rhetorical flourishes called for dedication and sacrifice, disdaining the "sunshine patriots" who would desert the cause in its darkest hour.

Newspapers sometimes provided an important venue for serious writers to develop their talent and display their wit; editorials sometimes rivaled the broadsides in their revolutionary (or counter-revolutionary) fervor. Occasionally their propagandistic efforts resulted in ribald humor, as when the *Philadelphia Packet* of August 29, 1778, chastised certain Tory ladies for "their late fondness for British debaucheries and macaronis."[2] The reference is to the most common verse of "Yankee Doodle," in which the Yankee hero sticks a feather in his hat and calls it macaroni—period slang for the eccentric fashions adopted by the foppish young men of England in imitation of the popular, flamboyant Italian styles.

Aside from broadsides and pamphlets of a political nature, America offered little chance for a professional writer to survive on literary efforts alone. Few if any American novels were being written, and none were being published; the professional theatres, which had thrived on British plays and were not yet outlets for American writers, were closed during the war. Paper became increasingly scarce as the war progressed. Further, the absence of copyright laws meant that virtually the entire proud tradition of British literature could be reprinted by American publishers without fee; American writers were essentially asked to compete with Shakespeare and Milton, but without hope of financial reward. In his *Autobiography* Benjamin Franklin related how his father warned him against devoting himself to a literary life, which the elder Franklin thought would lead to dissipation, dishonor, and inevitable destitution. These unfortunate circumstances were not to change for at least fifty years after the signing of the Declaration of Independence.

An important source for the era's pamphlets were the ministers and priests of the various religious sects, who were not slow to encourage their charges to flock to the war. A favorite text was "Cursed by he that keepeth back his sword from blood."[3] Many ministers permitted their churches to serve for political gatherings; it was in retribution for this that General Howe turned the Old South meeting house into a riding school and used some of its pews in a hog pen. The most popular politically based sermons were frequently printed off as pamphlets.

POETRY

Literate Americans of the Revolutionary era were frequently exposed to poetry, much of it anonymously published in newspapers. The age produced two talented and dedicated poets, Philip Freneau and Phyllis Wheatley, but newspapers frequently let lesser poets slip into print, especially if they celebrated rustic values. The best of these poems typically had a humorous thrust, like "The Tobacco Sot," which appeared in the *Pennsylvania Evening Post* on October 28, 1775:

Slap Jack, a dry consumptive smoking sot,
Whole months with weed is always glowing hot,
Where shall I go, alas, when Death shall come?

And with his raw bon'd clutches seal my doom?
Faith, replies Tom, there can no heaven be,
Without tobacco, for such sots as thee;
Nor need you fear a hell when you expire,
You deal so much on earth with smoke and fire.

Poets who were able to write without payment could count on a limited audience in the more interesting colonial newspapers and magazines, especially if they dealt with recent events and fitted their work into the neoclassical forms then monopolizing the literary marketplace.

Philip Freneau

Few of his contemporaries were as gifted as the poet Philip Freneau in exposing humorously the foibles of his countrymen before the war, and in celebrating the new nation even while its fate was still uncertain. A Princeton graduate, he briefly served the cause of American independence, first as a soldier and then as a seaman/smuggler. He was captured and confined for six weeks on a British prison ship in New York. Following his release in a prisoner exchange, he began writing for a Philadelphia newspaper, the *Freeman's Journal*, the beginning of his newspaper work, which culminated in his founding of the *National Gazette*, an important voice for a decentralized, Jeffersonian democracy.

The topicality and vehemence of Freneau's Revolutionary War poetry is striking; in the early (1775) poem "A Political Litany," he attacks (in lines 9 and 10) the

pirates sent out by command of the king
To murder and plunder, but never to swing.

For most of his writing career, Freneau needed a political targets upon which to vent his spleen. He was consistently democratic in orientation; he actively attacked the Tories in his college verse, the king and his minions during the Revolution, and thereafter centrists who sought to strengthen the national government at the expense of individual rights. In his generation, he came closest to the background of diverse experience that the nineteenth-century poets Ralph Waldo Emerson and Walt Whitman would think indispensable for their ideal American poet. After receiving an excellent collegiate education, he labored unhappily as a teacher, then more successfully as a sea captain in trade between the American coastal cities and the Caribbean Islands. As an editor, his work was more erudite and polished than that of most of his contemporaries. As a social commentator, his views were typically filtered through the lens of committed party politics.

As a poet, Freneau can be viewed as a transitional figure. His earliest surviving poems, fraught with stylish encomiums to Cynthia and other Roman figures, echo the neoclassical vogue that he picked up in his university courses. As interest grew in contemporary events, he was among the first to write poetry that sustained itself on purely American events and images. Thus in an early poem, "The Midnight Consultations" (1775), the British generals are more likely to consider their soldiers transported by Charon to the Stygian shore than merely to lie dead in the retreat from Concord or on the slopes of Breed's Hill. Soon, however, his poems contained fewer images or other content that could not have been furnished by the American landscape.

As a poet/propagandist of the Revolution, Freneau frequently used dramatic monologue, soliloquy, or imagined dialogues to unfairly blacken the reputations of British generals or statesmen. However his political assertions strike us today, they carried weight in an eighteenth century wedded to the literal truth of religious texts and with few sources of news. They reveal more about the biases and prejudices of his society than about the personalities he is supposedly revealing. His militantly Protestant audience, reading "General Gage's Confession" (1775), would probably have been most aghast at the speaker's Catholicism. A few might have also been disturbed by Gage's imagined communion with the spirit world, and many would have been amused at the general's being more troubled about ordering his men to steal sheep than about commanding them to kill other men. Freneau's most interesting poem is probably "The British Prison Ship," his account of the harrowing capture of an American vessel following its fight with a British ship and his subsequent incarceration as a prisoner of war.

Phillis Wheatley

The early work of Phillis Wheatley was an exception to general rule that a formal education was necessary to become a renowned poet in eighteenth-century America. Brought from Africa as a six-year-old slave, Wheatley had the extreme good fortune to land in a progressive Boston family. They nurtured her prodigious growth in language and sold subscriptions to enough of their friends to pay for the publishing of her first book of poetry. This was a tremendous boon; few other American books of poetry were being published under any circumstances.

Her work is predictably domestic; she not only shared the limited professional horizons of most women of her time but as a slave had absolutely no choice in the matter. Her most famous poems convert the theological arguments of an evangelistic Christianity into verse; the speaker of "On Being Brought from Africa to America" is not openly antagonistic toward the system that stripped her from her parents' arms and left her at the mercy of strangers a world away. Resigned to her faith, the speaker takes solace in the opportunity for Christian salvation that she likely would not have had if her childhood been less traumatic.

Wheatley's other poems in her first published collection suggest a satisfaction with her plight that undoubtedly won her many supporters among her benefactors. Perhaps the greatest trauma of Phillis Wheatley's adult life came as a result of her poetry, however. Perhaps her next volume of poetry would have been much better than the first; it definitely would have been longer. Unable to find a publisher or sufficient subscribers to pay for it, however, she burned her manuscripts in frustration. Her action is a bitterly eloquent statement about the barriers keeping American writers from supporting themselves with their literary work alone.

THE SLAVERY DEBATE

Debates over the abominable institution of slavery permeated the literature of the period. The most powerful religious objections came from the Society of Friends, popularly known as the Quakers, which early brought the weight of their entire sect to bear on the question. During the Revolutionary era, however, the abolitionists among Quakers formed the "still, small voice" of conscience; unfortunately, the circumspect nature of their faith sometimes led them to be less vociferous than the cause merited, and the question of independence from England tended to push all unrelated political and social issues from the stage. This was especially true if the issue in question had the potential to sever permanently the tentative union between the southern and northern colonies. Nevertheless, the arguments that individual Quaker leaders such as John Woolman began forming were to furnish the Civil War generation with the moral ammunition it would eventually need to settle the compelling issue of its day. Many of the leading founding fathers did what they could to set an example for the nation. Benjamin Franklin, for instance, eventually led the American Abolitionist Society, and his last words to be printed in his lifetime were against slavery. George Washington set many of his slaves free in his will. Thomas Jefferson tried to attack slavery in the Declaration of Independence, but these passages had to be dropped before the delegates from the southern colonies would sign the document.

Many writers tried to cast the issue in dramatic terms, but much of the resulting literature was overwrought. No less a writer than de Crèvecoeur overextended himself in depicting the plight of a rebellious slave being tortured for killing the overseer of a plantation. In his ninth letter from an American Farmer, Crèvecoeur claims to have found a slave suspended in a cage in which he was being consumed alive by birds and insects. While the injuries inflicted upon individual slaves were often brutal and sometimes deadly, this supposedly eyewitness account may leave the modern reader questioning what birds so eager to prey upon human flesh can be found in South Carolina. Crèvecoeur was more effective in contrasting the obvious wealth of Charleston with the abject poverty and coerced labor of the slaves at the base of the pyramid of which the affluent lawyers, planters and merchants formed the apex.

9

Music

Tastes in Revolutionary-era American music were as varied as one might expect among three million people from such diverse backgrounds. When Thomas Paine argued that all Europe, not just England, was the father of America, he understated the case. In music, rival rhythms from three continents enhanced life in southern manor houses and among the educated elite of the northern colonies, in the fields of the plantations, and in the deepest, wildest woods. Among the European colonists, the audiences ranged from the extremely sophisticated patrician classes on the eastern seaboard, where wealth brought contact with the highest achievements of European culture, to the untrained family ensembles of the frontier, where one was unlikely to hear the latest piano sonatas or Haydn string quartets that were elsewhere in vogue. The emotional scale of American music ranged from the reveries induced by the solemn hymns of a dozen religious denominations to the intense passion evidenced in the spirituals of the slave cabins and in the tribal songs of the various Indian tribes, and to the profane chanteys of the sailors on their vessels and in the coastal taverns they frequented. Charleston, South Carolina, already supported a professional orchestra, and the Moravians of Pennsylvania had their own musical college and amateur performers and composers, whose talents could approach those of the European peers.

AMERICAN INDIAN DANCES

In the slave quarters, on the frontiers, and in the Indian camps, music and dancing were typically informal affairs. Colonists were often at a loss trying to understand the songs and dances of the American Indians. Staid old Benjamin Franklin, in so many ways the Ideal American, could not interpret or appreciate the finer points of the celebrations of the Indian who gathered to negotiate a treaty of peace with the Pennsylvanians. The most hilarious moment in American dance must have come when Indian leaders woke Franklin and his delegation in the middle of the night in hopes of obtaining the wherewithal to continue their drunken reverie. In 1777, an army doctor was similarly unimpressed with the drinking and dancing following a treaty between the Iroquois confederation and Gen. Philip Schuyler. The dancers were colorfully dressed, painted their faces and hair red, white, and black, and wore little bells on their ankles that jingled as they danced to a small drum covered with a skin. The most memorable aspect of the scene for James Thacher was the rum that the Indians consumed, and that left many of them still drunk the next morning.[1]

In the South, the experience of William Bartram was similar. He once watched as an entire community of Creek Indians turned out to dance the night away in their town square. He made no mention of their drunkenness; apparently the renewal of normal relations with the white traders sufficiently elevated their spirits without artificial aid.[2] Later he watched an entire Cherokee Indian village turn out for a festival on the eve of an important ball game against another village, an evening that began with fiery oratory designed "to influence the passions of the young men present, excite them to emulation, and inspire them with ambition."[3] In Bartram's description, the proceedings sound like a combination homecoming rally and victory dance. A company of girls in clean white robes, beads, bracelets, and ribbons sang, accompanied by both instrumental and vocal music. For fifteen minutes they moved in two semicircles, until a war whoop signaled the entrance of the male dancers. Well dressed, painted, and ornamented with plumes, silver bracelets, gorgets, and wampum on their moccasins, the men rotated in a semicircle around that of the girls with precise steps and motions that Bartram thought required great attention and perseverance. Every other man gently rocked up on his toes while those on either side lowered themselves upon their heels, and their circle continued to rotate in a complex manner. At preset times they changed direction or switched positions with remarkable alertness and address, accompanied by a shrill whoop. At other times, the men danced with a variety of gesticulations and capers, some of them, in Bartram's words, "innocent and diverting enough," others emulating battle or the chase for game, or reenacting some tribal tragedy. All the dances were theatrical, and they were interrupted by comic and sometimes lascivious interludes. The women conducted themselves with becoming grace and decency, veiling themselves in amorous passages.

On the other hand, twice he witnessed the power that drink held over even these favored people. Encountering a small party of warriors returning from a successful hunt, Bartram's party was offered a fawn skin filled with honey; in return, the traders treated the Indians to liquor. His comment that the Indians entertained the white men during the night with their drum, flutes, and gourd rattle was without apparent irony.[4] Later he watched the most "ludicrous bacchanalian scenes" after a war party of forty Seminoles traded a herd of raided horses for a hundred gallons of liquor in five-gallon kegs but denied themselves a single drink before returning to the town with their prizes. For ten days white and red men and women frolicked together until the liquor dried up, leaving the Indians willing to pawn even their last possessions for a final drink to settle their stomachs.[5] Their next thought was to raid their Choctaw neighbors for the express purpose of raising more money; they set about negotiating with the traders to finance the expedition with loans for blankets, shirts, and other necessities. Many of the southern tribes, including the Choctaws, Chicasaws, and Muscogugles, made stipulations in their treaties with the colonial governments that alcohol was not to be sold in their towns.[6]

Before the disastrous effects of European alcohol could turn their ceremonies into bacchanalias, however, American Indian songs and dances perpetuated all other aspects of their culture. Some Indian tribes ascribed supernatural power to the acts of singing and dancing, and prolonged continuation of either or both might transport a performer into mystical realms that were unattainable by other means. Singing a particular song might put an Indian in contact with his ancestors, providing a warrior with inspiration from the immortalized exploits of his predecessors or reducing his fear of death by means of communication with the spirit world. Inability to write down lyrics, notate melodies, or in any other way to record music, kept the songs from being preserved or widely adopted outside tribal enclaves, however. In addition, the disruptions of tribal culture caused by alcoholism and other diseases resulting from exposure to European civilization eventually reduced the influence of most Native American music along the Atlantic shore to its immediate audience. The echoes of Native American music eventually died away, having made almost no impact on the musical heritage of the dominant culture.

AFRICAN AND AMERICAN SLAVE DANCING

Among many of the African tribes from whom the future slaves had been stolen, singing and dancing had historical as well as cultural and religious functions. The wisdom of generations of tribal life reverberated in their traditional songs, sometimes filling the night air to the accompaniment of percussion instruments so sophisticated as sometimes to convey actual human words. Skilled practitioners of "talking drums" to this day converse across long distances by beating out patterns that replicate human speech. Songs and dances provided ample opportunity for preserving and conveying cultural identity through traditional rhythms while at the same time facilitating individual expression. The overwhelming, transcendent nature of the experience was only possible if the entire tribe lent its support, training dancers to express themselves from their earliest experience of the traditional dances. Sometimes the entire tribe danced to a single drummer, or to several drummers performing synchronously.

The slaves hauled in chains to the New World were sometimes brought on deck and forced to dance in an attempt to keep them healthy. Stripped of its cultural significance, African dance wilted in the tropical heat. Misappropriated as a means of maintaining the dancers' bodies in marketable trim, dance fell from its pillar as the most sublime assertion of freedom to become a tool of their enslavement. The former spirit of the African dance, dependent upon the entire tribe's participation and one of their chief cultural bonds, could not survive the voyage because freedom had been at its core.

The Africans would typically be torn away from even those tribesmen who had been transported across the Atlantic with them when they were sold in the slave markets, and on the plantations they could be brought to the point of exhaustion under the watchful eyes of guards jealous of any vestige of cultural continuity that might undermine their authority. However, dance still provided one of the few opportunities for the oppressed people to transcend their bondage. Many Africans managed to preserve some strained continuity with their old dance communities. Above all, their love of dance and song were instrumental in forming a new, decidedly American identity among the slaves. Forced to adopt English by their need to communicate with slaves from other tribes as well as with their oppressors, they added another dimension to the language of the Revolution, with its enlightened arguments about liberty and the natural rights of men. Music could still set them free even as the plantation hierarchy tried to control its scope.

It would take time, even centuries, for the worlds of music and dance to appreciate fully the newer, uniquely American forms that sprang from the free African in American chains, but the new music would owe much to the passions and rhythms of the African music tradition. An important early example of the influence of the crossover from the plantation experience to the stage was Charles Dibdin's *The Padlock*, an opera that had its American debut in 1769.[7] It featured a role for a black performer, but the part was given to an Englishman in makeup, establishing a theatrical tradition that persisted until the twentieth century. This musical apartheid kept black musicians from reaching a wider audience and tended to relegate American music as a whole to the production of pale imitations of European compositions.

RELIGIOUS MUSIC

On Sundays, religious music reigned supreme throughout the colonies. Church choirs proved an important training ground for many American singers throughout the eighteenth century, and even die-hard Puritan communities slowly accepted music in the church. Services for most other sects routinely included singing and, occasionally, organ music; church organs gradually paved the way for other musical instruments. Worthy of special note is the organ of twenty-six stops built for New York's Trinity Parish in 1740.[8] Church bells had heralded great events, mourned the passing of parishioners, and announced Sunday services since the second half of the seventeenth century in New England, but the first chimes, a series of bells of varied size upon which tunes could be played, were imported from Gloucester, England, for Boston's Christ Church in 1744.[9]

By the Revolutionary era, musicians were still writing hymns, but many composers as well as singers were no longer constrained by piety. Nevertheless, the decidedly religious bent of *The New England Psalm Singer*, the first book of exclusively American songs to appear in the colonies, was evident even in its title.[10] Published in 1770, the volume includes hymns with tunes named in honor of churches of the Boston area; hence "Old South" and "Old North" take their places beside hymns like "Massachusetts." The principal artistic force behind the text was William Billings, a twenty-four-year-old native Bostonian (about whom more below) who devoted his life to music. He would publish *The New England Psalm Singer* and five other books of songs after it; the strength of the secular trend in music is evident in *The Psalm Singer's Amusement*, his 1781 title that suggests a frivolity that would have outraged the earliest New England colonists.

THE IMPORTATION OF MUSICAL INSTRUMENTS

The eighteenth-century household was typically dependent upon the individual talents of its members for musical entertainment. Those who had sufficient income and leisure could become quite proficient on their instruments. The love of music was so widespread that the delegates to the Continental Congresses would not have to look far to work up their own orchestra. Thomas Jefferson was an excellent violinist, and Benjamin Franklin invented a new instrument, the "armonica," to harness the sometimes eerie sounds produced by friction on cut glass. Although the level of talent is certain to have varied widely, some of the best musicians could render perfectly the European sheet music that was often available in coastal areas. While true American musical independence would have to wait for later centuries, music played a very important role in everyday life in the colonies.

Every popular musical instrument in Europe made an appearance somewhere in the American colonies, but the portability of the fiddle, drum, and fife helped ensure their wide distribution. The richest coastal homes could even have their harpsichords or spinets (small upright pianos). Pianofortes (an Italian word since shortened to piano) were manufactured in New England prior to the Revolutionary War. The first American-made violin was manufactured in Worcester, Massachusetts in 1776.[11]

On October 1, 1768, two regiments of British regulars paraded into Boston with fixed bayonets and full-dress uniforms; they introduced the colonists to bassoons, oboes, and French horns.[12] The dulcimer, spinet, and violin were also fairly well known on this side of the Atlantic, and Philadelphia's first music store included guitars, mandolins, clavichords, and flutes, and offered lessons on instruments as diverse as the cello and the French horn. An in-house scribe copied scores for anyone wanting to purchase only a single copy of a particular song instead of an entire book. To Giovanni Gualdo, the proprietor of the shop, goes the honor of introducing the clarinet on the Philadelphia concert stage in 1770, at a time when it was still rarely played even in Europe.[13] In a musical dictionary printed in the front of *The Singing Master's Assistant* (1778), Billings mentions the harp, harpsichord, lute, and organ, a suggestion that they were already present on American soil in substantial numbers. A steady market arose in the manor houses for teachers to train the inhabitants, especially children, in voice or instruments; music teachers sometimes roamed abroad in hopes of finding suitable patrons. Others hoped to capitalize on the public demand for secular as well as church music by opening their own singing and sometimes dancing schools.

SOCIAL DANCING

Social dancing was popular in New England throughout the period, often accompanied by itinerant fiddlers and whatever local talent was available. The first dance book published in the United States was *A Collection of the Newest and Most Fashionable Country Dances and Cotillions, by John Griffith of Providence, Rhode Island* in 1788. It was followed by *The Dance Instructor*, by W. J. Keene of New Hampshire, two years later. Although these volumes appeared long after the last shots had been fired, earlier references suggest that the same dances were performed during the Revolutionary War. From such sources, we learn that line dances were especially popular. The process by which a succession of couples assumed the leading, most active role, with everyone getting an equal opportunity, demonstrates a democratic impulse that was also making itself felt in most other aspects of American social life at the time.

In Philadelphia, dances and concerts were held in a warehouse prior to the opening of the spacious City Tavern early in 1773.[14] Such festivities were immensely popular in that city despite the Quaker majority's sanctions against dancing. The Methodist Church also prohibited dancing for its members, but the popularity of music among the cultural elite throughout the colonies provided a strong inducement for colonists of all backgrounds to savor the newest European sonatas as well as their own musical heritage.

Prior to the Revolution, dances were sometimes held in the mansions of the southern plantations. An evening's music often began with minuets, short pieces that allowed a succession of couples to exhibit quietly graceful dance sequences. The tone of the evening would gradually shift to more active music, frequently culminating in reels (the Virginia Reel is typical) and jigs. Country squires and their families might surprise and delight the urban graduates of dancing schools when they showed up at balls fully practiced in the latest steps. In many cases, they had been trained in private by itinerant dancing masters.

Throughout his life, no less a personage than George Washington was highly valued as a dance partner. Statuesque, handsome, vital, and well trained in the required movements, possessing a country squire's eye for expressive tailoring, and gallantly deferring to his partners, General Washington was a commanding presence at the ball even before gaining wealth, power, and immortality on the battlefield.

Even service in a military hospital could be enriched by dance. James Thacher noted the employment of one (appropriately named) John Trotter, a dance master who was to teach the good doctor and other gentlemen attached to the hospital how to dance every afternoon, beginning on February 4, 1778.[15] Master Trotter had reportedly for many years been teaching the art in New York City and had acquired great fame as a man of knowledge and experience in his profession. It is perhaps symptomatic of the displacements occasioned by the war that he would have found himself in a wilderness outpost attempting to teach a medical staff how to dance.

WILLIAM BILLINGS

Billings was the greatest composer, compiler, and advocate of American music in the second half of the eighteenth century. His remarkable career demonstrates the unexpected ways in which British colonial policy impinged upon the prerogatives of individual colonists, and how the frustrated goals and ambitions of the average citizen could build into the ground swell that fed the Revolutionary spirit. Born in Boston in 1746, Billings had been trained as a tanner of hides for shoes and other leather products. Early exhibiting an aptitude for music, he was fortunate that the rapidly expanding music industry offered commercial opportunities for his talent. Although he received no formal education in composition, he was tutored by a man who became his business partner. Billings was uniquely a man of his times, supporting himself through the increasingly popular institution of the singing school. He was capable of creating his own compositions as well as teaching others to sing, but problems arose when he tried to secure the legal rights to his songs.

Because of the strong religious traditions of New England, Billings could count on solid sales for his first published effort, an anthology of musical sermons that he edited and to which he added many of his own compositions. Without broadly applicable copyright protection, however, it was necessary for the Massachusetts composer to obtain legislative recognition of his work, which could then be protected as his property after the royal governor approved the legislative proposal.

William Billings, however, was repeatedly refused copyright for his songs despite the Massachusetts legislature's endorsement of his petitions. This meant that anyone could print and sell his work without royalty payments or even acknowledgment of the true author and composer of the work. Infuriated, Billings began serving the Patriot cause by hauling much-needed supplies to the army and penning many topical songs chronicling British infringements on American rights and celebrating American victories in the war. The fact that the frustrated Billings turned his considerable talents to the composition of revolutionary songs and ballads makes him useful for studying the ways in which the colonial government was inadequate for American conditions. As is frequently the case with such transitional figures, his creative impulse led him to pen patriotic lyrics for the musical airs with which he was most familiar, which happened to be hymns. His most successful of these initial efforts resulted in "Chester." The tune and its title were borrowed from *The New England Psalm Singer*, but Billings's topical references in the new lyrics gave the Americans a more respectable marching song to accompany "Yankee Doodle."[16] Billings was a prodigious talent; over three hundred of his songs have been preserved, mostly in his six published collections.

"YANKEE DOODLE" AND OTHER FOLK SONGS

As political fervor reached a fever pitch, music began to carry its share of propagandistic freight. On October 17, 1768, the *Boston Chronicle* ran an advertisement for "The New and Favourite Liberty Song." Its opening line began with the words "In freedom we're born."[17] The most famous song of the American Revolution, "Yankee Doodle Dandy," was initially played as a jeering reference to the colonials' lack of professional polish as military men and their audacity to challenge the crown. It was certainly in this derisive spirit that the relief column sent out to rescue the Concord expedition of April 18, 1775, marched to the tune. After the regulars were driven back to Boston, the song was embraced by the Patriots for the duration of the war. It was suitable for the drums and fifes of their armies and easily accommodated new verses as the war progressed. No other folk ballad rivaled its popularity, and it has come to symbolize the American Revolution in a way that no other songs and few other productions in any medium have approached. Few other songs in history have so thoroughly belonged to the people; countless verses and their local variations were penned by scores of anonymous wits. Many versions of its lyrics were published in the newspapers with the following notation: "Air—Yankee Doodle."[18] It is apparently a genuine folk song, for all attempts at definitively establishing its origin have been frustrated. Its ubiquity in the colonies probably forestalled its publication as music; despite many references to the tune throughout Revolutionary-era literature, the earliest surviving printing of the tune dates from *Scotland* in 1782.[19] Perhaps because many versions of the lyrics were ribald, the earliest American printing bears the late date of 1794.[20]

Many of the folk songs created during the period also celebrated the most recent political developments. It took a man of the cloth, Reverend Nathaniel Niles, to cast the British Army as the bloodhounds of war in "The American Hero," his 1775 reaction to the Battle of Bunker Hill. The text argues that all the horrors of war will fail to intimidate the speaker. The value of his life, soon forfeited in any case, will be redoubled if he survives the call to battle for "Fame and dear Freedom."[21] Throughout the colonies, Patriots were recognizing that their cause offered innumerable opportunities for social and economic mobility as well as political independence.

USES OF MUSIC IN WAR

On April 19, 1775, in what has been called the first overt act of the American Revolution, William Dimond, the drummer boy for the local militia, signaled the arrival of the British regiments into Lexington with a roll on his snare drum.[22] This very drum has been preserved by the Lexington Historical Society. Later in the war such instruments could be used to rouse the martial spirit of a town's residents, sending them scurrying to discover the cause of the commotion, which could be a recruiting party.[23]

The most enduring image of the American Revolution came from a nineteenth-century lithograph by Archibald Willard. Drums were used to organize troop movements on the battlefields and fifes lifted the spirits of marching men. Courtesy of the Library of Congress.

Once hostilities had begun, officers in both armies typically relied on their drummer boys to communicate commands amid the din of battle, where it was impossible to hear shouted commands. Different rhythms could be sounded to synchronize troop movements, reform lines, and signal retreat. Because many American officers had their first military experiences under British colors, drums could also be used to communicate with the enemy; a drummer might beat out a request to parley. Often accompanied by the white flags that in time became even more universally recognized as an invitation to negotiate, representatives from each army could discuss such things as the terms of surrender or a short truce to retrieve casualties. The drums were also used on more mundane occasions as well; a particular beat called "The General" alerted Continental troops that they were to strike their tents in preparation to march in Delaware in 1777, and it also sounded assembly.[24] Eventually, the sounds could be almost comforting; in his *Military Journal,* the army doctor James Thacher recalled how he felt about the drums and other musical instruments of war:

> What can compare with that martial band, the drum and fife, bugle-horn and shrill trumpet, which set the war-horse in motion, thrill through every fibre of the human frame, still the groans of the dying soldier, and stimulate the living to the noblest deeds of glory? The full roll of the drum, which salutes the commander-in-chief, the animating beat, which calls to arms for the battle, the reveille, which breaks our slumbers at dawn of day, with "come, strike your tents, and march away," and the evening tattoo, which commands to retirement and repose; these form incomparably the most enchanting music that has ever vibrated on my ear.[25]

It may have taken some time for new recruits to become so reconciled to the drums. With the passage of time, however, they might find this voice of the army reassuring; it told them precisely what to do and when to do it, and it enabled them to distinguish between the daily din of the army's breaking camp and a real emergency, such as the infiltration of the enemy within their ranks.

Fifers were almost as much in demand as drummers in the Revolutionary militias. Their flute-like tunes could take some of the drudgery out of marching, and many fifers, like John Greenwood, were chosen as much for their exemplary martial spirits as for their skill on the fife. In the era of the musket, musicians took as great a chance from a random shot or a lucky cannonball as any of the regular soldiers. Many fifers were too young to serve in an active combat role but became soldiers if they survived. John Greenwood was offered eight dollars a month and food for his services.[26] Promoted to fife major, Greenwood became responsible for assigning other fifers to detachments formed from his militia unit. On at least one occasion he assigned himself to such a unit. He was sent with it to Canada, where he witnessed scalping and the other unpleasantnesses of frontier warfare after weeks of privation that left many dead soldiers on the trail.

In combat, the drummers could add an air of normalcy in addition to conveying orders. They were a reassuring presence even as bullets whistled past their ears and cannonballs sailed overhead. When silence was desirable, musicians might assist with the baggage transports or the care of the sick and wounded. They could also be given the odious task of inflicting lashes as ordered by court-martial in the Continental Army; drum-majors had the responsibility of ensuring that such corporal punishment was properly administered.[27]

It is tempting to think of the British as cheerless curmudgeons intent on keeping the spirits of the people closely in check. A closer look at their activities when they were out of uniform reveals a startlingly different picture. It is clear by the social calendars kept by the British regulars in the occupied cities that the colonial love of music and dancing had its roots in England. British officers in Philadelphia staged amateur theatricals and a total of thirteen formal balls, attended by the cream of Tory society, in the six months they held the city.[28] The most famous Loyalist balladeers were Jonathan Odell and Joseph Stansbury.[29]

William Billings's "Chester," identified as a hymn when it appeared in his 1778 *Singing Master's Assistant*, incorporates the typical propagandist's ploy of painting the enemy with the broadest demonic brush while relying on his own side's allegiance to God to ensure its eventual victory. With Yankee pride, he argues that "New England's God forever reigns" (line 4), an assertion that echoed the notions of the early sixteenth-century Puritans who had come to America in part to found a City Upon a Hill, a New England Canaan that God would permit to flourish because the colonists pledged to live in accordance with His laws. In opposition, he named Howe, Burgoyne, Clinton, Prescott, and Cornwallis, five British generals who first combined in an "infernal league" (line 8) but were destined to "yield to beardless boys" (line 16), a reference to the relatively recent development of the colonial American army.

"Chester" begins with a statement of defiance against tyrants and the "galling chains" of slavery, a metaphor reflecting the author's New England prejudices. The song also envisions a Revolutionary battle; by 1778 the Continental Army was almost strong enough to win a European-style pitched battle, so dependent upon disciplined firing lines and synchronized troop movements. The poem also includes an account of ships of the Royal Navy being "shattered in our sight" (line 10); the ships of the day tended to fare poorly against shore batteries of approximately the same strength.

The songwriter captured the haughty strides with which the British Army marched into battle formation, but there were relatively few instances of their fleeing before a disciplined American advance at the time the song was written. The "martial noise" (lines 14–17) refers not only to the drums used to arouse the soldiers' spirits and to signal troop movements but also to the deafening roar of the battle. As hymns should, the last stanza praises the Lord for the victory. For its intended audience, the song's vision of several military miracles as well as its religious conclusion reinforced faith in the righteousness of the American cause.

Searching for an appropriate marching song for which to surrender, General Cornwallis's musicians at Yorktown in 1781 are reputed to have chosen "The World Turned Upside Down." The title of this children's verse as well as its lyrics suggests their astonishment at surrendering an entire European army to the less-disciplined Patriot forces and their French allies. They were, however, not the first large British army to surrender in this war; the Americans at Saratoga had captured Burgoyne and his five thousand men in 1777.

10

Performing Arts

It may surprise many modern Americans to learn that their celebrated freedom of speech has often been abrogated during times of national crisis, especially during the wars. In fact, prior to the passage of the Bill of Rights, there was no guarantee of freedom of speech throughout the colonies. Since liberty was such a catchphrase of the Revolution, one might expect the colonists to have held more progressive attitudes on this issue than their royalist counterparts, but tales abound of the tar-and-feathering of Loyalists throughout the era.

Things could turn ugly for the Patriots as well, with James Otis becoming one of the first martyrs for American independence. At one time the most famous lawyer in Boston, the Harvard-educated Otis was among the first American colonists to produce cogent arguments for separation from the mother country. He was also the first to experience fully the emotional implications of that step; it is possible to view Otis as an American Hamlet, driven toward Revolution by the fire of his own rhetoric but so steeped in British legal tradition that he sometimes wavered in his commitment to that goal. In 1764 he became head of the local Committee of Correspondence, an organization aimed at informing all the colonists about their political grievances. As an elected official, he did as much as Sam Adams to thwart the prerogatives of the governor of Massachusetts, but he was also instrumental in preventing the armed resistance to the British Army that Adams advocated in 1768. Outraged by a royal official's accusation that he was promoting treason, on September 5, 1769, he started a brawl in a Boston pub. He was so badly beaten that his mental as well as physical health were permanently impaired. The temper of the times dictated a certain circumspection before accepting political office or even making political statements as a private citizen.

A BAN ON PUBLIC PERFORMANCES

The sanctions against free expression extended to the performing arts. After the French and Indian War, theatres were built in New York City, Annapolis and Baltimore (Maryland), Williamsburg (Virginia), and Philadelphia, and plays were also held at the Bow Street Theatre in Portsmouth, New Hampshire. The history of the British theatre in America was not as rosy as the construction of new theatres would suggest, however. In fact, the subsequent history of the entire British colonial enterprise roughly followed the pattern established by their theatre. Banned first from the New England colonies, then kept alive only by the presence of the British Army in the larger cities of the middle colonies, the theatre was ultimately chased from the colonies entirely.

Whence sprang the American opposition to the stage? The traditions of censorship and even outright banning of theatrical entertainment are older

The American theatres had been closed during the war, practical photography was still fifty years off, and motion pictures would not be invented for over a century, but a German engraver named Carl Guttenberg imaginatively anticipated all of them in his 1778 cartoon. Courtesy of the Library of Congress.

than even the British theatre. After closing secular Roman plays in the sixth century, the Catholic Church maintained vigilant oversight of the stage for over a thousand years. Eventually traveling troupes of actors could reach their audience if they depicted heavily religious themes and biblical scenes, but their performances were even then frequently censored for the lewd and lascivious behavior of individual actors away from the stage. Henry VIII ended the Catholic Church's influence in England in 1533, but his own restrictions on dramatic performances extended censorship to control the stage for its potentially dangerous political content as well as its tendency to promote religious discord. Secular theater was not allowed in England until the last quarter of the sixteenth century, and performances were even then severely circumscribed and always subject to the royal pleasure.

In America, Puritan Massachusetts had an especially long history of antipathy toward stage productions as a result of the colony's having been founded as a religious experiment. New England clergy sometimes railed against the theatre as "chapels of Satan," charging that they emptied the churches and aided the pope.[1] Plays had long been censored throughout the northern colonies as frivolous diversions that distracted from the serious contemplation of the soul, and actors generally were not held in very high regard, because of their reputed immorality. In Philadelphia, the Quaker John Smith expressed his sorrow upon hearing the daughter of a friend being encouraged to waste her time on something as frivolous and fraught with temptation as seeing a play.[2] By the start of the American Revolution, the arguments on both sides of the censorship question were as sophisticated and as familiar as those for independence.

ECONOMIC AND POLITICAL REASONS FOR THE BAN

Economic problems also contributed to the closure of the theatres. On October 20, 1774, the Continental Congress passed a resolution to "discountenance and discourage . . . shows, plays, and other expensive diversions and entertainments." Under the pecuniary distress resulting from strained economic ties with Great Britain, it is easy to understand why a majority of the representatives from all the colonies would agree with the parsimonious Yankees that such *expensive* diversions should be prohibited.

In fact, the man who was shortly to be named the commander in chief of the Continental Army was such an inveterate theatergoer that the subsequent history of the entire Revolution might have turned out differently had the Continental Congress not raised its collective hand against theatrical performances. An entry in George Washington's diary illustrates how expensive they were. On April 9, 1774, he recorded that "sundry play tickets for myself and others" had set him back five pounds, twelve shillings six pence.[3] Prior to the war, Washington attended plays in

Philadelphia, Williamsburg, Annapolis, and Alexandria. He attended at least seven performances from March 11 to April 7, 1773, and four plays in five nights from the 5th through the 9th of October that same year. When Congress enacted this austerity measure, he was freed to concentrate on the theatres of war instead. He would eventually permit performances of *Cato* to help while away the tedium of Valley Forge, and at least one of his officers hoped that the theatres would remain open if the British abandoned Philadelphia.[4] This would not happen, however. Over the next four years, many of the colonies independently passed laws prohibiting staged performances, effectively darkening the professional stage in America until 1781.

There were also more broadly patriotic and even propagandistic reasons for the congressional theatre ban. The honor of being the first American-born professional actor may belong to Nancy George, who was listed among the principal players of the touring Murray and Kean Company when they moved from her native Philadelphia for the New York stage in 1750. Another candidate is Samuel Greville, who practiced medicine as well as performing on the Charleston stage.[5] It is significant that John Martin, more widely thought to have been the first American-born male professional actor, did not appear among the professional ranks until 1790. This means that almost all the plays and players on the professional American stage were British.

To this day, the excellence of Shakespeare and the other British dramatists remains a powerful inducement to attend the theatre, but the Bard of Avon frequently filled his scenes with celebrations of Englishness. The emerging nation's Patriots, among whom were many avid theatregoers, were very cognizant of that fact. The choice of exclusively British plays (at a time when no others were available) made New York's Sons of Liberty suspicious of the professional theatre. They got a decade's jump on the Continental Congress's ban on plays by "discountenancing" a performance of May 5, 1766. A mob overran the stage, terrorized the audience, and pulled down and burned the Chapel Street Theatre in the name of Liberty.[6]

Charleston had the most active stage in the pre-Revolutionary colonies. The last shot had barely been fired in the French and Indian War (1756–63) before Charleston resumed its theatre habit, and over 180 performances were staged in its 1773 season. Shakespeare was popular at other theatres as well, but he was never so well represented in a single American colonial theatre season as he was at Charleston that year. Productions included *Richard III, King Lear, Romeo and Juliet, Henry IV (Part One), Hamlet, Othello, King John, The Merchant of Venice, The Tempest, Julius Caesar,* and *MacBeth. Cymbeline* and *The Merry Wives of Windsor* were performed elsewhere, as was an adaptation of *The Taming of the Shrew.*[7] Most of the other productions could be classified as either comedies of manners, in which love triumphs over such artificial barriers as social class and parental opposition, or operas (twenty performances of thirteen different works). When Charleston's theatre was closed in accordance with the October 20, 1774, resolution, the theatrical center of the nation briefly shifted back to the North.

THE SCHOOL FOR SCANDAL

One of the most popular plays brought to the colonies from Britain was the ubiquitous *Tragedy of Cato*, by Joseph Addison. It was performed on every major stage in the colonies and holds the distinction of having been performed in the American camp at Valley Forge near the end of the army's frightful winter there. Set on the frontier of the Roman Republic, *Cato* celebrates the last stand of a doomed senator/general days before he must face Caesar's victorious hosts with the remnants of his own army and their African allies. Even as some of Cato's men show their weakness; the more passionate of his two sons pines after love; while his other son secretly hopes to undermine his sibling's chances of succeeding his father. One can easily imagine Washington's fascination with the tragedy; like the Numidian prince who models himself on Cato in the play, Washington was "transplanting . . . his bright perfections till I shine like him."[8] Like Cato, Washington had renounced his comfort in favor of his duty in the service of liberty, despite seemingly insurmountable odds. He learned to face physical hardship, desertions, and betrayals with Roman composure.

Having said all that, however, *Cato* seems a strange choice if Washington was trying to raise the morale of his troops. It not only portrays an army on the verge of annihilation; it talks openly about desertion even near the peak of the command structure. The politics of the play are also a bit questionable, from an American perspective. Although the charismatic Cato represents the last best hope of the republic, as a representative of the established government his situation is more akin to that of the Loyalists than that of their adversaries. At that moment in history, no one could be certain but that a successful conclusion of the war might result in a military dictatorship or the establishment of a new American royalty. Loyalist propagandists pointed out that the end result of all the colonists' sacrifices could be the substitution of one King George for another. In the play, Cato, before committing suicide, arranges clemency for such of his followers as will trust Caesar, and escape by ship for those who would rather face the open seas.

Perhaps the best that could be said for performing the play at Valley Forge is that its exaltation of Cato may have inspired Washington's troops to associate their goal of freedom with the personal success of their general. It could also have served as a cautionary tale for those who would plot against him. Just before making his own escape, the main leader of a mutiny within Cato's army sacrifices his minions with the explanation that lowly participants in a successful plot are disregarded if they succeed but suffer painful, ignominious deaths if they fail.[9]

The most popular comedies in America before the Revolution were George Farquhar's *The Recruiting Officer* and *The Beaux' Stratagem*, and the favorite musical romp was John Gay's *The Beggar's Opera*.[10] Even a casual glance at these works reveals their satirical content. While *The Beaux' Stratagem* is a comedy of manners, the other two works poke fun at the establishments of the army and the police, two institutions with which the conservative governments of the colonies were closely aligned. The risqué nature of *The Recruiting Officer* is evident from the opening act; the officers are reported to leave a bastard in the district for every soldier they take from it. Their military strategies inform their courtships, and the women to whom they lay siege take as much pleasure in temporarily defeating their stratagems as they do in capitulation. The major difference between the way the genders play their respective roles in this play is that the men form alliances with each other to further their amorous designs, while the women campaign even more fiercely against each other than they do against the men. The officers find willing sergeants to marry such lower-class women as they impregnate and are not above enlisting their new-born offspring as recruits, on furlough, so that the army will provide funds for the child while the enlistment helps fulfill the natural father's recruitment goals. A thinly veiled prostitution seems to flourish throughout the play; the officers are able to corrupt a servant girl with promises of upward social mobility, and a rustic lass with Flanders lace. Their recruitment of soldiers is conducted with even fewer scruples.

The Beaux' Stratagem revolves around the adventures of two men with education but no property who have turned to the countryside to acquire their fortunes. By taking turns playing master and servant as they move from one town to the next, they hope to gain access to provincial women of property. Each man attempts to work his charms upon women of his own apparent class. The language and manners of the man acting like a servant give him away; the pair attract the attention of an innkeeper who plots with highwaymen, and also of an unhappily married woman who begins to voice her fantasies. To such Puritans as still lingered in Massachusetts by the middle of the nineteenth century, the play presents a society without a moral bottom.

The women of *The Beggar's Opera* are portrayed as almost universally wanton, and the law and the class system are shown to be equally to blame for it. The toughest job in the kingdom belonged to the "child-getter" of the prison; his job was to impregnate condemned female prisoners to forestall their appointments with the gallows.

The Beggar's Opera turns the rules of straight society upon their head; a crooked husband and wife plot to have their son-in-law arrested before he can turn their daughter away from a life of crime. At the center of the controversy is the scoundrel Macheath, a small-time criminal conspirator. If there is a moral lesson in the opera it lies in the treacherous nature of the criminal milieu. Macheath is surprised by his betrayal to the police by first the men and then the women he trusted, but he had provided everyone with ample evidence that he was himself not to be trusted. The likeable rogue owes his ultimate release to the public's preference for happy endings; Macheath learns nothing from his near hanging and is last seen plying one of his wives with the same lies that had been his undoing throughout the play. Taken collectively, the opera and two comedies suggest that the mid- and late-eighteenth-century theatre was a School for Scandal, to co-opt the title of Richard Brinsley Sheridan's immensely popular (in Britain) 1777 play. It is easy to see why the New England churchmen and their governmental allies sought to keep the theatre out of their colonies.

AMATEUR THEATRICALS BY THE BRITISH ARMY

The highest-ranking British officers came from the theatrical center of the world. As famous as Shakespeare remains today, he was only one of many Elizabethan dramatists, and the outstanding British dramatic tradition did not end with Shakespeare and his contemporaries. Except when the Puritans briefly gained power and closed the theatres in England during the Commonwealth of Oliver Cromwell, the British stage continued to flourish. Until the American Revolution, many of the most popular plays of the day were eventually performed on both sides of the Atlantic.

One of the ironies of the political scene in Boston is that since 1750 until the British Army's theatricals of 1775, plays were banned in the city.[11] It took the armed representatives of what many colonists viewed as an oppressive government to bring the freedom of the stage to Boston. During the early years of the war, the British Army briefly held Boston and was subsequently able to drive the Continental Army from New York and even Philadelphia, the de facto capital of the new nation (because the Continental Congress met there). The fact that the British officers felt comfortable enough to stage amateur theatricals in these occupied cities underscores the essential problem of British strategy for the conduct of the war. Their senior officers were gentlemen in the Old World sense, landed aristocrats born to privilege, accustomed to luxury, and proud of their connections to the empire. They could be fearless on the battlefield, but felt it adequate to sweep the amateur American army from the field or wait for it to melt away in the face of what they considered intolerably harsh winters. Attendance at the theatre was one of the many ways in which they could pass the time while they awaited these seemingly inevitable results. As we have seen, Maj. Gen. John Burgoyne found time to write plays, and Maj. John Andre found time to organize the *Mischianza* (Philadelphia, May 18, 1778), a spectacle in honor of the departure of Gen. William Howe as commander in chief of the British forces in America.[12] British soldiers also performed at the John Street Theatre in New York City and the Southwark Theatre in Philadelphia during the war.[13]

After the British were forced from Boston on March 17, 1776, plays were not allowed in the city again until 1792.[14] The American Company, the only prewar company of professional actors to resume performances after the Revolution, weathered the storm by keeping active in the Caribbean until it was welcomed back to the Continent.

AMERICAN PUPPET THEATRE

While amateur theatricals by the British Army were possible because they were beyond the control of the colonists, the American public had not yet embraced another form of dramatic production. It is tempting to think of the role a little Punch or Judy could have played in the American Revolution. Revolutionary fervor could have reached fever pitch as the blue-uniformed hero battered his red-coated nemesis in retaliation for the latter's insults of our heroine, or her flag. Judy's spangled and starred dress could have made her stand for more than just affrighted innocence; she could have represented no less a personage than America herself.

Alas, it was not to be. Puppetry had yet to achieve the widespread popularity in England that would have made for an effortless jump across the sea. The few puppets and their masters who did make it to America were silenced during the crisis. This was perhaps fortunate; popular sentiment was so divided as practically to guarantee a hostile reaction by one faction of a crowd or the other, regardless of the political spin the puppeteer attempted. Master and puppet might have languished in a city jail for sedition or found themselves uncomfortably sharing the same rail as they were ridden out of town, blackened with pitch and covered with feathers by the revolutionaries.

Nor were nonpolitical themes safe. The widely held belief in the fallen nature of theatre folk in general begot widespread church opposition to their craft, and if some church fathers felt that performances by human players were devilry, nonhuman actors enraged them.

Even had puppetry found a more receptive soil prior to the outbreak of hostilities, the puppet theatre fell under the same proscriptions that closed other theatres until after the war. America would have to wait until

the last two decades of the eighteenth century for the tiny foot of a mari-
onette to leave more than an ephemeral impression on our shores.

AMERICAN PLAYS WRITTEN DURING THE REVOLUTIONARY ERA

Only two plays written by Americans were performed before the start
of the American Revolution, and both appeared on the Philadelphia stage.
The Prince of Parthia was presented on April 24, 1767, by subscription as
part of a tribute to the late Thomas Godfrey, Jr., a nascent poet as well as
playwright who died in 1763 at the tender age of twenty-seven.[15] Its subject, the palace intrigues among Old World royalty, reveals much about
the state of American drama prior to the Revolution; its mimicry of Elizabethan revenge tragedies places it at least fifty years behind the London
stage. One of the things it shared with Shakespeare's plays is the stage
villainy of the queen Thermusa, but the title character's jealous younger
brother Vardanes, and Lysias, a plotting courtier, and even worse. As in
Cato, the younger brother's jealousy extended even to his sibling's courtship of a beautiful girl. Women are the root of all discord in the play; even
the title character's love interest had been in love with Thermusa's rebellious son Vonones, whom the prince had recently killed in battle. Despite
its reliance on the shopworn device of a second brother's schemes to usurp
the eldest brother's birthright by preventing his ascendance to the throne,
the characters are frequently delineated well enough to be engaging. It is
a tale of princely courage and honor amid the chaos fomented by mal-
contents and intriguers.

The greatest tragedy of *The Prince of Parthia,* however, is that its playwright died so young. Here was an American writer unafraid to write in
the storied tradition of the British stage, who worked out a full-length play
in the colonial backwaters. The play's exotic and antique setting is not a
slavish copying of European materials; rather, it reflects the classicism then
in vogue among his countrymen. In other words, his demonstrated preference for antiquity was not a pretense; the artist was engaged in American materials precisely in that his aesthetic choices reflect the genuine
preferences held by men of his class, training, and background prior to
the Revolutionary War. Only an audience from the distant future would
chastise Godfrey for not making the play more "American." His immediate audience understood that his aesthetic choices reflected the hopes,
ambitions, and ideals of the educated elite of his generation.

The most interesting American play written before the start of widespread protest against British colonial policy was Robert Rogers's *Ponteach*
(1766). The play indicts the entire British enterprise in America for its scandalous treatment of the Indians, whose causes are ably advanced by their

great chief Pontiac, as modern transliteration would render his name. Rogers condemns British traders for their doctored scales and rum, adulterated with drugs to increase its potency at the start of trade negotiations, and with water afterwards to decrease its expense. Such shenanigans bring to mind a scene the inveterate traveler William Bartram witnessed in Georgia. As discussed in the following chapter, he watched as government agents negotiated two million acres away from the Indians in exchange for the trading debts they had accumulated. He once met two young traders whose forty kegs of Jamaican spirits had been destroyed by Creek Indians desperate to keep liquor from their towns; Bartram noted that they could have made eighty kegs by "dashing," watering down the rum.[16] Yet a third source verifies the same phenomenon; the pious John Woolman recorded a conversation with a trader of Pennsylvania who knew of the selling of rum to the Indians in order to profit by their inebriation when bartering for their hides.[17]

The profit motive provokes two hunters in Rogers's play to shift from preying on animals to killing Indians. They justify their descent into robbery and murder as revenge against the losses their families sustained at the hands of other Indians, and they take their scalps to sell in the next Indian war. Their racist remarks are echoed by two army officers at an English fort; they condescendingly dismiss Pontiac as a "cursed old thief" despite the eloquence of his appeals for justice. Pontiac fares no better with the king's emissaries, three English governors who make him wait outside while they divide the king's gifts among themselves before passing a scant remainder to the intended recipient. The Indians openly question the governors' pledges of peace and brotherhood, and the governors ignore Pontiac's refusal to honor them by smoking the *calument,* and his obvious displeasure with their actions. Reflecting that the king is not a hatter and hence would have no use for the hides and pelts Pontiac had brought, they decide to divide this loot as well. Even the Catholic Church is assailed; in asides the priest eventually reveals the political machinations behind his dealings with Pontiac and his own ambition to become pope.

Ponteach was the work of a sensitive young man of thirty-four with more than a passing familiarity with the western frontier. In fact, its major incidents were practically current events, as Pontiac's War had ended just two years before.

Surviving accounts of the playwright's own life seem as dramatic as anything he ever wrote. It is tempting to blame his subsequent career on his early exposure to human duplicity and depravity in the French and Indian War, but he joined his first regiment to escape prosecution.[18] He quickly distinguished himself with his daring and, rising to the rank of captain, led several successful raids. A tendency to misappropriate funds kept him from ultimately prospering in such governmental offices as he was subsequently able to obtain. He has the dubious distinction of not only having his services refused by both armies during the Revolutionary War but also of being imprisoned on both sides of the Atlantic (for suspicion of espionage on the American side, and for debts in London). At a time in American history when divorce was extremely rare, his wife, a preacher's daughter, obtained one. While such anecdotes no doubt provide insights into the man's character and partially explain his skill at fathoming his villains' hearts, they do not diminish the effectiveness of his play or the originality he showed in portraying the Pontiac War from the Indians' perspective.

As the play progresses, however, it depends more on the author's observations of other performances than on his observations of Indians. The intensity with which Pontiac's sons focus on their father's distemper and their suggestion that he may be as provoked by his own wounded vanity as by practical concerns of state reflect an awareness of Elizabethan and Reformation drama. Nor was the author immune from the religious prejudices of his native New England; the tremendous distance the colonies had yet to travel on the road to religious tolerance is evident in the priest's designs on the beautiful Monelia. Only the timely arrival of Pontiac's son prevents the priest from raping the woman, a situation and rescue reminiscent of similar scenes in *Cato*. *Pontiac*'s greatest debt to *Cato*, however, is the rivalry between the title character's sons. In both plays, the honesty of the passionate son and his overpowering love for a girl are manipulated by his conniving brother. A few late twists keep *Pontiac* interesting as a revenge tragedy, but the Native American elements have been left far behind.

A slightly more topical drama, George Cockings's *The Conquest of Canada; or, The Siege of Quebec*, was first staged in 1773. It dealt with the British conquest of French Canada in the French and Indian War.

Because of the British origins of the plays and players on the colonial stage, it was natural for the Tories to use the theatre in the propaganda war, as demonstrated by the appearance of "A Dialogue, Between a Southern Delegate and his spouse, on his return from the Grand Continental Congress" in 1774. The word "Grand" in the title was intended as sarcasm; the play makes much of a delegate who neglects his own farm to attend the affair. Much of this comedy's humor lies in the hackneyed figure of the henpecked spouse, who begs his wife to keep up appearances before the neighbors.

The play commences with the return of a southern delegate to his farm, from which he had hastened to Congress in order to have his voice heard. His wife suggests that only the serious drinking rumored (and to a certain extent, known) to have occurred could have so emboldened some of the delegates to stand up to Parliament. The contemporary audience would have recognized this as an implied attack on the delegate's manliness, since he is unable to control his wife. The twenty-first-century reader, however, is more likely to note her eloquent rebuttal of his defense of his actions. Her assertion of feminine power conflicts with the playwright's implied notion that the delegate's ideas are suspect precisely because of his lack of manly fortitude. The author, identified as only as "Mary V.V." on the title page, dedicated the pamphlet to the married ladies of America, but the humor of this comedy largely springs from its ad hominem fallacy—the serious grievances outlined by Congress are suspect because of this representative's inability to control his wife. This jest, and her dismissive assertion that the empress of England would be elected president at the next Congress, no doubt seemed so ridiculous to the play's initial audience as to guarantee a laugh. Antifeminist attitudes flourished during that era.

The play was written in rhymed couplets; many of the lines could have provided the smart Tory set with epigrams attacking the pretentiousness of the delegates in challenging Britain's might. The author was prescient in depicting the husband as a delegate from a southern state; only as the struggle assumed the character of a civil war in some southern states did the destruction descend to the levels predicted by the wife.

PROPAGANDA IN WARTIME DRAMA

While there was no market for publishing or performing American plays until long after the war, several individuals continued writing them. The surviving scripts, many of which owe their continued existence to their publication and dissemination in pamphlet form, typically held more propagandistic than aesthetic value. It seems likely that most of the pamphlets never aspired to more than being closet dramas, lacking any realistic prospect of ever reaching the stage; the most the authors could hope for was an audience of private readers. Most of the pamphlet/plays were published anonymously, not only for fear of a distant indictment for treason but in recognition of the more immediate threat of partisan retribution.

An important American female playwright was Mercy Otis Warren, the author of a two-act farce called *The Group*, which was printed anonymously in 1775.

Propagandists on both sides were quick to churn out plays commemorating their most recent victories in the war. To preserve the reader's sense of chronology, the discussion that follows observes the sequence in which the depicted battles were actually fought, not that in which the plays appeared.

The Fall of British Tyranny, or American Liberty Triumphant (1776) was penned while the British still occupied Boston. Although the colonials had had success at Concord, had stood up to the British regulars at Bunker

Hill, and now kept the largest British army on the continent bottled up in Boston, the play's title was prematurely optimistic, unification of all American colonies not having been achieved. Two attempts were made to add Canada to the rebellion. The haphazard efforts of Ethan Allen and John Brown led to the former's defeat and capture at Montreal on September 25, 1775. News of this recent disaster informs the fifth act of the play, but the playwright nevertheless drew upon all the rumors and anti-British propaganda then current to cast aspersions on the competence of the highest British officers.

The much larger and better organized second colonial assault on Canada met with more success, initially. The colonial generals Richard Montgomery and Benedict Arnold swept the small British outposts from their path, even taking Montreal on November 13, 1775. By New Year's Eve, they were attacking Quebec. Unfortunately, they ran into an entrenched army twice the size of their own. On New Year's Day, 1776, Arnold was wounded and Montgomery was killed, and all American hopes for bringing Canada to their side died with him. The theatrical result was Hugh Henry Brackenridge's *The Death of General Montgomery, in Storming the City of Quebec* (1777). The imagined speeches attempt heights reminiscent of earlier playwrights. There is even an appearance by the ghost of James Wolfe, the British general who died heroically while defeating the French at Quebec during the French and Indian War. Now the Patriot propagandist makes him take sides against his murderous countrymen and predict the future glory of America. More to the point are the play's indictments of the maltreatment of prisoners of war, some of whom were designated for the "slow-scorching fires" of the Indian allies as recompense for their help in the battle. The remainder were to languish in British prisons despite Gen. Sir Guy Carleton's promises of fair treatment if they surrendered.

There were colonial military successes to celebrate even in 1776, however. The British position in Boston had become untenable when the rebels surprised the garrison at Fort Ticonderoga in upstate New York and hauled the captured cannons down to Boston. The heavy losses the British Army suffered in frontal assaults at Bunker Hill may have also discouraged the British officers; in any case, they withdrew by sea on March 17, 1776, inspiring *The Blockheads, or The Affrighted Officers*, attributed to Mercy Otis Warren. The play dramatizes the alleged malfeasance, incompetence, and even cowardice of the British officers. Many Loyalist families joined the soldiers on this shipboard exodus, and the playwright took special delight in describing the discomfiture of these refugees.

After the Continental Army narrowly escaped annihilation in the disastrous battle of Brooklyn Heights on August 27, 1776, the British seized control of New York City for the duration of the war. *The Battle of Brooklyn: A Farce in Two Acts* (1776) was the Loyalist response to the British victory. The principal, nearly universal charge against the American generals in the play is thievery, a natural enough accusation for a loyal citizen to make against the rebels who would deny the king's ownership of the colonies. The play suggests that they were waging war for merely personal, essentially criminal reasons. The play is remarkable for the speed with which it appeared; it castigated American military incompetence even as Washington and his officers were struggling to keep their army in the field after what could easily have been a death blow.

Like the actual battle, the two-act play opens with the too-confident American generals awaiting the British army they are certain to defeat. In the play, provision has already been made for the prisoners shortly expected; General Washington's greatest concern is that the American people will discover his own tyranny before the Revolution succeeds. His junior officers are most concerned about preserving their spoils from each other's depredations.

Many of the plays written in America before and during the Revolution tried to adapt the most popular British dramatic forms of the day to American materials, but their efforts were hindered by weight of their politics. The result was plays that typically contained more diatribes than dialogue. The two most important exceptions to this rule were *Ponteach* and Robert Munford's *The Patriots* (c. 1778–79).

The Patriots directs its attacks against those who would force American loyalty oaths on even the ideologically neutral as well as the Tories. It bemoans the discrimination and prejudice so harmful to Americans of Scot ancestry, and it attacks the recruiting practices of unscrupulous officers. The play also combines two of the most popular genres of the era, the twisted-courtship comedy and the patriotic (or more broadly, nationalistic) interpretation of current events. Although several characters are but pale imitations of Shakespeare's originals, as is the subplot involving recovered identities and noble births, enough new twists are provided to keep the audience involved.

Aside from the insights they provide into the political and social climate of the American Revolution, several of the plays written in this era are remarkable for their consideration of the major issues that still plagued America as late as the twentieth century. *The Patriots,* for example, censures discrimination based on race and national origin, which later caused the outrages against Japanese-Americans at the start of the Second World War, and it attacks the guilt by association and jingoism that marked Joseph McCarthy's attacks on free speech in the 1950s. Similarly, *Ponteach*'s concern for the just treatment of Native Americans and its indictment of the racism that sanctioned their extermination introduced national problems that have yet to be solved.

The acts of Congress that closed the theatres during the war, along with other austerity measures, helped alleviate some of the unrelenting financial pressure on the new government. More important, however, was the symbolism of the gesture. Forcing even the distant Carolinians to forego their entertainment had a unifying effect on the colonies, involving all of them in the struggle for independence, in the same way that aluminum and steel drives connected their World War II descendents on the home front with the soldiers in the field.

What was lost when the lights were turned off on all the professional stages in America? The luckiest of the professional actors went with the Royal Company of Actors to the West Indies for the duration, returning with their renamed American Company in 1782. Other actors returned to England, but more than a few careers were ruined, and the American theatrical tradition was set back a generation. Although disastrous for some of the individuals involved, however, the new national consciousness that developed after the war soon spawned great popular demand for plays based on Revolutionary events, especially those celebrating Washington and his military triumphs. This helped the theatre expand far beyond its probable dimensions had its prewar, colonial development continued uninterrupted.

American writers were still some generations away from being able to earn a living with their pens, but the new national consciousness, expanded interest in all things American, and steady economic growth were slowly creating an economically reliable basis for their work. It would take more than a century before American dramatists could create first-rate works, however.

11

Travel

Throughout the Revolutionary era, the only power available for transportation or any other task sprang from biological, solar, and water sources. A colonist could harness the first of these by walking, riding horses, or hitching draft animals to his conveyances or other machines. This made traveling by land laborious, time-consuming, and relatively expensive. Although constant use for centuries had turned a few Indian paths into permanent, easily discernable trails, these paths tended to lead into the hinterlands and away from the relative safety and profitable trading with Europe of the coastal cities. There simply were not enough European settlers away from the coast to share the expense of creating practical roads on a modern European or American scale, and the lakes and rivers that facilitated travel by boat or canoe were impediments to travel by other means. Crèvecoeur claimed that Americans from West Florida to Nova Scotia communicated with each other on good roads and navigable rivers, but this was true only in some of the more advanced colonies. It was still impractical for colonists from West Florida to communicate with those of Nova Scotia by traveling exclusively on roads and rivers. Even travel from Philadelphia to Maryland required a ferry ride over the Susquehanna River, during which the winds could make it difficult for a horse to keep its feet.[1] It took the Marquis de Lafayette and the other French volunteers who accompanied him thirty-three days to travel from Charleston, South Carolina, to Philadelphia in 1777. The roads seemed impassable and soon broke the primitive carriages they had acquired; part of their baggage and their horses were lost; and most of the men ended up walking all the way. Two of the men died and were buried where they fell.[2] From an economic standpoint, the prospect of building even a single adequate road from

Massachusetts to Charleston was an expensive proposition rightly left to the nation-building efforts of later generations. Access to the coast was still far more important than connecting distant inland points.

Most Americans still did not travel very far or very often, but those who did journey through the countryside did so for a number of reasons. Much travel was prompted by financial considerations. It was possible to make a killing by trading with the Indians, and an even easier fortune could be garnered by seizing their land in payment for their trading debts, by force following a militia victory, or through governmental negotiation. Such lands had to be surveyed before the speculators could make their profits, so crews of surveyors joined frontiersmen and settlers already encountered on the road. Scientific curiosity led William Bartram to explore the frontier areas beyond the southern colonies, while John Woolman felt compelled to carry his testimony of God to the Indians as well as the Quakers of the middle colonies and North Carolina. Some of the most prominent men in the colonies found themselves traveling for days and even weeks for political purposes after they were summoned to Philadelphia for the Continental Congresses. Still other colonists traveled for their health, for a pleasurable change of scene, or just for leisure, as Philip Freneau remarked in his "Expedition of Timothy Taurus."

Military experience also exposed many men to regions they had only heard of before. John Woolman relates how the military officers of his Pennsylvania community drafted local militiamen to relieve Fort William Henry in New York in September 1757. The French destroyed the fort before the Pennsylvanians arrived, but it was an instance in which militia obligations forced colonists to travel. Few whose state militias were absorbed into the Continental Army and who survived the fighting for six years could boast of more travel than their commander in chief; probably only the Generals Horatio Gates and Nathanael Greene, with their deeper forays into the southern colonies, covered more ground than George Washington. Washington rode up from his Virginia estate to take his seat at both Continental Congresses, left the second to take charge of the Boston siege, fought the British from New York to Philadelphia and back again, then rode with his army to Virginia to capture Cornwallis at Yorktown—to mention only his longest treks.

Benjamin Franklin probably traveled more extensively than any American of his time who was not engaged in whaling, commercial shipping, or in a navy, but most of his mileage was transatlantic. On the British side, the two transatlantic voyages required to complete an enlistment meant that the average redcoat covered more miles than his Yankee counterpart during the war. Most of these were nautical miles, however. British armies in America tended to operate out of urban centers and move by sea if they were needed elsewhere. Of course, one's travels in either army could come to an abrupt halt.

Although trade between the colonies was gradually becoming more important as the eighteenth century progressed, trade with England still presented the best market opportunities. Although the well-traveled Great Wagon Road connected Philadelphia with Virginia and the Carolinas, travel overland from Massachusetts to Philadelphia was still so novel that John Adams took exhaustive notes on his cross-country journey to the first Continental Congress. The lack of infrastructure soon becomes evident in the travel narratives of the era. Trading companies and emigrants could start on well-established Indian trails, but they soon encountered difficulties in determining which unmarked path to take, and even the best-equipped and most-knowledgeable travelers had to pause before rain-swollen creeks or rivers.

Before the Revolutionary War, limited overland postal service was established in both the northern and southern colonies, but it was typically more dependent upon the relay rider's familiarity with the local landscape than on clearly marked turnpikes. While he was postmaster general of the northern colonies, Benjamin Franklin began the pioneering effort of placing milestones along the routes his riders had to travel. This greatly alleviated navigational anxieties in the North, but the forest still began at the western edge of town in many places. The ability to find one's way was a necessity for anyone contemplating a cross-country jaunt; otherwise the adventure could quickly turn into a test of survival skills.

HOSPITALITY EXTENDED TO TRAVELERS

It was common for people traveling before the war to stay at the homes of whatever prosperous settlers they encountered en route. This tradition of providing hospitality to strangers on the frontier had its roots in the Bible, a settler's memory of difficulties he had encountered in his own travels, and the rarity of meeting new people. In his *Letters from an American Farmer,* St. Jean de Crèvecoeur wrote effusively of his happiness when travelers chose to stop at his farm instead of a neighbor's. He found this tribute gratifying and claimed to have been more pleased than astonished to find whole families scattered about the two rooms of his home.[3] He found reciprocal hosts when it was his turn to travel; he noted his comfort traveling two hundred miles from his home to Philadelphia. Each night he retired as the guest of friends living along the way.[4] He boasted that such hospitality could be found throughout America and was sure such neighborliness would facilitate the excursions of any learned men who chose to study life on this side of the Atlantic.

In the southern colonies, the inveterate traveler and botanist William Bartram was occasionally hosted by Indians as well as white homesteaders, so there was some truth to Crèvecoeur's boast. The term "hotel" was not used in America until the Revolutionary War had nearly ended.[5]

A growing number of taverns or inns provided travelers with rooms (or shared accommodations, which sometimes meant climbing into a bed already occupied by a complete stranger of the same gender), in addition to their offerings of food and beverage.[6] The inns often had such colorful names as The Practical Farmer, The White Horse, The Three Tunns, The Fleece, or The Red Lion.[7] Other's took their names from their proprietors, such as Hollingsworth's or Currey's in Pennsylvania.[8] Pleased with his accommodations, a colonial guest would report that a tavern "keeps good entertainment."[9] Elsewhere, a luckless traveler could find himself sharing a bed with a legion of bloodsuckers, probably fleas.[10]

The increased interest in distant colonies resulting from the war helped propagate popular demand for travel narratives, a literary genre that would grow throughout the American experience. During the war, however, travel could be exceptionally hazardous. Even before the political controversies began, Benjamin Mifflin was roughly handled for letting his horse graze in a tavern yard.[11] As controversies surrounding British policies in America grew more heated, a traveler had to be careful that his host's casual conversation did not lead him into betraying his own sentiments. The suspicions cast upon any stranger tended to limit travel for any but the most serious reasons once the war had begun. Freebooter cowboys (with British sympathies) and skinners (those with sometimes nominal allegiance to the patriotic cause) occasionally helped themselves to the personal belongings of the travelers encountered, although they claimed to be helping their respective causes by interfering with the movements of their political opponents and catching spies. One such group was instrumental in capturing Major John Andre as he attempted to return to British lines after facilitating Benedict Arnold's treason. By 1781, the prevalence of such irregular forces meant it took two months for two men to carry dispatches on a roundtrip from New York City to Quebec, a distance of only 559 miles if one were not obliged to avoid enemy checkpoints and freebooting patrols.[12] At least the messengers finally made it through on that occasion; on March 29, 1781, a post boy was intercepted just five miles from his destination by three members of the New Jersey Volunteers (a Loyalist militia). Among the letters were several from George Washington with information the British found useful.[13]

After the British blockade of Boston closed that port in 1775, the colonial army's siege of the city kept most Tory traffic from getting in by overland routes. Throughout the war, naval blockades and occupation by the British Army had as dampening an effect on colonial travel as on commercial traffic. Paper shortages and public focus on military events also kept travel narratives and other literary endeavors from being printed during the war.

Once the war commenced, American hospitality took a decided turn for the worse. Questions had to be answered correctly before doors were opened. Hence, the Baroness von Riedesel and her family, traveling to Virginia with the remnant of Burgoyne's surrendered army in 1778, were refused meat for the children despite her offer to pay for it. The housewife whom she asked acknowledged that she had beef, veal, and mutton, but none for people who had come to the America to kill the inhabitants.[14] General Lafayette himself seemed set for an even worse reception upon arriving in Winneah harbor as a French volunteer in 1777, but the threatening men they encountered took them to a Major Huger's house, where they were given the traditional warm welcome.[15]

Even the best-connected strangers could no longer depend upon even an official warm reception. So many French freebooters had hastened to Philadelphia to obtain commissions in the American army that Congress tried to turn away even those who arrived with Lafayette in 1777. Only their persistence and General Washington's intercession after meeting Lafayette weeks later brought them into the Continental Army.[16]

INDIAN GUIDES IN THE FORESTS

Both armies and individual travelers sometimes depended upon Indian guides. Although a fascination with massacres infests the colonial countryside in the modern mind with wild, nearly genocidal Indians, normal intercourse with the Indians included widespread trading and, sometimes, treaties of mutual defense. It is important to differentiate among the many tribes with which the settlers came into contact at different points in tribal and colonial history. The most powerful southeastern tribes had long histories of dealing with other tribes as well as a century and a half of usually benign interaction with the colonists; they tended to tolerate and sometimes assist travelers passing through their territories. Sometimes local Indians would advise traders and settlers of impending encroachments by hostile war parties from other tribes, thus averting massacres. Both Bartram and John Woolman interacted with the Indians on a daily basis and were kept informed of imminent warfare in plenty of time to change their plans (Bartram) or resign themselves to their fate (Woolman). In peaceful pre-Revolutionary times, it was normally safe for individual travelers to journey through the North American forests east of the Alleghenies, insofar as safety from the Indians was concerned.

Such daily interaction as William Bartram recorded in his journals during his extensive travel through the southern colonies reveals quite a different aspect of tribal society than that immortalized in nineteenth-century novels such as James Fenimore Cooper's "Pathfinder" series and in twentieth-century western cinema. The British Army captain Jonathan Carver, undertaking a journey of discovery from Boston westward, covered nearly seven thousand miles, much of it by canoe, in less than two and a half years. Laden with gifts, he encountered twelve tribes of Indians and waited out two winters as a guest of two separate tribes. Neither Bartram nor Carver could have survived if the Indian tribes had been as unrelentingly ferocious as they are frequently portrayed, and as some could actually become in and after battles against their colonial persecutors. By 1776, the hostile tribes that had come into frequent contact with the colonists and tried to resist them with continuous open warfare had been annihilated.

WILLIAM BARTRAM'S TRAVELS AMONG THE INDIANS

Historians concerned with the southern colonies owe a tremendous debt to William Bartram, an amateur but gifted botanist who recorded his travels on horseback from North Carolina to what is now southern Mississippi from April 1773 to 1777. Although his narrative is often slowed by rhapsodies over exotic plants, his enthusiasm ultimately becomes contagious. He may also rightly be considered the first in a long line of southern humorists, for his highly skilled pen animates many of the people whom he accompanied in their trading caravans or in whose tribal villages he sometimes lingered. He was as keen an observer of human nature as of vegetative nature; one of the touchstones of his work is a refusal to dismiss entire groups of people with a few stereotypical phrases. Each individual person is appraised (and usually appreciated) regardless of racial background. He describes racially mixed marriages with an absence of vituperation that is remarkable for an eighteenth-century American. Remarking that the Creek Indian who ferries him across a river was married to a white woman, he praises the man's civility and common sense. Another interracial marriage had less happy results; Bartram recorded the plight of a genteel North Carolinian who had amassed a fortune in dealing with Florida's Seminole Indians only to have it squandered in gifts to her relatives by the exceedingly beautiful Indian he married.[17]

William Bartram was one Pennsylvanian for whom the woods held no terror; indeed, he welcomed the sudden change from the rice fields and other cultivated lands to the unplowed pine forests of the West, for the opportunities it afforded him to view new flora. He was equally fond of the fauna, devoting nearly as much space to the habits of gopher turtles and the size and danger of alligators as to the hibiscus and other colorful flowers. Witty and sensitive as well as intelligent, he studied the Indians and at least some of their languages. Invited to a ceremonial dance on the eve of a ball game between two Indian villages, he noted that the festivities began with a long harangue by an aged chief on the benefits of exercise and on the town's many victories, "not forgetting or neglecting to recite his own exploits."[18]

Sometimes travel in the colonies was possible only because of the ingenuity and guidance of friendly Indians. William Bartram and a Mustee

Indian once built a raft twelve feet long and nine feet wide by binding logs with grape vines to ford a raging river. Although it was a novel experience for the white man, the pair ferried all the horses and goods of an entire trading caravan across. Immediately they faced another challenge and were forced to cross a "raccoon bridge," a sapling felled to span a branch of the river. This primitive bridge was so high that Bartram described it as "resting in the air." They each packed a hundred pounds of goods; Bartram admired the ease with which his companion crossed, contrasting it with his own sideways shuffling over the chasm.

Stopping with a succession of white settlers in the woods, he was pleasantly surprised at being offered fresh milk, butter, and cheese; the coastal towns lacked such commodities. Horses and cattle, owned and herded by the Indians, were almost as frequently encountered as deer, turkey, and quail, and peach trees stood beside fields of corn, rice, indigo, and cotton.

The unarmed Bartram found his passage among the Indians almost unhindered. Only once did he express fear from that quarter; he was riding alone when an obviously enraged Indian charged up to his horse with his rifle at the ready. Appeased by the cordiality with which this white man greeted him, he provided directions to a house some ten miles distant, despite having left the place swearing to kill the next white man he met. While acknowledging the luck involved with his escape, Bartram nevertheless attributes it to the native nobility of the untutored Indian. The passage is reminiscent of Jean Jacques Rousseau's celebrations of the "noble savage." Bartram's account has the advantage that its author encountered Indians on a daily basis, whereas the French philosopher's largely conjectural arguments had been advanced despite the well-known tortured martyrdoms of several early Catholic fathers who had approached the northern tribes with missionary zeal. On the other hand, Bartram was no fool; he had the good sense to put off part of his journey when the Indians seemed unsettled and out of humor.[19] He frequently attached himself to trading caravans, realizing that even the Choctaws, who were at war at the time, never attacked traders on the road.[20]

Bartram once joined a peace delegation designed to pacify the Creek and Cherokee tribes while negotiating the transfer of two million acres of their land. This transaction would discharge the debts they had accrued with white traders, so the aged chiefs, perhaps also influenced by liberal presents they received, finally agreed. Surveyors were immediately dispatched, and Bartram quickly received permission to join approximately ninety mounted men on the trail. The composition of the group suggests that of similar expeditions throughout the colonies. Among the technical crew were surveyors, artists to render the distinctive attributes of various landmarks, astronomers to determine their exact longitude and latitude, chain carriers to help measure distances, and markers. Guides, hunters, about a dozen Indians and one disinterested, altruistic amateur botanist completed this mounted caravan, for which twenty or thirty pack animals carried provisions and camp equipment. They split into three teams at Wrightsborough, a Quaker settlement on forty thousand acres in Georgia.

Bartram was so enamored of the Seminole Indians that he listed their vices so as to avoid seeming overly biased in his descriptions of what seemed to him joyous, contented, loving, and guileless people. They made war from the same erroneous motives as the rest of mankind. He had never heard of the Seminoles or Creeks burning or torturing their captives or killing women and children, an assertion he makes to counter tales of Indian atrocities based on accounts of warfare as it was practiced among certain northern Indian tribes or by the colonial militia mobs occasionally gathered to suppress them. They gave into the temptations of adultery and fornication to a greater extent than other nations, but they punished the guilty parties whenever they were caught by cutting off their ears. They had also begun to over-hunt since the traders began dazzling their eyes with "foreign superfluities," taking such large amounts of game that their traditional means of sustenance were endangered.[21] Although courageous in war, they were skittish around snakes; they would avoid killing a rattle-snake for fear of retribution from the snake's family. They sought out Bartram, a collector and handler of wild things, to remove a rattlesnake from their village.

JOHN WOOLMAN'S TRAVELS AMONG THE INDIANS

While William Bartram's travels were largely prompted by his scientific curiosity about the botany of the southern Indian territories, John Woolman traveled west for the sake of testifying his Quaker faith before the northern Indians. While Bartram was apt to fall into rhapsodies about a flowering shrub and, one suspects, only secondarily recorded his impressions of the people he met, Woolman was primarily concerned with the area's inhabitants and the state of his own soul. Because their reasons for traveling were so different, each approached the necessity of travel differently. For Bartram, it was a welcome opportunity to be surrounded by natural beauty. He was so practiced at camping and in such good shape that he wore out horses instead of being ground down himself. In a storm, his first concern was helping the traders protect their goods from rain damage.

As for Woolman, however, it took considerable soul-searching and remonstration with his wife before he could bring himself to leave the safety and comfort of his home for the uncertainties of travel and the dangers of the wilderness. He suffered miserably from the cold, distempers, and sleepless nights on the trail. Both Bartram and Woolman discovered Indian artifacts; as one might expect, Bartram was keenly interested in the mounds and other ways Indians had changed the topographical features of the South. When Woolman came across a group of hieroglyphics painted on trees from which the bark had been peeled, he studied the red or black pictures of warriors to gain some insight into their warlike spirits. Feeling their need to experience the love and peace his religion had brought into his life, he advanced more than ever dedicated to sharing it with them.

As one of the tenets of his faith was that no single man possessed all truth, he was as anxious to learn about their beliefs as he was to bring his religion to them. Because Bartram's practice of botany occurred early in that science's development in America, he was mostly concerned with collecting and cataloging the various plant species. Woolman, on the other hand, could see the harm done by such intrusive and acquisitive practices; his moral sense led him to some of the first pronouncements in favor of habitat preservation. He understood how wanton hunting and white claims of land ownership had forced the Indians into ever more difficult terrain, and he sympathized with their plight.

CRÈVECOEUR'S AND WOOLMAN'S CRITICISMS OF THE SOUTH

In his *Letters from an American Farmer,* Crèvecoeur related how he journeyed to Charleston, South Carolina, the richest city in the American colonies. Two navigable rivers carried all the produce of the surrounding countryside, especially rice and indigo, to its docks, and the most affluent planters of the colony congregated in its mansions in search of health and pleasure. Crèvecoeur was far less sanguine about the city's lawyers, however, finding them far too abundant and acquisitive. He thought the privileged classes in general were too detached from the abject misery that their expenses necessarily brought to their slaves. Charleston's gold ripped children from their mothers in Africa and brought them to incessant daily labor under a sun as fierce, Crèvecoeur argued, as that of their native regions. At the same time Charleston's rapacity also deprived them of the wholesome food and drink necessary to function in such an extreme climate. Unlike northern slaves, whom he found enjoying nearly as much freedom as their masters and who were allowed to visit their wives once a week, southern slaves would have been foolish to develop emotional ties with men or women they might never see again.[22] In Crèvecoeur's account, the fat, healthy, and hearty northern slaves think themselves happier than the poor whites they encounter, and many continue to serve their benevolent Quaker masters even if they are set free.[23] In sharp contrast, Crèvecoeur claimed that the worst imaginable cruelty was practiced on a southern slave he encountered. That unfortunate had been left suspended in a cage to be eaten by the birds and insects for the crime of murdering his overseer.[24]

John Woolman's experience with southern slavery, although less literary than Crèvecoeur's account, seems decidedly more heartfelt. To Crèvecoeur's notion of a compassionate northern slavery, Woolman would reply that the institution, and ultimately the individual slaveholders, were to blame for all the murders committed in Africa to acquire the human chattel. He once argued that if the blood shed there were sprinkled on the garments of every colonist who profited from it, slavery would cease to exist.[25] At the age of thirty-seven, when he was mustering his strength to denounce slavery within his church, Woolman traveled to the southern colonies. Although voicing opposition to slavery was the chief reason for his journey, he felt ambivalent about offending his various hosts and uneasy as to whether his real motivation was self-aggrandizement, or just a chance to argue. His knowledge of scripture helped him win several private disputes in which his adversaries tried to justify slavery on biblical grounds, but his arguments generally had an intellectual rather than an emotional basis. In North Carolina, torn between reluctance to give offense and eagerness to do what he could to alleviate the great evil of slavery, he chose silence. He was relieved when the Carolinians themselves brought up the question of educating their slaves, especially about religion.

Whatever his inner turmoil about the slave question, he was affirmed by the renewals of pure love at a Virginia meeting. At yet another Quaker meeting, he rejoiced at the story of a Mennonite who, traveling past the house of an acquaintance, chose to camp in the woods rather than be accommodated in luxury obviously earned by the sweat of the man's overworked slaves.[26] Even more cheering was the fact that Woolman heard the tale in Virginia, the entire economy of which was based on slave labor. His Quaker reticence kept him from making similar avowals of his antislavery beliefs, but other Quakers were obviously arriving at the same view. The Quakers were among the first religious groups in America to oppose the institution of slavery, passing a resolution to discourage the practice at their yearly meeting in 1758.[27]

HORSE POWER

Horses could be expensive to purchase and maintain, as documented by Benjamin Mifflin in his travels from Philadelphia to Delaware and Maryland, from July 26 to August 14, 1762. He recorded virtually every time he had to feed (or "bate") the animal. His horse ate at least twice a day on the road in addition to the oats and hay it consumed in the evenings, fodder that his owner was able to purchase from farmers or inn-

Horses provided the easiest means of covering long distances, but most of an army would travel on their feet. Travelers were forced to ford rivers or pay to be ferried across them. Courtesy of the Library of Congress.

keepers. The prudent traveler, Mifflin noted, considered taking good care of horses as the most material factor in traveling;[28] he would personally make sure that his horse received good fodder, instead of entrusting his care to an innkeeper.[29]

William Bartram estimated that his horse carried him at least six thousand miles in three years of travel on the southern trails. It was not until he attached himself to yet another caravan of serious traders that his "trusty old slave," as he referred to the animal, had to be replaced. Although he had had the foresight to bring sufficient presents for the Indians to purchase another horse, at that point he found himself facing the unpleasant alternatives of falling behind his temporary companions in hostile Indian territory or hiring them to take him farther and then turning the animal loose in the woods. Luckily they encountered another caravan, and he was able to purchase a strong young horse for ten pounds sterling and his own mount.[30]

John Woolman also rode out to the Indians but was far more inconvenienced by the experience than the naturalist had been. Soaked by cold, torrential rains, challenged by the terrain of the Blue Ridge Mountains, and wary of the increasing likelihood of a frontier war, he meditated until he could accept the physical hardships as the means by which the Father of Mercies was bringing him into closer sympathy with the Indians.

Woolman's trip to the southern Friends included another daring (for him) hundred-mile side jaunt to Goose Creek. He spent the first night in a public house, the second in the woods, and reached Goose Creek on the third.[31] Lying sleeplessly on the damp ground and feeding the mosquitoes throughout the second night led him to contemplate the expulsion of Adam and Eve from Eden. In two months, he covered about 1,150 miles, an average of over nineteen miles a day despite frequent meetings and other delays. On another occasion, he traveled two hundred miles in two weeks on Pennsylvania roads.[32] On a trip to Boston in hot weather, he and another traveler, moved by compassion, excused the heavy guide they had engaged and the over-burdened horse that had to bear him. This is one of the few references in travel narratives or journals of the period to the suffering the horses sometimes endured. Most accounts noted only when they were unable to continue their work.

The two most famous horseback rides of the Revolutionary War were those of Paul Revere and Caesar Rodney. Revere's nocturnal ride on April 18, 1775, was immortalized as "Paul Revere's Ride" in a famous poem written by Henry Wadsworth Longfellow in 1860. Military secrets were hard to keep in a heavily politicized town like Boston in 1775, where at least half the citizenry were silently (and often openly) opposed to the British occupation. Housing soldiers in private homes as well as in commandeered public buildings increased their intimacy with the residents, who after all were still subjects of His Majesty. Such intimacy encouraged spies to inform the army that seditious figures like Sam Adams and John Hancock might be captured in Lexington and that the increasingly hostile local militia had stockpiled weapons and ammunition in Concord. Spies for the other side passed knowledge of the British plans to the Patriots, and Revere was instrumental in organizing the other messengers and personally warning Adams and Hancock in advance of the British approach. Billy Dawes and Dr. Samuel Prescott joined Revere on the road that night, and only Prescott made it all the way to Concord. While it may seem that Revere's later notoriety was mostly the result of the greater ease with which rhymes could be found for his last name, he deserves his fame as a messenger. On at least five other occasions, Revere carried important messages over long distances for the Patriot cause, once averaging over sixty miles per day to inform Philadelphia and New York of the events unfolding in Boston.[33]

Caesar Rodney's ride was even more critical than Revere's most famous trip; he was the only man in the world who could have performed his role at a crucial moment in history. On June 7, 1776, Richard Henry Lee, a delegate from Virginia, acting on instructions from his state's elected assembly, introduced a resolution for independence. A committee was formed to frame a document announcing American independence to the world, but the final vote on the measure was postponed until its exact wording could be determined and the required unanimity of state's delegations could be obtained. Delaware had named three delegates to the Second Continental Congress, but Caesar Rodney became ill and had returned home during the session. The other two delegates, George Read and Thomas McKean, split their votes on the critical question, with Read arguing that the step was premature. Informed of their deadlock, Rodney raised himself from his sickbed and rode from Delaware to Philadelphia to break the tie within his delegation. On July 2, 1776, his crucial vote on the floor of the Continental Congress made the resolution for independence official, and on July 4 Congress voted to accept the Declaration of Independence in the form that has been preserved. Without Rodney's heroics, and the efforts of his horse, the opportunity for the required unanimity might have passed. Delegates might have been recalled, or instructed by their state assemblies to oppose the measure, or individually changed their minds.

Horses could be expensive, but sometimes the services of a single horse could be stretched to transport two men by means of the "ride and tie," well known in the colonies. John Greenwood and another fifer had one eight-dollar horse to carry them the 350 miles to Boston. One man would ride for two miles and then tie the horse. The other would walk to the horse, mount him, proceed another two miles after overtaking his partner, and leave the horse tied up and resting behind him as he again proceeded on foot.[34]

When Horatio Gates fled from the catastrophe at Camden, South Carolina, in August of 1780, the fifty-two-year-old general rode a single horse sixty miles in one day and covered 120 additional miles on relayed horses over the next two days. A soldier, John Slover, a stole a horse in 1781 from Indians who had already burned his fellow captives at the stake; he covered eighty miles on horseback and another twenty miles running in a single day. By comparison, an army on good roads in its own country could manage forced marches of sixty miles per day, as the combined French and American forces sometimes did when hastening from New York to surround Cornwallis in Virginia.[35]

Horse theft probably motivated some of the 465 militiamen who assembled forty miles from Fort Pitt in Pennsylvania on May 20, 1781. Each was told to bring a horse, a gun, and a month's provisions. Those who had earlier lost horses would be able to reclaim them if they were found in the Indian villages, and those whose horses were lost during the expedition were to be given the opportunity to replace them from among the horses taken from the Indians. Some of the men lost their horses before serious marching had even begun, and others begged off on account of having only brought five days' provision. The unluckiest found themselves caught in a precipitous retreat on mounts that were not up to the task, and many militiamen lost their lives.

In times of peace, a variety of carriages and wagons were available to the wealthy colonist who desired to be seen about town in a fancy rig. The very wealthiest would have a six-horse team driven and served by liveried servants, but only gradually did such vehicles become available for public transport even between the most populous northern cities. The smallest carriages were called "chairs," but southern plantation owners were likely to travel more elegantly. Hence, Janet Schaw found herself spirited along the North Carolina roads in a "phaeton" pulled by four horses and attended by several servants on horseback.[36] To accompany her husband, the Baroness von Riedesel started off from Canada in Burgoyne's army in a "calash" large enough for her children and servants.[37]

In combat, especially when the enemy singled out the British officers as targets, the horses that bore them also frequently suffered. Many others died during transport from England, including forty-six horses of a light dragoon regiment that arrived in October of 1776 after an eleven-week crossing.[38] The surviving horses arrived sick and in generally poor condition.

MESSENGERS AND POST RIDERS

Important, time-sensitive messages—such as warning of the advance of the British Army toward Lexington and Concord—were sent via mounted messenger.

The idea of entrusting people with urgent messages was in place before the Europeans came. The Iroquois sent runners throughout their confederation. Before the Revolutionary War, John Woolman recorded that such messengers arrived in the settlement of Wyoming, Pennsylvania, with news that a British fort farther west had fallen; the next night another runner reported that Indian warriors with scalps had arrived just ten miles away. The war was clearly traveling east faster than Woolman was traveling west.[39] In fact, a faster-riding Moravian passed Woolman on his way to visit the same Indian village. The two exchanged pleasantries on the road and later listened tolerantly to each other as they took turns talking to the Indians about their respective beliefs.

Less urgent messages could be entrusted to the continental postal services, for which Benjamin Franklin provided an early model of efficiency and leadership. His initial interest in the postmaster job was to ensure that the post riders could deliver his newspaper, though he was civil (and politically adept) enough to permit them to carry rival newspapers as well as his own. Suspecting that Franklin had intercepted public letters from a colonial governor and forwarded copies to political enemies, who had published them, the British authorities took the office from him; the later offer of the post of the first postmaster general of the United States represented such a delicious irony that he immediately accepted it. During the war each side developed its own postal services and frequently intercepted the enemy's mail in hopes of obtaining tactical information.

Postmaster R. Bache placed an advertisement in the *Pennsylvania Evening Post* on October 28, 1775, to announce the establishment of a thrice-weekly post from Philadelphia to New York; it was to leave the former city every Tuesday, Thursday, and Saturday. Twice each week the post was to be dispatched to the east as far as Portsmouth, and every Tuesday and Saturday it was sent as far south as Savannah, Georgia. Although the journey still required weeks, the fact that such posts were scheduled so frequently suggests that the colonies were neither as isolated nor as uninterested and ill informed about each other as they had been in the prior century.

INLAND WATERWAYS

The value of America's lakes and rivers as inland waterways had been recognized by even the earliest colonists. Most of the forts built in America during the eighteenth century, including Fort Ticonderoga and West Point, guarded access to major waterways. Wherever it was feasible, and frequently where it was not, wharfs were thrown up along the riverbanks between the major American cities and the sea in hopes of luring oceangoing commercial vessels.[40]

The famous Erie Canal would not open for another fifty years, but turnpikes and minor portages between rivers connected upstate New York with the coast. Most of the present Canadian/American border region could be traversed by canoe, but nothing larger. In a sufficiently cold winter, the rivers could become highways; the guns captured at Ticonderoga were brought across the ice to the Patriot forces surrounding Boston to break the British fleet's blockade of that port. The frozen rivers also offered recreational opportunities; Crèvecoeur bragged of running his horse-driven sleigh over the ice at twelve miles an hour.[41] In the South, the waterways were less useful, because the fall line, above which rivers are no longer navigable, was much closer to the coast.

Several significant moments in colonial American history were possible only because of the access provided by small boats. Paul Revere began his famous midnight ride by rowing past the British ships anchored at the mouth of the Charles River. Whenever secrecy was paramount, as it was on that night, rags could be wrapped around the blades of the oars to muffle the sound as they splashed into the water. The most famous crossing was Washington's risking of his army as well as his life on the icy Delaware River, under the cover of darkness and a winter storm, to attack the Hessian troops in Trenton, New Jersey, on the day after Christmas in 1776.

Elsewhere rivers were used tactically. Armies strove to collect all available boats to stop any pursuit by an enemy or to ferry their own forces across the obstacle that separated them. The decisive American victory at Yorktown was only possible because the British were not able to cross the York River, and the French fleet unexpectedly kept the Royal Navy from coming to their rescue.

LOGISTICAL PROBLEMS OVERLAND

Nature provided the only running water for everyone in the colonies, but those who stayed home had a better chance of finding drinkable water. Clear, fresh water was the most abundant natural resource east of the Mississippi River, but fear of contagion kept many people from drinking it.

During the war, the British Army's relative lack of mobility on land played to the Continental Army's advantage whenever the colonial troops could draw it into a lengthy campaign far away from reinforcement by sea. For all its advantages in armaments, training, and tradition, and its frequent numerical superiority on the battlefield, the British Army deployed far less rapidly than the relatively unorganized militias it frequently faced. The absence of rapid response options proved deadly to the British soldiers waiting for support during their long retreat from Concord, although they did manage to cover around thirty miles in less than twenty hours.[42] Lack of mobility and indecisive tactics also kept the British Army from following up on its victories to crush the Continental Army in New York in 1776. In the fall of 1777, it was the main ingredient in the rout at Saratoga. Burgoyne wasted valuable weeks trying to develop adequate roads for his army. It took General Howe and his army sixty-five days after leaving New York to arrive at Philadelphia on September 26, 1777, including an entire month, marching and counter-marching in response to Washington's maneuvers, to cover the last fifty-four miles.[43] Burgoyne's army was even slower; it took twenty-four days to move twenty-six miles, building its road as it went.[44] From September 20 to October 7 he was entirely stopped; discovering no way out of the morass, he surrendered on October 17.[45]

The lack of overland mobility also forced the British to post garrisons of several thousand men. These forces were too small to subjugate the countryside but large and widely scattered enough to be objectives, as General Washington proved in his victories at Trenton in 1776 and at Princeton a few days later. In the southern colonies, the lack of adequate roads allowed the colonists to harass and eventually exhaust the British armies sent to subdue them.

OCEANIC TRAVEL

The sea provided the colonists with whatever finished goods they could not manufacture themselves, but they unfortunately also brought regiments of British soldiers and artillery, first from England, and then from one colony to another as the focus of the war shifted. Replacements and orders had to come from New York City or from London, across three thousand nautical miles of open ocean. The naval connection occasionally offered tactical advantages to the British Army, as when General Clinton sailed in 1777 from New York with an army and left the American generals guessing as to his probable routes and destination; in the end, he occupied Philadelphia. Access to the sea rarely helped the American military until the French fleet from the Bahamas kept a smaller British fleet from relieving Cornwallis at Yorktown in 1781.

While movement on land required human or animal exertion, coastal traders and Atlantic merchant ships filled many seaports with life and energy. Pictured here is Salem, Massachusetts, around 1771. Courtesy of the Library of Congress.

The trip across the Atlantic, at least a two-month voyage, was always fraught with peril. Not just seamen but traders, immigrants, slaves, and students bound for university studies in London made the trip. By the middle of the eighteenth century, such voyages were so commonplace that accounts were published only when things went wrong. During the Revolutionary War, attack by pirates or ships of hostile navies sometimes added spice to such narratives. Vessels could be captured as contraband by the Royal Navy on one side and by congressionally authorized (or freelancing) privateers on the other. Adding to the confusion was the fact that privateers on both sides sometimes flew their enemy's flags in the hope of luring their intending prizes. In 1781, for example, the *Quebec,* a British ship, gave chase to what was thought to be a Dutch ship. As it grew close, the *Quebec* unfurled an American flag, and the quarry broke out its Swedish ensign. Undeterred, the British captain forced the other ship to heave to, only to learn it was a British merchant ship with salt and coffee bound for Danzig.[46]

The exploits of John Paul Jones in British home waters provided American popular culture with its first universally heralded naval hero, especially when he captured a British warship as his own was sinking. The Royal Navy, however, was able to establish a full-scale, and effective, blockade against most American ports it targeted. It even captured Henry Laurens, recently the second president of the Continental Congress, en route to Holland to negotiate a treaty and a loan, in 1780. Such privateers and naval ships as the Americans possessed became increasingly bold and successful as the war wore on; one captured dispatches that revealed the British war aims in 1781.[47]

Disruptions in international shipping could sometimes reach ludicrous lengths, as when in July 1781 a Spanish ship bound for New York was captured by two American privateers and redirected to Philadelphia. On their way, however, the vessel was captured by a British privateer, which redirected it to New York. Just outside of New York Harbor it was boarded a third time, but the rebels only took off the five prisoners taken when the royal privateer had captured the vessel. It was finally allowed into New York, as it may not have been able to do had it not belonged to neutral Spain.[48] Two days later another ship arrived safely after being taken by an American privateer, only to be retaken by a British ship. To one British captain, it seemed as though the coast swarmed with privateers.[49] The absence of British naval force in the theater greatly encouraged the privateers of several nations and discouraged merchants who would have preferred to make money more honestly.

Regardless of where in Europe a transatlantic voyage commenced, the first challenge facing its passengers was seasickness. Almost everyone on board the vessel conducting General Lafayette to America in 1777 suffered from this calamity, though the weather was good.[50] On the British side, a

Hessian mercenary recorded in his journal that his entire company on the ship transporting them to England on the first leg of their trip to America staggered about as if they were drunk.[51] The enforced idleness (for passengers) of shipboard life, compounded by narrow confines and the necessity of keeping out of the crew's way in general and below decks in inclement weather, and the poor quality of food on most vessels (salt pork and dry biscuits, by most accounts) meant that most travelers were in worse physical shape upon their arrival in America than when they had embarked. Such close quarters also allowed contagious disease to spread quickly. In addition to all that, wartime voyagers faced the threat of capture on the open ocean. Most accounts after the war began include sightings of enemy frigates and ensuing races with every man's liberty at stake.

Most problems, however, were caused by capricious winds, which could becalm vessels on the open sea, prevent them from making progress on the desired course, or force them to stay in port until the wind changed to a favorable direction. Slack winds allowed Woolman's party of Quakers to advance only to Tarpawling Cove in a whole day; a few acquired beds in a public house, and the rest were obliged to sleep on its floor.[52] Another full day's sailing in light winds brought them only within four miles of Nantucket, close enough for ten of them to row ashore. It took Benjamin Mifflin a full day to sail across fourteen miles of open bay from Annapolis, and the passage for man and horse cost twelve shillings six pence.[53]

At the other extreme were the North Atlantic squalls and ice, which added peril in winter, and the hurricanes of the late summer months. Either of these extreme weather conditions could snap even the thickest masts like toothpicks or toss about the heaviest ships of the line. The dispersion of Admiral John Byron's royal fleet in 1778 could serve as an example. All the ships were supposed to arrive in New York together, but the *Russel* turned back for England, the *Invincible* made Newfoundland, the *Albion* limped to Lisbon, the *Princess Royal* and *Culloden* made it to Halifax, and only the *Cornwall* and the lesser ships of the fleet arrived in New York.[54] In 1781, a hurricane dismasted most of an English squadron in Jamaica.[55] Ships leaving too early in the year could also encounter icebergs; in March 1776 a transport ferrying troops encountered numerous islands of ice, one of them a mile in circumference and sixty feet high. The next day the ship encountered an iceberg so long that its far end could not be seen. A thick fog encased the same vessel in ropes of crystal as the water vapor froze on the rigging, but the beauty of the scene was diminished by the necessity of having to break up the ice before the tackle could be used.[56]

Despite their ordeals, however, transatlantic crossings frequently spurred the popularity of nautical scenes in folk art. Even passengers whose voyages ended with indentured servitude might have fond memories of the weeks spent in relative idleness on the open seas, especially if the water supplies stayed clean, they did not tire of sometimes moldy biscuits and salt beef, and the vessel was not plagued by disease. Even a relatively uneventful crossing could provide a shock at the end; Janet Schaw could only imagine bears and wolves prowling as her ship approached Cape Fear, North Carolina, on February 14, 1775.[57] It was characteristic of the times that a British officer would be especially pleased upon finding that of the 2,283 embarked from Ireland on one voyage, only sixty arrived sick, and only five died.[58] More typical were the five hundred soldiers who had to be hospitalized for "scurvy and itch" out of 2,750 Germans who arrived in New York on August 11, 1781.[59] For the Hessian mercenaries who had never been at sea before, the most shocking events were the burials at sea. One diarist thought that he could see the fish and lobsters tearing at the flesh of a cadaver as soon as it hit the water.[60]

Three or four hundred Africans, facing a transatlantic journey against their will, were sometimes confined in cramped holds on the slave ships. Although the discovery of germs and bacteria still lay in the future, some hint of their power was observed in the contemporary references to bad air, from which distempers arose, killing many in the ships.

An enlightening prewar journal reveals the breadth of international trade and how active merchant shipping had become. Benjamin Mifflin recorded seeing in 1762 one ship loaded with lye and five with tobacco in Baltimore in 1762.[61] He also learned that a schooner loaded with salt from St. Martins had been taken by a Rhode Island privateer; an admiralty court in Virginia awarded the privateer three shillings for his work and allowed the vessel to continue back to Baltimore. While Mifflin found no seagoing ships at Annapolis, he did find three under construction at the city's wharves—a thirty-eight-foot sloop, a brigantine of fifty feet, and a ship of sixty feet. Keels for two other ships, of forty-five and seventy feet, had already been laid.[62]

NANTUCKET WHALING

Nantucket whalers found the best lumber in Massachusetts, pitch and tar in North Carolina, flour and biscuits in Philadelphia, and meat in Connecticut.[63] A typical whaling ship was manned by a crew of thirteen on a brig capable of carrying 150 tons.[64] Its complement was dispatched in two crews of four oarsmen, one harpooner, and a helmsman, in small whaleboats to pursue their prey whenever it was sighted. Rowed to within fifteen feet of the enormous animals, the harpooner, one of the strongest men in the crew, tried to wound it mortally. Ideally the animal died quickly and close to the ship; otherwise it dived or attempted to outrun the menace. If poorly struck or exceptionally strong, a whale could pull the boat at high speed across the waves—a "Nantucket sleigh ride." A St. Laurence whale, seventy-five feet long, weighed about three thousand pounds and yielded 180 barrels of oil. In 1770, 2,158 men were dispatched from Nantucket in 135 whaling ships of various sizes.[65] All had signed on to remain at sea at least until they had filled their ship to its capacity with whale oil, and some could stay out nearly twice as long if they managed to offload their barrels onto a ship that would carry their oil to England and sell it there.

12

Visual Arts

By 1783, the greatest names in eighteenth-century American art—West, Copley, Peale, Trumbull, and Stuart—had independently recognized the need to cross the Atlantic to obtain first-class training and were already making their work known in Europe. Their aims and achievements were foreign to the great majority of Americans, however. Although a plantation owner might hang a huge likeness of his sire or grandsire in the parlor to reinforce his claim of nobility among the tidewater gentry, most people lacked the time, money, and education to appreciate anything beyond a slavish imitation of the portraits they had viewed in England or in finer homes on this side of the Atlantic. The tastes of the art-commissioning public had long since settled on English models of portraiture, which demanded a certain elegance of pose, costuming, and execution, and any artist deviating from these standards was unlikely to have the wealthiest patrons. Still, the fact that the colonies could produce five painters of such surpassing quality suggests a far more vital community of working artists and a far more supportive market for their art by the time the revolution began than could have been found in colonial America prior to 1763.

Once the fighting for independence began in earnest, patriotic and economic pressures combined to force upon the American people an austerity that prevented them from acquiring additional paintings or supporting more artists. Commissions for portraits rendered in the traditional style dried up even faster than the supply of hard cash; the marginal artist was forced to return to painting houses or shoulder his musket to fight on one side or the other. The colonial printers still lacked resources to enhance their newspapers with pictures or illustrations, although a few broadsides made use of engravings of simple line drawings to broaden their appeal.

As for sculpture, after a statue of George III, horse and all, was pulled from its pedestal and melted down for cannonballs, it would take seven years of fighting before an American public clamoring for its own heroes would desire new statues; in the meantime, the nation's foundries had more pressing business. At a time when people were burying their silverware, plates, and service to protect it from looters and thieves, few were in the mood to commission more of the same, no matter how accomplished and famous the silversmith. A few isolated individuals still turned to such folk arts as woodcarving or needlepoint to express their frustrations with their present circumstances or their hopes for the future, but in general, production in the visual arts declined in the United States during the Revolutionary War years.

MYTHICAL MEN AND TRANSCENDENT ART

With the notable exception of Paul Revere's rendering of the Boston Massacre, the images of the American Revolution most likely to spring into the modern mind are largely those of artists of much later eras. Unfortunately, they are usually as remarkable for their historical inaccuracy as they are for their patriotic fervor. For example, John Trumbull's famous *The Signing of the Declaration of Independence, July 4, 1776*, has reinforced the erroneous belief held by generations of Americans that the document was actually signed on the date announced in its opening line. Almost all the signers added their names on August 2, 1776, and even "Matthew Thornton" signed even though he did not join the Continental Congress until November 4, 1776.[1] At least six other names were added as late as January of the next year.

Perpetuating the myth that the signing took place on the Fourth of July increases the dramatic poignancy of the signing, but it distorts the historical record and actually diminishes the courage it took for some of the richest and best-educated men in the colonies to commit what amounted to an open act of treason. Their fortunes and even their lives would probably have been forfeit had their bid for independence not succeeded. The actual votes for independence came on July 2, 1776, but the necessary political will had built up over a dozen years. The members of the Continental Congress were marked men even before July of 1776, but signing took even more courage in 1777 than it would have half a year earlier, for the war had taken several disastrous turns in the six months before Christmas of 1776—the invasion of Canada, a British offensive toward Ticonderoga, and the loss of Long Island.

Arguably the single most patriotic image of the American Revolution comes from a painting of a drummer, a fifer, and a flag-bearer marching past a wounded soldier on a Revolutionary War battlefield. It was created by Archibald McNeal Willard for the centennial of the Declaration of

Independence in 1876. The fifer has a bandaged head, which unites his suffering with that of the wounded man. The prostrate figure determinedly raises his cap in salute. Few icons of the Revolution have been so frequently and even lovingly parodied—most famously by Walt Disney—as Willard's *The Spirit of '76*.

Rivaling the Willard painting in popularity is Emanuel Leutze's *Washington Crossing the Delaware*, finished in 1851. It commemorates the night of December 25, 1776, when the general risked his entire army in an attack designed to engender new support for the cause. Washington is depicted almost as if he were a statue, a solid presence, seemingly the figurehead of the army. No painter was on hand to record the actual emotions that may have been visible on his face on that wretched night, when he was gambling not only his own life but the success of the entire war, but it seems an injustice to his humanity and intelligence to suggest that he was unaware of the risks or emotionally unaffected by them.

Leutze's worst anachronism in the *Delaware* painting is the flag, with its famous Stars and Stripes, a design that would not be adopted by Congress until June 14, 1777.[2] The absence of shadow in the painting demonstrates the artist's knowledge that the actual crossing occurred at night, but the clearly delineated facial features and colors suggest a very transparent night indeed. It is also doubtful that Washington and those under his immediate command would have assumed such heroic postures when the whole point of the maneuver was to avoid being seen until the surprise attack could be launched in force. Despite its by now well-documented inaccuracies, however, the painting conveys the dangers of crossing the ice-choked river and celebrates the heroic efforts of the common men who put their backs into bringing the American cause to fruition.

Leutze also created a companion piece in which the general is portrayed rallying his troops at Monmouth (June 28, 1778). It was a curious moment for the artist to choose; at first glance it seems a battle scene, in which both lines are on the point of attacking. In reality, only colonial forces are portrayed; Washington, despite the sweep of his sword and his imperious carriage, is busily correcting a communications error, not preparing to charge an entrenched enemy at the head of his troops (having ordered a full-scale attack on the British as they marched from Philadelphia to New York, Washington had been surprised to learn that his subordinate, Gen. Charles Lee, had ordered his main force to retreat instead). Both of Leutze's paintings reflect the aesthetics of the artist's time more than those of the American Revolution. For one thing, each painting is an enormous, impetuously flamboyant conception that the artist might not have had the nerve to execute had not the famous French painter Jacques Louis David already done similar work.

If Leutze's *Washington Crossing the Delaware* captured perhaps the most desperate moment of the American Revolution, John Trumbull rendered its proudest moment in his *Surrender of Cornwallis*. Executed intermittently from 1787 to 1828, it depicts the events of October 19, 1781, and is remarkable (as well as accurate) in not portraying Cornwallis as present; he had had a subordinate surrender on his behalf. Even more memorable is Trumbull's large painting of Washington returning his commission to Congress, a scene unprecedented in world history. That historical event happened on December 23, 1783, in Annapolis, Maryland, where Congress had migrated to prevent further embarrassment at the hands of returning veterans demanding back pay. Few painters had Trumbull's persistence or his access to the historical figures involved.

Nearly as famous as these paintings is one by Charles H. Weisgerber, *The Birth of Our Nation's Flag*. Weisgerber portrays Betsy Ross sewing the stars on the national flag, but the familiar pattern on which she is working may not in fact have been her original design. The painting was executed for Chicago's Columbian Exhibition of 1893 (and was commemorated in 1952 by a three-cent postage stamp). Debunking historians have argued that the story is based on Ross family legend, first made public by the seamstress's grandson in 1870, and that very little physical evidence exists that Betsy Ross did indeed design the definitive five-pointed stars or sew them on a flag like that shown in the painting.

There are several reasons why the iconography of the American Revolution has largely been defined by the images created in later eras. First of all, most colonial painters were more inclined to work in the lucrative field of portraiture than in landscapes, and very few of them had the talent or resources to attempt large-scale paintings of battle scenes. Secondly, it seems to have taken about a decade after the Revolutionary War before prosperity returned sufficiently to support the arts and for the sacrifices and ordeals of the conflict to fade enough to allow people to become nostalgic about it. Finally, photography would not be invented for about sixty years after the war, and only well into the twentieth century before it reached a stage of technological advancement that allowed active battlefield photography.

LEARNING TO PAINT IN AMERICA

Prior to the American Revolution, most people of substance thought of themselves as British citizens, whether they were of English, Scotch, Welsh, or Irish lineage, or from one of the other European states that contributed to the rapid growth of the colonies. British victories in the Seven Years' War, of which the French and Indian War was only the North American theatre, made the United Kingdom the world's greatest military power, and the ascendancy of its navy channeled the wealth of the world through London. A strong new English advance in the plastic arts encouraged colonial expression in paint, but colonists who made the leap

Most Americans thought the repeal of the Stamp Act would end
the disharmony between Britain and her colonies. The rare
public monument depicted here, designed by Paul Revere and
erected in Boston in 1766, pointedly celebrates the restoration
of American liberty rather than the spirit of reconciliation.
Courtesy of the Library of Congress.

from house to portrait painting found themselves at a competitive disadvantage. Not only did native English and other European rivals have the
opportunity to view far more paintings and other art, but they could more
easily apprentice themselves to master artists or even attend art schools.

It is doubtful that the average American of 1776 would have been able
to view more than a handful of paintings in his lifetime. The first American art museum was opened in Charleston, South Carolina, in 1773, and
the Philadelphia artist Charles Willson Peale did not open his portrait
gallery in Philadelphia until 1782. Most of the portraits now viewed as
the masterpieces of early American art were widely scattered and in private hands until much later in American history. The few paintings the
average man might have come across would probably have been the privately commissioned portraits of wealthy men or their immediate ancestors hung in their homes. Benjamin West was the first American artist to
overcome his initial lack of advanced training and limited exposure to
European models to achieve an international reputation in painting, but
the promise evident in his earliest years of portraiture might not have been
fully realized had he not left for Italy at the age of twenty-two.

Of course there were exceptions. As a young man, John Trumbull sought out John Singleton Copley and marveled at his paintings, then "tutored himself in the fine arts by studying the works that hung on [Harvard's] chamber walls" and reading books on the subject in the college library.[3] After the war began, he came across a few copies of European works, and he found his way to London to study with Benjamin West before the war was over. John Singleton Copley supported himself with his portraiture after his stepfather died when he was only fifteen;[4] he regularly met with older artists like John Smibert, John Greenwood, and Robert Feke, and admired the original work and copies in their Boston studies.[5] Copley also yielded to the inevitable necessity of studying in Europe, in 1773, a removal that was probably given as much impetus by the unpleasant atmosphere of Boston for a Tory like him as by the call of the muse. Gilbert Stuart apprenticed himself to a Scottish painter named Cosmo Alexander at the age of fourteen and was off to the more painter-friendly pastures of England by age twenty-one.[6] Charles Willson Peale studied briefly with a local painter named John Hesselius and with Copley in Boston before sailing for England at the age of twenty-five to study with Benjamin West in London.[7]

Each of these famous painters brought his proficiency to an acceptable level by copying the work of other artists, quickly rose to the forefront among the provincial painters who surrounded him, sought what aid he could at the hands of more established artists, profited by whatever copied paintings he could find, and left to acquire the polish of Europe as soon as he had the time, money, and confidence in his talent to do so. The work of each artist underwent a marked change soon after his European studies began. Although each was still very young when he crossed the Atlantic and his art would probably have continued to develop had he not made the voyage, for most of them the experience broadened their choice of subject, improved their technique, and reinforced their devotion to their art.

FIVE AMERICAN MASTERS IN EUROPE

Benjamin West was the pioneer among the five men who became the most prominent American painters of the eighteenth century; he found his way to Europe in 1760 when he was twenty-two. A devout Christian, he went to Italy for three years to soak up the Italian devotional paintings before becoming a permanent resident of England. In America, the products of his precocious talent were mostly portraits, but in nearly every one a marked advance in the painter's ability can readily be discerned. Unlike most colonial portrait painters, West typically went beyond head-and-shoulders or three-quarter portrayals of his subjects to include details of the subject's environment.

Landscape with Cow, finished when West was only fifteen, is usually dismissed as "childish" in manner (a remark by the painter William Dunlop in 1814).[8] Still, it might be taken as a blueprint for the artist's life. In the foreground are twisted trees, a road so poorly executed it would fit better in an abstract painting, and several men engaged in pursuits like those West probably witnessed on a daily basis in the colonies. In the lower left corner is an interestingly painted cow that draws attention away from the rest of the painting. Foremost among the human figures in the painting is the man on a bridge; he seems to be looking wistfully at the ship that could transport him to the land of windmills and Italianesque towers on the far shore. The choices the painter faced seem clear; he could remain on this side of the water and paint cows and the occasional fisherman, or he could take passage to a Europe that seems magical in comparison. His rendering of the European landscape clearly indicates that he had before him copies or at least engravings of the paintings that had been made there. Seven years later he made the trip, and within a decade after that he was receiving regular commissions for portraits and other paintings from no less a personage than the king of England. From 1768 to 1801 he sold at least seventy-five pictures, cartoons, drawings, and sketches to his royal patron.[9] He spent the Revolutionary War years mostly in his English studios, where he entertained and encouraged other colonial painters.

John Singleton Copley was born in the same year as West but had the good fortune to belong to a family in which his stepfather, Peter Pellham, made his living as a painter and engraver.[10] Copley was as precocious as West but received formal training in his art throughout his childhood. There is a vitality to his portraiture even as, like West, he showed marked improvement with each painting. Unlike West's early interest in the sitter's environment, Copley preferred a dark background or generalized landscape that functioned almost like wallpaper and against which his subjects stood out in bold color. His early work is marked by poses and gestures copied from European masters, the original faces replaced with those of his patrons—a method that illustrates a way in which provincial painters could school themselves in their craft. By the mid-1760s, however, he was beginning to add props to suggest the sitter's work, although the backgrounds were still nondescript. His 1765 portrait of his brother attracted favorable attention from the British cultural elite, but his American practice was going so well that he had all the work he needed in Boston and during the seven months he spent in New York in 1771. In addition to renovating a mansion on Beacon Hill, Copley found time to visit Philadelphia, where he admired copies of work by such European masters as Titian that had been collected by the chief justice of Pennsylvania, William Allen.[11]

The politics of the era forced people to take sides, and the choice was not easy for the five painters. Their customers typically came from the moneyed classes, among whom in many areas were more Tories than

Patriots. West and Copley were already well on their way to becoming wealthy because of their art, but the younger painters had to make choices that could have serious and immediate effects on their income as well as long-range impacts on their future opportunities.

John Trumbull chose to throw in his fortunes with the Patriots, and as a recent Harvard graduate with a knack for drawing and a brother who was commissary general for the entire army, he rapidly became an aide-de-camp to General Washington and then a colonel serving as deputy adjutant-general for General Gates. Such easily gained rank was probably not properly valued, and he resigned early in 1777 when Congress dated his commission from September 1776 instead of June (costing him three months' seniority). By 1780, he was in London at the very center of American painting, the studio of Benjamin West, but by November the recent colonel of the Continental Army was in a British prison for treason; there he stayed for eight months. Finally released, he made his way to New York. After the war, in 1784, he returned to London.[12]

As the only one of the five painters with a college education, Trumbull began his serious work with large paintings of subjects from antiquity, but by 1885 he was working on the first of his paintings of important scenes from the American Revolution: *The Death of General Warren at the Battle of Bunker Hill, June 17, 1775* (1786); *The Death of General Montgomery in the Attack on Quebec, December 31, 1775* (1786); *The Declaration of Independence, July 4, 1776* (1787); *The Capture of the Hessians at Trenton, December 26, 1776* (begun 1786); *The Death of General Mercer at the Battle of Princeton, January 3, 1777* (1789); *The Surrender of General Burgoyne at Saratoga, October 16, 1777* (1822); *The Surrender of Lord Cornwallis at Yorktown, October 19, 1781* (1787); and *The Resignation of General Washington, December 23, 1783* (1824).

Trumbull's portraits included, a 1780 full-length George Washington, in which the face and uniform were painted from memory but the pose and background were rendered in the popular British style of the age.[13] It was the first of a long series of portraits of the general and other heroes of the early American republic that were widely copied, printed, and disseminated throughout the triumphant nation until the Civil War provided a new pantheon of popular icons.

Charles Willson Peale, born in 1741, was only a dilettante until he made his trip to London, where he stayed from 1767 to 1769. Setting himself up in England seemed to release a major force within Peale; he blossomed under the tutelage of Benjamin West and from exposure to the artist community to which he was introduced. Because there were as yet no public art museums in the colonies, Peale's heady experience of seeing his work appear on museum walls soon after he began painting was almost unprecedented for an American. He received his first major commissions during his short stay in England, and although the proceeds were not enough to pay his living expenses, one of them demonstrates the way in which the American political environment shaped even painting at this point.

A few Virginians tried to order a portrait of Lord Camden, an outspoken opponent of the Stamp Act, but Peale found the British politician unwilling to pose for the painting. As a substitute, an American lawyer practicing in London requested a portrait of William Pitt; when that luminary was also unwilling to sit for a painting, Peale took his likeness from a sculpture.[14] Returning to America, he produced museum-quality portraits that typically featured the sitters' sumptuous clothing and objects that suggested their work, although just as often his backgrounds were studio backdrops. His talent soon attracted the attention of a Virginia planter who later became famous, and this acquaintance resulted in the only portrait of George Washington painted before the Revolution.[15] The sitter chose to wear his Virginia Regiment uniform, despite the fact that he was now forty and the French and Indian War had been over for a decade. The painting hints that the agreeable life of a country squire had broadened his beam a bit; the fourth button from the bottom of his waistcoat had already been forced to withdraw from the line, and the fabric is so stretched around the last three that there seems little hope that they can hold out much longer. A gratuitous purple sash divides the figure from the lower left corner to the upper right; above this line is the competent military leader, on whom only the slightest double chin suggests any concession to age and good living. The angles that extend downward from his gun barrel and from the top of the marching orders so prominently and strategically placed in the lower pocket of the waistcoat suggest the virility of the man who would someday, and quite properly, be referred to as the father of his country. Washington liked the painting so much that he posed for six more portraits by the same artist in the course of the next twenty-seven years.

Peale was also fascinated by American fauna. When he opened his famous museum in 1787, its main attraction for most Americans was his collection of carefully taxidermied native animals.

Gilbert Stuart arrived in London in 1775 at not quite twenty. Although he had been studying art with a Rhode Island painter named Cosmo Alexander and had even ventured across the Atlantic with him in 1771, it was not until he placed himself in Benjamin West's studio that his portraiture excelled that of almost all his contemporaries. Stuart worked throughout almost all the war years in West's studio, leaving only in 1782. Although his best work, in which the facial features of his subjects are so distinctly and brilliantly rendered, still lay ahead of him, it was probably his 1782 portrait of William Grant on ice skates and the commissions it brought him that gave him the financial independence necessary to set up his own successful studio.

RALPH EARL, TORY PAINTER

A few colonial painters chose to maintain their British identities despite the revolutionary currents that swirled around them, and the most accomplished of these was Ralph Earl. He stayed in Connecticut even after the war began in earnest until forced to abandon the colonies because of his Tory sympathies; he may have saved several lives by alerting the British to a planned ambush. Arriving in London in 1778, he too sought out Benjamin West; he returned to New York in 1785 with such skill that several patrons sat for him even when he was in jail for debt.[16] His portraits tend to emphasize the sitter, placed against a nondescript background, and his best work belongs to the postwar era.

FORMAL PORTRAITURE

All of the famous Revolutionary-era battlefield paintings, such as Washington's confrontation with Lee, were painted after the war, in some cases several generations later. The paintings actually turned out in the Revolutionary era did not have the psychological or propagandistic impact of these later works. The most typical painting of the period was a privately commissioned three-quarters or head-and-shoulders portrait of a wealthy man. Prior to the war, successful lawyers, businessmen, and planters could become fixtures on the colonial landscape, but it is doubtful that they could realistically expect their portraits to hold the interest of anyone beyond their immediate circles, with the possible exception of their heirs. After the Revolution, these men found themselves suddenly belonging to the ages. The demand for portraiture skyrocketed with the ambitions of men newly freed from the limits imposed by colonialism and Old World emphasis on noble birth.

George Washington, for example, sat for the best American portraitists of his day. Most of the formal portraits for which he sat were eventually commemorated by the U.S. Postal Service. Such portraits were not entirely an issue of vanity. Photography had yet to be invented, so there was no other way for the richest or otherwise most important colonists to preserve their images. Because family relationships were among the most important aspects of American life at the time, such portraits might show subsequent generations what their grandparents or great-grandparents looked like and how substantial they had been.

It was no easy thing to acquire a formal portrait. First of all, one had to find a capable painter, preferably with European training; many house painters, who might better have stayed with their main line, offered their services as limners or portraitists. The artist might require many modeling sessions, for which the subject might have to maintain the same posture for hours on end. This limited the range of facial expressions to those

Franklin was already the most famous American
when he posed for this 1761 painting by
Benjamin Wilson. The vitality and topicality of
its background were highly unusual among
the staid portraits of the day. Courtesy of
the Library of Congress.

that could be held for long stretches and resumed upon demand; sitters
tended to have frowning, studious looks, or worse. The cost of the portrait could be prohibitive, and if dissatisfied the customer had little re-
course beyond a refusal to pay or submitting to the whole process a second
time.

Surprisingly frequently, however, the painter's efforts were crowned
with success that increased the popularity of both subject and artist.
Charles Willson Peale's portrait of John Inglis, for example, hung at the
entrance of the tremendously popular dance hall on the second floor of
Philadelphia's City Tavern.[17] At a time when there were no art galleries
or public collections, the exposure to the buying public guaranteed by
such prominent wall space (from 1773 to 1790, the tavern served as

Philadelphia's social center) must have seemed priceless.[18] Skill in portraiture gave employment to numerous artists and lasting fame to a few men like Stuart and Peale. During the Revolutionary War, however, the increased hazards of travel, a shortage of ready money in the weakened economy, and patriotic pleas against extravagance combined to limit the demand for portraiture. After the war, the demand for such art outstripped the economic recovery, because battlefield exploits had made some men famous and the new government had created posts of previously unavailable prominence. The painter's potential clients included Philadelphia's elite as well as the most important men of the colonies who had gathered for the Continental Congresses.

SILHOUETTES

Another, cheaper form of preserving one's likeness was the popular practice of tracing a subject's silhouette as it was projected onto white or black paper by a strong lamp. As a halfway measure, it was far cheaper than the oil portrait, but it was correspondingly less detailed and permanent. Many prominent men posed for silhouettes. They would be stationed with their heads on the same level as the bright light. A craftsman would then carefully trace the outline of the profile the subject's shadow formed on a piece of paper. The resulting silhouettes, for which even such luminaries as Washington and Franklin posed, came closest to negating the subjective hand of an artist of any medium then in existence.

STATUES, CARVINGS, AND ENGRAVINGS

A fascination with celebrity is not solely an American trait, and among the first things one asks about famous people is what they looked like. Small porcelain statues of Benjamin Franklin could be purchased in London; the same image was reissued with the name "Washington" replacing "Franklin" on its base.

Perhaps the depth of the sentiment against the Stamp Act can best be fathomed by considering the fact that a monument designed by Paul Revere was erected in Boston to commemorate its repeal. The concept of an obelisk, a four-sided monument with sculptures in relief and metal plaques, was borrowed from Egyptian antiquity.

Engravings could sometimes fill the role later assumed by photographs, providing readers of the colonial broadsides and newspapers with an artist's interpretation of an event. The same method was used for producing cartoons, which were largely political in nature throughout this period. The honor of having produced the first famous, widely recognized and reprinted cartoon in an American newspaper falls to Benjamin

Because Greek and Latin were the mainstays of a college
education in pre-Revolutionary America, allegorical
representations and classical allusions were common in the
visual as well as in the literary arts. This painting was made in
1781. Courtesy of the Library of Congress.

Franklin; its emphasis on uniting the colonies is remarkable because of its early date, 1754. Paul Revere's engravings of the Boston Massacre were also very influential. The interpretation of this event as a cold-blooded killing of innocent civilians popularized by his widely reprinted propagandistic rendering distorts the historical record of the largely accidental deaths of several members of what was essentially a mob on March 5, 1770.

Prints made from engravings sometimes also helped fill the popular demand for information about the great men in other colonies as well as in England. No American was more famous prior to the Revolutionary War than Benjamin Franklin, and prints of his likeness, especially the famous one that Edward Fisher developed based on an oil portrait by Mason Chamberlin, enabled distant admirers to associate a face with the great man's reputation. Franklin's stature was such that his portrait probably graced many walls in colonial family rooms heated by Franklin stoves and protected by lightning rods, two of his inventions. After the war began, the hanging of Franklin's portrait or those of other Revolutionary War figures helped patriots feel connected with their political and military leaders. The numerous battlefield scenes increasingly available after the war sometimes provided households with chances to make a private political statement of allegiance or to express their solidarity with friends or family who had served on the depicted battlefield.

Engravers also had official roles during this period; all paper currency had to include elaborate script in its design to discourage counterfeiters. No less a personage than Benjamin Franklin profited doubly from his role as an official state printer by using it to enlarge his acquaintance with, and currying the favor of, the most influential and trusted men of the assembly. It was their job to ensure that he did not print more money than was ordered and that he destroyed the plates after use. Of course, Paul Revere is considered the preeminent engraver of his time; his most powerful political work has already been discussed.

Surviving engravings make it easy to see how they could fill the role of decorative art in colonial American homes. Prints were not only far cheaper than the oil paintings of the period but many times more interesting in the breadth of their subject and treatment. Sometimes beginning painters would study whatever prints came to hand to work out technical problems in their own work, study that occasionally gave them a two-dimensional, linear, and flawed rendering of perspective.

CARTOONS AND CARICATURES

Although the first American cartoon, published in 1747, was a depiction of Hercules in Benjamin Franklin's *Plain Truth*, the first cartoon to be widely circulated in America had the surprising aim of uniting the colonies in 1755.[19] Benjamin Franklin pictured a snake that had been cut into thirteen pieces, each of which was labeled with the name of a state, above the legend "Join or Die." Although he may have erred in his choice of subject from a modern marketing perspective, his visual message was both clear and powerful. Several later cartoonists and sometimes even flag designers remembered Franklin's drawing and used snakes to suggest the colonies.

As its areas of conflict with Britain multiplied, America was typically caricatured as a woman in classical clothing remarkably similar to that worn by representations of the mother country. Gradually an Indian maiden gained prominence in the iconography of the era—a brilliant visual metaphor, because it insisted on the differences between the old country and the new. Using a woman to represent the colonies had the added advantage of conveying moral outrage and political imposition because the garments, often already little more than drapes used to suggest the classical robes favored in the period, frequently slipped. The original viewer was likely to transfer embarrassment to indignation for a mishandling of colonial affairs.

NEEDLEPOINT PANELS

The few surviving needlepoint panels created before the Revolution are as astonishing for their subjects as for their high production values. These direct relatives of the extraordinary tapestries still being created in Europe at the time filled the wall space later occupied by landscape paintings. In contrast to the narrow scope of oil painting in the era, Mrs. (Benjamin) Love Rawlins Pickman created matched panels of two rustic scenes and two harbor landscapes. One of her designs is based on a popular French engraving, a medium to which other women might turn for inspiration for their needlework projects. Other women were creating still lifes of fruits or flowers or replicating their family's coats of arms.[20] Although these specific items were mostly created in the 1740s, they would have still graced the walls of Revolutionary-era homes as family heirlooms. The best surviving examples are part of the M. and M. Karolik Collection and can be seen at the Boston Museum of Fine Arts. Each of the four panels by Rawlings Pickman featured extremely colorful silk threads on a background and base of black silk. The effect of their bright reflective fabrics on a continental wall must have been stunning, and the fine detail with which she worked the ships, buildings, human figures, and exotic birds make it difficult to imagine a more accomplished craftsman in her chosen medium.

The expensive materials woven into the surviving needlework, which sometimes included threads of silver as well as the finest silk, usually meant that the creators of museum-quality work were often part of the richest families. It should come as no surprise, therefore, that a family's coat of arms was a popular design choice. This was especially true since they typically featured foreground figures and elaborate borders without the gradations in shading found in other media that would be especially difficult to produce in needlepoint. Women in less affluent households would work with baser materials, such as satin and wool.

Cost of Products During the Revolutionary War Era

Determining the value of money was problematic for colonial Americans even before the Revolutionary War began. British currency was in such short supply that several colonies hit upon the expedient of printing their own money, and coins from other European countries sometimes made their way inland from the port cities. Individual merchants would sometimes develop their own exchange rates, discounting the funds a customer might offer in response to the perceived strength of a particular currency. In 1764, Parliament tried to stop the confusion with the Currency Act, which kept American colonies from printing their own money. The act would have had an adverse effect on the money supply had the colonists fully complied with it.

Once the war began, the Continental Congress began printing the American dollar. It was initially accepted at face value, which meant that a ten-dollar bill had the same purchasing power as the same sum of silver coins would have had. People gradually began discounting paper currency as Congress authorized additional printings that were not backed by gold or silver reserves equal to the total face value of the paper money in circulation. Confidence in the new currency gradually eroded with each additional printing; the saying that something was "not worth a continental" underscored the fact that the dollar was very nearly worthless in the last years of the war.

In sharp contrast to the American dollar, the official British currency still maintained most of its value during the era. Each pound sterling could be divided into twenty shillings, each of which could be further divided into twelve pence. Even when the government tried to regulate prices—a policy attempted by Governor William Tryon in New York—the effort was quickly undermined by market forces. The *New York Gazette,* which ran an announcement of the official prices for certain commodities, such as a pound of tea (ten shillings) or coffee (two shillings six pence), among other advertisements, continued in the same issue its practice of printing the going rates for a short list of commodities on page 1, immediately under its masthead. Here, tea was priced at ten shillings per pound and coffee at one shilling six pence.

Modern historians and economists who want to determine the actual price of a commodity are hampered by the fact that contemporary advertisements very rarely listed prices. This leaves scholars dependent upon such things as journal entries in which a diarist occasionally recorded a price or the purchases that led to the day's total expenditure, usually listed as only the final sum.

ADVERTISING AND NEWSPAPER SUBSCRIPTIONS

Newspaper: ten shillings for a yearly subscription to the *Pennsylvania Evening Post* in 1775 (Quarterly subscriptions were three shillings, individual issues two pennies each)

ANIMALS

Cow: Thirteen Pennsylvania dollars in 1774

Mare: Twenty-five Pennsylvania dollars in 1774

BOOKS AND PAMPHLETS

Pamphlet: two shillings (price of *Common Sense,* the forty-six-page pamphlet by Thomas Paine that became a best seller in the colonies when it appeared in 1776)

Book: thirty-six shillings for all three volumes "with neat bindings" of *Political Disquisitions* by J. Burgh, Gentleman, in 1775

ENTERTAINMENT

Concert tickets: one dollar each for an evening's vocal and instrumental selections in South Carolina in 1767[1]

Theatre tickets: box six shillings, pit four shillings, gallery two shillings, for *Venice Preserved; or, A Plot Discovered* at the Hospital in Albany in 1769[2]

FOOD AND DRINK

Beef: from two shillings four pence to three shillings per pound in New York in 1781[3] (In Boston, 1777, the same source listed beef at 18 pence per pound, while beef was only 8 pence per pound in Rhode Island)[4]

Chickens: twenty-five to forty shillings per dozen in Rhode Island in 1778[5]

Coffee: one shilling six pence in New York in 1777[6] Corn: four shillings six pence per bushel in Rhode Island in 1777[7]

Fish: eight pence to two shillings each for mackerel or sea bass in New York in 1781 (Sturgeon were held in such low esteem that 4 pounds of their flesh brought only six pence)[8] Lamb: from fourteen to twenty-four shillings per quarter in New York in 1781[9]

Pigs: four pence per pound, live weight in Rhode Island in 1778

Potatoes: two pence per pound in Rhode Island in 1777

Radishes: four pence per bunch in New York in 1781[10] Rum: six shillings six pence per gallon in Rhode Island 1781[11] Spinage: one shilling six pence in New York in 1781[12] Tea, green: six dollars per pound in 1777[13] Tea, Bohea: six shillings six pence in New York in 1777[14] Tobacco: one shilling per pound in New York in 1781[15] Turkeys: eight to fourteen shillings in Rhode Island in 1778

HORSE RACING PRIZES

Purse for both the Flatbush Races on September 10, 1777, and the Powles-Hook Races on August 17: one hundred pounds[16]

Purse for the winner of the best of three two-mile heats in 1780: fifty pounds in New York, second place ten pounds[17]

LAND

Rural: thirty-five shillings an acre, payable in seven years, in prewar Pennsylvania[18]

Urban: one hundred pounds for an acre of urban lots in Baltimore in 1762

TRAVEL AND TRANSPORTATION

Stagecoach, New York to Philadelphia in 1774: thirty shillings for passengers on the inside seats, twenty shillings for those who sat on top[19]

Stage wagon, New York to Morristown, New Jersey in 1774: four shillings[20]

TUITION

Course in language or higher branches of mathematics at Hughes's English Grammar School in New York City in 1773: five pounds per year, for other courses three pounds/year[21]

Notes

CHAPTER 1: EVERYDAY AMERICA

1. Alexander Hamilton, "A Full Vindication of Congress from the Calumnies of their Enemies . . ." in *The Works of Alexander Hamilton*, ed. Henry Cabot Lodge (London and New York: G. P. Putnam's Sons, 1904), vol. 1, 17.

2. Robert Rogers, *A Concise Account of North America* (London: J. Millan, 1765; repr. Yorkshire: S.R. Publishers, 1966), 121.

3. Friederich von Riedesel, *Memoirs and Letters and Journals of Major General Riedesel*, tr. William L. Stone (Albany, N.Y.: J. Munsell, 1868; repr. New York Times and Arno, 1969), vol. 2, 54.

4. Frederick Mackenzie, *The Diary* (Cambridge, Mass.: Harvard University Press, 1930; repr. New York: New York Times and Arno, 1968), 131.

5. Janet Schaw, "Janet Schaw, Caught in a Revolution," in *With Women's Eyes: Visitors to the New World 1775–1918*, ed. Marion Tinling (Hamden, Conn.: Archon, 1993), 4.

6. Ibid., 7.

7. Benjamin Mifflin, *The Journal of Benjamin Mifflin*, ed. Victor Hugo Paltsits (New York: New York Public Library, 1935), 8.

8. Mackenzie, 145.

9. Jean Baptiste Donatien de Vimeur, Count de Rochambeau, *Memoirs of the Count de Rouchambeau*, tr. M. W. E. Wright (Paris: French, English and American Library, 1838; repr. New York: New York Times and Arno Press, 1971), 10.

10. Ibid., 32.

11. Ibid., 53.

12. Mackenzie, 520.

13. Rochambeau, 16.

14. Ibid., 104.

15. Mackenzie, 146.

16. Ibid., 148.

17. Ibid., 185.

18. Gaston and Helene de Maussion, *They Knew the Washingtons: Letters from a French Soldier with Lafayette and from His Family in Virginia*, tr.: Princess Radziwill (Indianapolis: Bobbs-Merrill, 1926), 34.

19. Mackenzie, 517.

20. Hamilton, 43.

CHAPTER 2: WORLD OF YOUTH

1. Jeremiah Greenman, *Diary of a Common Soldier in the American Revolution, 1775–1783*, ed. Robert C. Bray and Paul E. Bushnell (De Kalb: Northern Illinois University Press, 1978), 39.

2. Philip Freneau, "The Silent Academy," in *The Poems of Philip Freneau: Poet of the American Revolution,* vol. 1 (Princeton, N.J.: University Library, 1902), 182–3.

3. Michel Guillaume Jean de Crèvecoeur, *Letters from an American Farmer* (Gloucester, MA: Peter Smith, 1968), 206.

4. Ibid.

5. Ibid., 210.

6. Ibid., 38.

7. Gaston and Helene de Maussion, *They Knew the Washingtons: Letters from a French Soldier with Lafayette and from His Family in Virginia,* tr. M. W. E. Wright (N.p.: n.p., 1838; repr. New York: New York Times and Arno Press, 1971), 138.

8. Ibid.

9. de Maussion, 139.

10. Ibid.

11. St. John de Crèvecoeur, "A Snow Storm as it Affects the American Farmer." in *Sketches of Eighteenth Century America,* ed. Henri L. Bourdin, Ralph H. Gabriel and Stanley T. Williams (New Haven: Yale University Press, 1925), 41.

12. Crèvecoeur, *Letters*, 30.

13. Ibid., 43.

14. de Maussion, 139.

15. Mary V. V. [pseud.], "A Dialogue, between a Southern Delegate, and his Spouse, on his return from the Grand Continental Congress" (1774), in Norman Philbrick, *Trumpets Sounding: Propaganda Plays of the American Revolution* (New York: Arno, 1976), 36, 38.

16. Friederich von Riedesel [Major General], *Memoirs and Letters and Journals of Major General Riedesel,* tr. William L. Stone (Albany, N.Y.: J. Munsell, 1868; repr. New York Times and Arno, 1969), vol. 2, 55.

17. Benhamin Mifflin, *The Journal of Benjamin Mifflin,* ed. Victor Hugo Paltsits (New York: New York Public Library, 1935), 16

18. James Thacher, *The American Revolution: from the commencement to the disbanding of the American army; given in the form of a daily journal* (Cincinnati: M. R. Barnitz, 1856), 352.

19. de Maussion, 185.

20. Crèvecoeur, *Letters,* 81.

21. Ibid., 120–21.

22. John Woolman, *The Journal with Other Writings of John Woolman* (London and Toronto: J.M. Dent & Sons, 1922), 90.

23. Jefferson, Thomas, *Notes on the State of Virginia* (Richmond, VA: J.W. Randolph, 1853), 97.

24. William Bartram, *The Travels of William Bartram* (New York: Macy-Masius, 1928), 355.

25. Ibid., 402.

26. de Maussion, 46.

27. Crèvecoeur, "A Snow Storm," 44.

28. Ibid., 46.

29. Michel Guillaume Jean de Crèvecoeur, "Thoughts of an American Farmer on Various Rural Subjects," in *Sketches of Eighteenth Century America*, ed. Henri L. Bourdin, Ralph H. Gabriel and Stanley T. Williams (New Haven: Yale University Press), 148.

30. Crèvecoeur, *Letters*, 25.

31. Crèvecoeur, "Thoughts . . . on Various Rural Subjects," 148.

32. Janet Schaw, "Janet Schaw, Caught in a Revolution," in *With Women's Eyes: Visitors to the New World 1775–1918*, ed. Marion Tinling (Hamden, Conn.: Archon, 1993), 5.

33. Johann Conrad Dohla, *A Hessian Diary of the American Revolution*, tr. Bruce E. Burgoyne (Norman: University of Oklahoma Press, 1999), 36.

34. Frederick Mackenzie, *The Diary* (Cambridge, Mass.: Harvard University Press, 1390; repr. New York: New York Times and Arno, 1968), 326.

35. Ibid., 329.

36. Ibid., 145.

37. Crèvecoeur, "A Snow Storm," 40.

38. Mifflin, 16.

39. Crèvecoeur, *Letters*, 16.

40. Ibid., 66.

41. Ibid., 72.

42. Mackenzie, 6.

43. Ibid., 9.

44. Ibid., 468.

45. Ibid., 7.

46. Dohla, 69.

47. Ibid., 23.

48. Mackenzie, 145.

49. Ibid., 390.

50. Dohla, 76.

51. Mackenzie, 517.

52. Ibid., 429, 456.

53. Ibid., 361.

54. For the national debt, James Thacher. *The American Revolution: from the commencement to the disbanding of the American army; given in the form of a daily journal* (Cincinnati: M. R. Barnitz, 1856), 350.

CHAPTER 3: ADVERTISING

1. Frederick Mackenzie, *The Diary* (Cambridge, Mass.: Harvard University Press, 1930; repr. New York: New York Times and Arno, 1968), 68–72.

2. James Thacher, *The American Revolution: from the commencement to the disbanding of the American army; given in the form of a daily journal* (Cincinnati: M. R. Barnitz, 1856), 31.

3. Jean Baptiste Donatien de Vimeur, Count de Rochambeau, *Memoirs of the Count de Rouchambeau,* tr. M. W. E. Wright (Paris: French, English and American Library, 1838; repr. New York: New York Times and Arno Press, 1971), 10.

4. Ibid., 32.

5. Ibid., 53.

CHAPTER 4: ARCHITECTURE

1. A. Lawrence Kocher and Howard Dearstyne, *Colonial Williamsburg: Its Buildings and Gardens* (Williamsburg, Va.: Colonial Williamsburg, 1949), 11.

2. Michel Guillaume Jean de Crèvecoeur, *Letters from an American Farmer* (Gloucester, MA: Peter Smith, 1968.), 127.

3. Mark Gelernter, *A History of American Architecture* (London and Hanover: University Press of New England, 1999), 85.

4. Crèvecoeur, *Letters,* 79.

5. Jeremiah Greenman, *Diary of a Common Soldier in the American Revolution, 1775–1783,* ed. Robert C. Bray and Paul E. Bushnell (De Kalb: Northern Illinois University Press, 1978), 88.

6. Emerson D. Fite and Archibald Freeman, *A Book of Old Maps Delineating American History* (New York: Dover, 1969), 248.

7. Ibid.

8. Ibid.

9. Ibid.

10. Ibid.

11. Michel Guillaume Jean de Crèvecoeur, "Thoughts of an American Farmer on Various Rural Subjects," in *Sketches of Eighteenth Century America,* ed. Henri L. Bourdin, Ralph H. Gabriel and Stanley T. Williams (New Haven: Yale University Press), 142–43.

12. Benhamin Mifflin, *Journal* (New York: New York Public Library, 1935), 8.

13. Janet Schaw, "Janet Schaw, Caught in a Revolution," in *With Women's Eyes: Visitors to the New World 1775–1918,* ed. Marion Tinling (Hamden, Conn.: Archon, 1993), 25.

14. Ibid., 65.

15. Fite and Freeman, 248.

16. Mifflin, 8, 9.

17. Ibid., 10.

18. Johann Conrad Dohla, *A Hessian Diary of the American Revolution,* tr. Bruce E. Burgoyne (Norman: University of Oklahoma Press, 1999), 187.

19. William Bartram, *The Travels of William Bartram* (New York: Macy-Masius, 1928), 168–9.

20. Ibid., 284.
21. Ibid., 296.
22. Ibid., 354.
23. Ibid., 402.
24. John Woolman, *The Journal with Other Writings of John Woolman* (London and Toronto: J.M. Dent & Sons, 1922), 116.
25. Crèvecoeur, *Letters,* 46.
26. Ibid., 88.
27. Gaston de Maussion, *They Knew the Washingtons: Letters from a French Soldier with Lafayette and from His Family in Virginia* (Indianapolis: Bobbs-Merrill, 1926), 36.

CHAPTER 5: FASHION

1. *New York Gazette,* November 10, 1774.
2. Johann Conrad Dohla, *A Hessian Diary of the American Revolution,* tr. Bruce E. Burgoyne (Norman: University of Oklahoma Press, 1999), 71.
3. Frederick Mackenzie, *The Diary* (Cambridge, Mass.: Harvard University Press, 1930; repr. New York: New York Times and Arno, 1968), 589.
4. James Thacher, *The American Revolution: From the commencement to the disbanding of the American army; given in the form of a daily journal* (Cincinnati: M. R. Barnitz, 1856), 30.
5. Ibid., 205.
6. John Greenwood, *The Wartime Services of John Greenwood: A Patriot in the American Revolution* (No city: Westvaco, 1981), 69.
7. Thacher, 241.
8. Mackenzie, 98.
9. Thacher, 266.
10. Jean Baptiste Donatien de Vimeur, Count de Rochambeau, *Memoirs of the Count de Rouchambeau,* tr. M. W. E. Wright (Paris: French, English and American Library, 1838; repr. New York: New York Times and Arno Press, 1971), 90.
11. Greenman, *Diary of a Common Soldier in the American Revolution, 1775–1783,* ed. Robert C. Bray and Paul E. Bushnell (De Kalb: Northern Illinois University Press, 1978), 116.
12. Ibid., 270.

CHAPTER 6: FOOD

1. John Slover, "Narrative," in *Indian Atrocities: Narratives of the Perils and Sufferings of Dr. Knight and John Slover, Among the Indians, During the Revolutionary War* (Cincinnati: U. P. James, 1867; repr. [as *Captivity Tales*]. New York: Arno Press, 1974), 57–60.
2. David Ramsey, *The History of the American Revolution* (London: n.p., 1793; repr. New York: Russell and Russell, 1968), vol. 2, 99.
3. Michel Guillaume Jean de Crèvecoeur, *Letters from an American Farmer* (Gloucester, MA: Peter Smith, 1968), 125.
4. Ibid., 38.

5. Robert Rogers, *A Concise Account of North America* (London: J. Millan, 1765; repr. Yorkshire: S.R. Publishers, 1966), 254.

6. Ibid., 262.

7. Johann Conrad Dohla, *A Hessian Diary of the American Revolution,* tr. Bruce E. Burgoyne (Norman: University of Oklahoma Press, 1999), 67.

8. Pettengill, R. W., ed. and tr. *Letters from America, 1776–1779* (Port Washington, N.Y.: Kennikat Press, 1964), 78.

9. Jeremiah Greenman, *Diary of a Common Soldier in the American Revolution, 1775–1783*, ed. Robert C. Bray and Paul E. Bushnell (De Kalb: Northern Illinois University Press, 1978), 14.

10. Ramsey, vol. 1, 188.

11. John Greenwood, *The Wartime Services of John Greenwood: A Patriot in the American Revolution* (No city: Westvaco, 1981), 58.

12. James Thacher, *The American Revolution: from the commencement to the disbanding of the American army; given in the form of a daily journal* (Cincinnati: M. R. Barnitz, 1856), 34.

13. Ramsay, vol. 2, 267.

14. John Enys, *The American Journals of Lt. John Enys. ed. Elizabeth Cometti* (Syracuse, N.Y.: Syracuse University Press, 1976), 26.

15. Ibid., 28.

16. Dohla, 40.

17. Greenman, 18.

18. Greenwood, 89.

19. Ibid., 78.

20. Thacher, 260.

21. Dr. Knight, "The Narrative of Dr. Knight," in *Indian Atrocities: Narratives of the Perils and Sufferings of Dr. Knight and John Slover, Among the Indians, During the Revolutionary War* (Cincinnati: U. P. James, 1867; repr. [as *Captivity Tales*], New York: Arno, 1974), 10.

22. Philip Freneau, *The Poems of Philip Freneau. ed. Fred Lewis Pattee.* (Princeton, N.J.: The University Library, 1903), v.2, 84. cf. Pattee's footnote for the Freneau poem "A New York Tory." The date was January 5, 1781.

23. Crèvecoeur, *Letters,* 51.

24. Ibid., 36–37.

25. Amelia Simmons, *American Cookery* (Hartford, Conn.: Hudson and Goodwin, 1796; repr. New York: Oxford University Press, 1958), 34.

26. Ibid., 10–16.

27. Ibid., 13–17, 24, 32, 41–42.

28. Ibid., 16.

29. Rogers, *A Concise Account,* 139.

30. Crèvecoeur, *Letters,* 127.

31. Ibid., 105–7.

32. Ibid., 142.

33. Benhamin Mifflin, *The Journal of Benjamin Mifflin,* ed. Victor Hugo Paltsits. (New York: New York Public Library, 1935), 8.

34. Enys, 76.

35. William Bartram, *The Travels of William Bartram* (New York: Macy-Masius, 1928), 164.

36. Ibid., 168, 200.
37. Ibid., 203–204.
38. Ibid., 285.
39. Crèvecoeur, *Letters*, 58.
40. Ibid., *Letters*, 37–8.
41. Frederick Mackenzie, *The Diary* (Cambridge, Mass.: Harvard University Press, 1930; repr. New York: New York Times and Arno, 1968), 6.
42. Thacher, 58.
43. Mifflin, 7–8.
44. Greenman, 249.
45. Ibid., 266.
46. Dohla, 127.
47. Ibid., 8.
48. Philip Freneau, "The British Prison Ship," in *The Poems of Philip Freneau: Poet of the American Revolution* (Princeton, N.J.: University Library, 1903), vol. 2, 31.
49. Dohla, 191–92.
50. Crèvecoeur, *Letters*, 154–5.
51. Ibid., 155.
52. Ibid., 41.
53. Simmons, 6, 7.
54. Jean Baptiste Donatien de Vimeur, Count de Rochambeau, *Memoirs of the Count de Rouchambeau*, tr. M. W. E. Wright (Paris: French, English and American Library, 1838; repr. New York: New York Times and Arno Press, 1971), 43.
55. Dohla, 12.
56. Greenman, 30.
57. Freneau, "The British Prison Ship," 37.
58. Mifflin, 7.
59. Gaston de Maussion, *They Knew the Washingtons: Letters from a French Soldier with Lafayette and from His Family in Virginia* (Indianapolis: Bobbs-Merrill, 1926), 93.
60. Thacher, 10.
61. de Maussion, 131.
62. David Ramsey, *The History of the American Revolution* (London: n.p., 1793; repr. New York: Russell and Russell, 1968), vol. 1, 315.

CHAPTER 7: LEISURE ACTIVITIES

1. James Thacher, *The American Revolution: from the commencement to the disbanding of the American army; given in the form of a daily journal)* Cincinnati: M. R. Barnitz, 1856), 33.
2. Johann Conrad Dohla, *A Hessian Diary of the American Revolution,* tr. Bruce E. Burgoyne (Norman: University of Oklahoma Press, 1999), 69.
3. Jeremiah Greenman, *Diary of a Common Soldier in the American Revolution, 1775–1783*, ed. Robert C. Bray and Paul E. Bushnell (De Kalb: Northern Illinois University Press, 1978), 248.
4. Thacher, 39.

5. Ibid., 29.

6. Robert W. Henderson, comp., *Early American Sport: A Checklist of Books by American and Foreign Authors Published in America prior to 1860* (Madison, N.J.: Fairleigh Dickinson University Press, 1977), 117.

7. Dohla, 68.

8. Thacher, 140.

9. Friederich von Riedesel, *Memoirs and Letters and Journals of Major General Riedesel,* trans. William L. Stone (Albany, N.Y.: J. Munsell, 1868; repr. New York Times and Arno, 1969), vol. 2, 17.

10. Jeremiah Greenman, *Diary of a Common Soldier in the American Revolution, 1775–1783,* ed. Robert C. Bray and Paul E. Bushnell (De Kalb: Northern Illinois University Press, 1978), 247.

11. *New York Gazette,* July 1, 1768.

12. Dohla, 121.

CHAPTER 8: LITERATURE

1. John Trumbull, *M'Fingal: An Epic Poem,* intro. Benson J. Lossing (New York: G. P. Putnam; Hurd & Houghton, 1864), 9–10.

2. Sterling E. Murray, "Music and Dance in Philadelphia's City Tavern, 1773–1790," in *American Musical Life in Context and Practice to 1865* (New York and London: Garland Publishing, 1994), 29.

3. Norman Philbrick, *Trumpets Sounding: Propaganda Plays of the American Revolution* (New York: Arno, 1976), 80.

CHAPTER 9: MUSIC

1. James Thacher, *The American Revolution: from the commencement to the disbanding of the American army; given in the form of a daily journal* (Cincinnati: M. R. Barnitz, 1856), 115–16.

2. William Bartram, *The Travels of William Bartram* (New York: Macy-Masius, 1928), 200.

3. Ibid., 298.

4. Ibid., 206.

5. Ibid., 215–16.

6. Ibid., 386.

7. Irving Sablosky, *American Music* (Chicago: University of Chicago Press, 1969), 46.

8. Edward C. Wolf, "Peter Erben and America's First Lutheran Tunebook in America," in *American Musical Life in Context and Practice to 1865,* ed. James R. Heintze (New York and London: Garland Publishing, Inc., 1994), 51.

9. Christine Merrick Ayars, *Contributions to the Art of Music in America by the Music Industries of Boston 1640–1936* (New York: H. W. Wilson, 1937), 298.

10. William Arms Fisher, *Notes on Music in Old Boston* (Boston: Oliver Ditson, 1918; repr. New York: AMS, 1976), 11.

11. Ayars, 194.

12. Russell Sanjek, *American Popular Music and Its Business: The First Four Hundred Years* (New York: Oxford University Press, 1988), 279–280.

13. Karl Krueger, *The Musical Heritage of the United States: The Unknown Portion* (New York: Society for the Preservation of the American Musical Heritage, 1973), 134–35.

14. Sterling E. Murray, "Music and Dance in Philadelphia's City Tavern, 1773–1790," in *American Musical Life in Context and Practice to 1865* (New York and London: Garland Publishing, 1994), 9.

15. Thacher, 122.

16. Sablosky, 29.

17. Fisher, 17–18.

18. Irving Lowens, *Music and Musicians in Early America* (New York: W. W. Norton, 1964), 92.

19. Ibid.

20. Ibid., 91–92.

21. Nathaniel Niles, "The American Hero," in Frederick C. Prescott and John H. Nelson, *Prose and Poetry of the Revolution* (Port Washington, N.Y.: Kennikat, 1969), 84–86.

22. Ayars, 305.

23. Jeremiah Greenman, *Diary of a Common Soldier in the American Revolution, 1775–1783*, ed. Robert C. Bray and Paul E. Bushnell (De Kalb: Northern Illinois University Press, 1978), 111.

24. Ibid., 75.

25. Thacher, 264.

26. John Greenwood, *The Wartime Services of John Greenwood: A Patriot in the American Revolution* (No city: Westvaco, 1981), 45.

27. Thacher, 186.

28. Murray, 26–27.

29. Prescott and Nelson, 84.

CHAPTER 10: PERFORMING ARTS

1. Hugh F. Rankin, *The Theater in Colonial America* (Chapel Hill: University of North Carolina Press, 1965), 2.

2. Ibid., 31.

3. Paul Leicester Ford, *Washington and the Theatre* (1899; repr. New York: Benjamin Blom, [1967]), 22.

4. Ibid., 25–26; and Thomas Clark Pollock, *The Philadelphia Theatre in the Eighteenth Century, Together with the Day Book of the Same Period* (New York: Greenwood, 1968), 36–39.

5. Rankin, 199.

6. Ibid., 109–10.

7. Ibid., 192; and Pollock, 33.

8. Joseph Addison, *Cato*, in *The Works of Joseph Addison* (Philadelphia: J.B. Lippincott & Co., 1883), 404.

9. Ibid., 439.

10. Rankin, 192.

11. William W. Clapp, Jr., *A Record of the Boston Stage* (Boston and Cambridge: James Munroe & Co., 1853. repr. New York: Benjamin Blom, 1968), 2–4.

12. Mark Mayo Boatner, III, *Encyclopedia of the American Revolution* (New York: David McCay, 1966), 710.

13. David Ritchey, comp. and ed., *A Guide to the Baltimore Stage in the Eighteenth Century: A History and Day Book Calendar* (Westport, Conn.: Greenwood, 1982), 4.

14. Clapp, 5–7.

15. Moses Coit Tyler, *The Literary History of the American Revolution, 1763–1781* (New York: G. P. Putnam's Sons, 1897), 24.

16. William Bartram, *The Travels of William Bartram* (New York: Macy-Masius, 1928), 387.

17. John Woolman, *The Journal with Other Writings of John Woolman* (London and Toronto: J.M. Dent & Sons, 1922), 105.

18. Robert Rogers, *Ponteach*, 22.

CHAPTER 11: TRAVEL

1. Benjamin Mifflin, *Journal* (New York: New York Public Library, 1935), 8.

2. Gaston de Maussion, *They Knew the Washingtons: Letters from a French Soldier with Lafayette and from His Family in Virginia* (Indianapolis: Bobbs-Merrill, 1926), 41–2.

3. Michel Guillaume Jean de Crèvecoeur, "Thoughts of an American Farmer on Various Rural Subjects," in *Sketches of Eighteenth Century America,* ed. Henri L. Bourdin, Ralph H. Gabriel and Stanley T. Williams (New Haven: Yale University Press), 148.

4. Crèvecoeur, *Letters*, 76.

5. Sterling E. Murray, "Music and Dance in Philadelphia's City Tavern, 1773–1790," in *American Musical Life in Context and Practice to 1865* (New York and London: Garland Publishing, 1994), 47.

6. Ibid., 4–5.

7. Mifflin, 7, 8, 18.

8. Ibid., 7.

9. Ibid., 11.

10. Ibid., 15.

11. Ibid., 15.

12. Frederick Mackenzie, *The Diary* (Cambridge, Mass.: Harvard University Press, 1930; repr. New York: New York Times and Arno, 1968), 467–68.

13. Ibid., 498.

14. Friederich von Riedesel, *Memoirs and Letters and Journals of Major General Riedesel,* trans. William L. Stone (Albany, N.Y.: J. Munsell, 1868; repr. New York Times and Arno, 1969), vol. 2, 14.

15. de Maussion, 36.

16. Ibid., 41.

17. William Bartram, *The Travels of William Bartram* (New York: Macy-Masius, 1928), 110.

18. Ibid., 298.

19. Ibid., 300,

20. Ibid., 351.

21. Ibid., 184.

22. Crèvecoeur, *Letters*, 166–7.

23. Ibid., 169.

24. Ibid., 177–8.

25. John Woolman, "Remarks on Sundry Subjects," in *The Journal with Other Writings of John Woolman* (London and Toronto: J. M. Dent & Sons, 1922), 233.

26. Ibid., 67.

27. Ibid., 71.

28. Mifflin, 7.

29. Ibid., 15.

30. Bartram, 352.

31. Woolman, 66.

32. Ibid., 71.

33. William Pierce Randel, *The American Revolution: Mirror of a People* (Maplewood, N.J.: Rutledge, 1773), 204.

34. John Greenwood, *The Wartime Services of John Greenwood: A Patriot in the American Revolution* (No city: Westvaco, 1981), 86–88.

35. Jean Baptiste Donatien de Vimeur, Count de Rochambeau, *Memoirs of the Count de Rouchambeau*, tr. M. W. E. Wright (Paris: French, English and American Library, 1838; repr. New York: New York Times and Arno Press, 1971), 64.

36. Janet Schaw, "Janet Schaw, Caught in a Revolution," in *With Women's Eyes: Visitors to the New World 1775–1918*, ed. Marion Tinling (Hamden, Conn.: Archon, 1993), 2.

37. Friederich von Riedesel, *Memoirs and Letters and Journals of Major General Riedesel*, trans. William L. Stone (Albany, N.Y.: J. Munsell, 1868; repr. New York Times and Arno, 1969), vol. 2, 10.

38. Frederick Mackenzie, *The Diary* (Cambridge, Mass.: Harvard University Press, 1930; repr. New York: New York Times and Arno, 1968), 72.

39. Woolman, 110.

40. Mifflin, 7–9.

41. Crèvecoeur, "Various Rural Subject," 33–34.

42. Emerson D. Fite and Archibald Freeman, *A Book of Old Maps Delineating American History* (New York: Dover, 1969), 255.

43. Ibid., 265.

44. Ibid., 270.

45. Ibid.

46. John Enys, *The American Journals of Lt. John Enys,* ed. Elizabeth Cometti (Syracuse, N.Y.: Syracuse University Press, 1976), 62.

47. Rochambeau, 52.

48. Mackenzie, 578.

49. Ibid., 598.

50. de Maussion, 32.

51. Johann Conrad Dohla, *A Hessian Diary of the American Revolution*, tr. Bruce E. Burgoyne (Norman: University of Oklahoma Press, 1999), 12.

52. Woolman, 93.

53. Mifflin, 14.

54. Mackenzie, 427–28.

55. Ibid., 472.
56. Enys, 4.
57. Schaw, 1.
58. Mackenzie, 554.
59. Ibid., 585–86.
60. Dohla, 20.
61. Mifflin, 11.
62. Ibid., 12.
63. Crèvecoeur, *Letters*, 124.
64. Ibid., 127.
65. Ibid., 130–32.

CHAPTER 12: VISUAL ARTS

1. Mark Mayo Boatner, *Encyclopedia of the American Revolution* (New York: D. McKay Co., 1966), 540, 1007.

2. James Thacher, *The American Revolution: from the commencement to the disbanding of the American army; given in the form of a daily journal* (Cincinnati: M. R. Barnitz, 1856), 87.

3. Helen A. Cooper, *John Trumbull: The Hand and Spirit of a Painter* (New Haven, Conn.: Yale University Art Gallery, 1982), 2–3.

4. Alfred Frankenstein and Editors of Time-Life Books, *The World of Copley 1738–1815* (New York: Time-Life Books, 1970), 30.

5. Ibid., 39–40.

6. Rhode Island School of Design Museum of Art, *Gilbert Stuart: Portraitist of the Young Republic* (Washington, D.C.: National Gallery of Art, 1967), 10–11.

7. Edgar P. Richardson, Brooke Hindle, and Lillian B. Miller, *Charles Willson Peale and His World* (New York: Harry N. Abrams, 1982), 17.

8. Helmut von Erffa and Allen Staley, *The Paintings of Benjamin West* (New Haven: Yale University Press, 1986), 435.

9. John Dillenberger, *Benjamin West* (San Antonio, Tex.: Trinity University Press, 1977), 133–35.

10. Frankenstein, 39.

11. Ibid., 69.

12. Cooper, 3–7.

13. Ibid., 97.

14. Richardson, 30–31.

15. Ibid., 44–45.

16. Frankenstein, 93.

17. Sterling E. Murray, "Music and Dance in Philadelphia's City Tavern, 1773–1790," in *American Musical Life in Context and Practice* (New York and London: Garland Publishing, 1994), 29.

18. Ibid., 32.

19. Michael Wynn Jones, *The Cartoon History of the American Revolution* (New York: G. P. Putnam's Sons, 1975), 13.

20. Edwin J. Hipkiss, *Eighteenth-Century American Arts: The M. and M. Karolik Collection* (Cambridge, Mass.: Harvard University Press, 1941), 273–82.

COST OF PRODUCTS DURING
THE REVOLUTIONARY WAR ERA

1. O. G. Sonneck, *Early Concert Life in America (1731–1800)* (Leipzig, Germany: Breitkopf & Hartel, 1907), 20.

2. *New York Gazette & Mercury,* July 3, 1769.

3. Frederick Mackenzie, *The Diary* (Cambridge, Mass.: Harvard University Press, 1390; repr. New York: New York Times and Arno, 1968), 529.

4. Ibid., 157.

5. Ibid., 413.

6. *New York Gazette,* October 25, 1777.

7. Mackenzie, 165

8. Ibid., 531.

9. Ibid., 529.

10. Ibid., 529.

11. Ibid., 165.

12. Ibid., 529.

13. Ibid., 165.

14. *New York Gazette,* October 25, 1777.

15. Mackenzie, 470.

16. *New York Gazette*, July 1, 1771.

17. *New York Gazette*, November 11, 1780.

18. Michel Guillaume Jean de Crèvecoeur, *Letters from an American Farmer,* Gloucester, MA: Peter Smith, 1968), 69.

19. *New York Gazette*, November 10, 1774.

20. Ibid.

21. *New York Gazette,* November 11, 1773.

Further Reading

Abrams, Ann Uhry. *The Valiant Hero: Benjamin West and Grand-Style History Painting.* Washington, D.C.: Smithsonian Institution, 1985.

Adams, Abigail, and John Adams. *Familiar Letters of John Adams and His Wife Abigail Adams, during the Revolution.* Boston: Houghton Mifflin, 1875.

Addison, Joseph. *Cato.* in *The Works of John Addison...in Six Volumes.* Philadelphia: J.B. Lippincott & Co., 1883.

Anderson, Madge. *The Heroes of the Puppet Stage.* New York: Harcourt, Brace, 1923.

Ayars, Christine Merrick. *Contributions to the Art of Music in America by the Music Industries of Boston 1640–1936.* New York: H. W. Wilson, 1937.

Bartram, William. *The Travels of William Bartram.* New York: Macy-Masius, 1928.

"The Battle of Brooklyn" (1776). In Norman Philbrick, *Trumpets Sounding: Propaganda Plays of the American Revolution.* New York: Arno, 1976.

Boatner, Mark Mayo III. *Encyclopedia of the American Revolution.* New York: David McCay, 1966.

Brackenridge, Hugh Henry. "The Death of General Montgomery, in Storming the City of Quebec" (1777). In Norman Philbrick, *Trumpets Sounding: Propaganda Plays of the American Revolution.* New York: Arno, 1976.

Carver, Jonathan. *Travels through the Interior Parts of North America in the Years 1766, 1777 and 1778.* Minneapolis, Minn: Ross & Haines, 1956.

Clapp, William W., Jr. *A Record of the Boston Stage.* Boston and Cambridge: James Munroe & Co., 1853; repr. New York: Johnson Reprint Co., 1968.

Clarke, Garry. *Essays on American Music.* Westport, Conn.: Greenwood, 1977.

Cooper, Helen A. *John Trumbull: The Hand and Spirit of a Painter.* New Haven, Conn.: Yale University Art Gallery, 1982.

Crèvecoeur, Michel Guillaume Jean de. *Letters from an American Farmer.* Gloucester, MA: Peter Smith, 1968.

———. "Thoughts of an American Farmer on Various Rural Subjects." In *Sketches of Eighteenth Century America.* ed. Henri L. Bourdin, Ralph H. Gabriel and Stanley T. Williams (New Haven: Yale University Press).

Dillenberger, John. *Benjamin West: The Content of His Life's Work*. San Antonio, Tex.: Trinity University Press, 1977.

Dohla, Johann Conrad. *A Hessian Diary of the American Revolution*, ed. and tr. Bruce Burgoyne. Norman: University of Oklahoma Press, 1976.

Dolmetsch, Joan D. *Rebellion and Reconciliation: Satirical Prints on the Revolution at Williamsburg*. Williamsburg, VA: The Colonial Williamsburg Foundation, 1976.

Earle, Alice Morse. *Two Centuries of Costume in America, 1620-1820, vol. 2*. New York and London: Benjamin Blom, 1968.

Enys, John. *The American Journals of Lt. John Enys*. Syracuse, N.Y.: Syracuse University Press, 1976.

Erffa, Helmut von, and Allen Staley. *The Paintings of Benjamin West*. New Haven, Conn.: Yale University Press, 1986.

Fisher, William Arms. *Notes on Music in Old Boston*. Boston: Oliver Ditson, 1918; repr. New York: AMS, 1976.

Fite, Emerson D., and Archibald Freeman. *A Book of Old Maps Delineating American History*. New York: Dover, 1969.

Ford, Paul Leicester. *Washington and the Theatre*. (1899) repr. New York: Benjamin Blom, 1967.

Frankenstein, Alfred, and Editors of Time-Life Books. *The World of Copley 1738–1815*. New York: Time-Life Books, 1970.

Freneau, Philip. "The British Prison Ship." In *The Poems of Philip Freneau: Poet of the American Revolution*, vol. 2. Princeton, N.J.: University Library, 1903.

———. "Expedition of Timothy Taurus." In *The Poems of Philip Freneau: Poet of the American Revolution*, vol. 1. Princeton, N.J.: University Library, 1902.

———. *The Poems of Philip Freneau: Poet of the American Revolution*. Princeton, N.J.: University Library, 1902.

———. "Mars and Hymen." In *The Poems of Philip Freneau: Poet of the American Revolution*, vol. 1. Princeton, N.J.: University Library, 1902.

———. "The Silent Academy." In *The Poems of Philip Freneau: Poet of the American Revolution*, vol. 1. Princeton, N.J.: University Library, 1902.

Gelernter, Mark. *A History of American Architecture*. London and Hanover: University Press of New England, 1999.

Greenman, Jeremiah. *Diary of a Common Soldier in the American Revolution, 1775–1783*, ed. Robert C. Bray and Paul E. Bushnell. De Kalb: Northern Illinois University Press, 1978.

Greenwood, John. *The Wartime Services of John Greenwood: A Patriot in the American Revolution*. No city: Westvaco, 1981.

Hamilton, Alexander. "A Full Vindication of Congress from the Calumnies of their Enemies . . ." In *The Works of Alexander Hamilton*, ed. Henry Cabot Lodge (London and New York: G. P. Putnam's Sons, 1904), vol. 1, 17.

Henderson, Robert W., comp. *Early American Sport: A Checklist of Books by American and Foreign Authors Published in America prior to 1860*. Rutherford, Madison and Teaneck, N.J.: Fairleigh Dickinson University Press, 1977.

Hipkiss, Edwin J. *Eighteenth-Century American Arts: The M. and M. Karolik Collection*. Cambridge, Mass.: Harvard University Press, 1941.

Hitchcock, H. Wiley. *Music in the United States: A Historical Introduction*. Englewood Cliffs, N.J.: Prentice-Hall, 1969.

Howard, John Tasker, and George Kent Bellows. *A Short History of Music in America*. New York: Thomas Y. Crowell, 1957.

Jefferson, Thomas. *Notes on the State of Virginia*. Richmond, VA: J.W. Randolph, 1853.

Jones, Michael Wynn. *The Cartoon History of the American Revolution*. New York: G.P. Putnam's Sons, 1975.

Knight, Dr. "Narrative." In *Captivity Tales*. New York: Arno Press, 1974.

Kocher, A. Lawrence, and Howard Dearstyne. *Colonial Williamsburg: Its Buildings and Gardens*. Williamsburg, Va.: Colonial Williamsburg, 1949.

Krueger, Karl. *The Musical Heritage of the United States: The Unknown Portion*. New York: Society for the Preservation of the American Musical Heritage, 1973.

Lahee, Henry. *Annals of Music in America*. Boston: Marshall Jones, 1922.

Leacock, John (attributed). "The Fall of British Tyranny: or American Liberty Triumphant" (1776). In Norman Philbrick, *Trumpets Sounding: Propaganda Plays of the American Revolution*. New York: Arno, 1976.

Lowance, Mason I., Jr., and Georgia B. Bumgardner, eds. *Massachusetts Broadsides of the American Revolution*. Amherst: University of Massachusetts Press, 1976.

Lowens, Irving. *Music and Musicians in Early America*. New York: W. W. Norton, 1964.

Mackenzie, Frederick. *The Diary of Frederick Mackenzie*. Cambridge, Mass.: Harvard University Press, 1930; repr. New York: New York Times and Arno, 1968.

Mary, V. V. [pseud.]. "A Dialogue, between a Southern Delegate, and his Spouse, on his return from the Grand Continental Congress" (1774). In Norman Philbrick, *Trumpets Sounding: Propaganda Plays of the American Revolution*. New York: Arno, 1976.

Maussion, Gaston de and Helene Maussion. *They Knew the Washingtons: Letters from a French Soldier with Lafayette and from His Family in Virginia*, tr. Princess Radziwill. Indianapolis: Bobbs-Merrill, 1926

McClellan, Elisabeth. *History of American Costume, 1607-1870*. New York: Tudor Publishing, 1969.

McPharlin, Paul. *The Puppet Theatre in America*. New York: Harper and Brothers, 1949.

Mifflin, Benjamin. *The Journal of Benjamin Mifflin*, ed. Victor Hugo Paltsits. New York: New York Public Library, 1935.

Miles, Ellen G. *American Paintings of the Eighteenth Century*. New York: Oxford University Press, 1995.

Moore, Frank. *Songs and Ballads of the American Revolution*. New York: D. Appleton, 1861.

Munford, Robert. "The Patriots" (1798). In Norman Philbrick, *Trumpets Sounding: Propaganda Plays of the American Revolution*. New York: Arno, 1976.

Murray, Sterling E. "Music and Dance in Philadelphia's City Tavern, 1773-1790." In *America's Musical Life in Context and Practice to 1865*. New York and London: Garland Publishing, 1994.

National Gallery of Art (U.S.). *Gilbert Stuart: Portraitist of the Young Republic*. Washington, D.C. and Providence, R.I.: National Gallery of Art and Museum of Art at Rhode Island School of Design, 1967.

Niles, Nathaniel. "The American Hero." In Frederick C. Prescott and John H. Nelson, *Prose and Poetry of the Revolution* (Port Washington, N.Y.: Kennikat, 1969), 84-86.

Odell, George C. C. *Annals of the New York Stage*. New York: Columbia University Press, 1927.

Pearson, William H. *American Buildings and Their Architects: The Colonial and Neo-classical Styles*. Garden City, New York: Doubleday, 1970.

Pettengill, R. W., ed. and tr. *Letters from America, 1776-1779*. Port Washington, N.Y.: Kennikat Press, 1964.

Philbrick, Norman. *Trumpets Sounding: Propaganda Plays of the American Revolution*. New York: Arno, 1976.

Pierson, William H. *American Buildings and Their Architects: The Colonial and Neo-classical Styles*. Garden City, New York: Doubleday, 1970.

Pollock, Thomas Clark. *The Philadelphia Theatre in the Eighteenth Century, Together with the Day Book of the Same Period*. New York: Greenwood, 1968.

Prescott, Frederick C., and John H. Nelson. *Prose and Poetry of the Revolution*. Port Washington, N.Y.: Kennikat, 1969.

Ramsey, David. *The History of the American Revolution*. London: n.p., 1793; repr. New York: Russell and Russell, 1968.

Randel, William Pierce. *The American Revolution: Mirror of a People*. New York: Rutledge, 1973.

Rankin, Hugh F. *The Theater in Colonial America*. Chapel Hill: University of North Carolina Press, 1965.

Rhode Island School of Design Museum of Art. *Gilbert Stuart: Portraitist of the Young Republic*. Washington, D.C.: National Gallery of Art, 1967.

Richardson, Edgar P., Brooke Hindle, and Lillian B. Miller. *Charles Willson Peale and His World*. New York: Harry N. Abrams, 1982.

Riedesel, Frederica von (Baroness)."Madame Riedesel at the Battle of Saratoga." In *With Women's Eyes: Visitors to the New World, 1775-1918*, ed. Marion Tinling. Hamden, CT: Archon, 1993.

Riedesel, Friederich Aldophus von. *Memoirs and Letters and Journals of Major General Riedesel*, tr. William L. Stone. Albany, N.Y.: J. Munsell, 1868; repr. New York Times and Arno Press, 1969.

Rifkind, Carole. *A Field Guide to American Architecture*. New York: New American Library, 1980.

Ritchey, David, comp. and ed. *A Guide to the Baltimore Stage in the Eighteenth Century: A History and Day Book Calendar*. Westport, Conn.: Greenwood, 1982.

Rochambeau, Jean Baptiste Donatien de Vimeur, Count de. *Memoirs of the Count de Rouchambeau*, tr. M. W. E. Wright. Paris: French, English and American Library, 1838; repr. New York: New York Times and Arno Press, 1971

Rogers, Robert. *A Concise Account of North America*. London: J. Millan, 1765; repr. Yorkshire: S.R. Publishers, 1966, 121.

———. *Ponteach; or the Savages of America*. In *Representative Plays by American Dramatists*, ed. Montrose J. Moses. N.Y.: E. P. Dutton & Co., 1918–1925.

Sablosky, Irving. *American Music*. Chicago: University of Chicago Press, 1969.

Sanjek, Russell. *American Popular Music and Its Business: The First Four Hundred Years*. New York and Oxford: Oxford University Press, 1988.

Schaw, Janet. "Janet Schaw, Caught in a Revolution." In *With Women's Eyes: Visitors to the New World 1775–1918*, ed. Marion Tinling. Hamden, Conn.: Archon, 1993.

Seilhamer, George O. *History of the American Theatre*. Vol. 1, *Before the Revolution*. Vol. 2, *During the Revolution and After*. New York: Benjamin Blom, 1968.

Simmons, Amelia, *American Cookery*. Hartford, Conn.: Hudson and Goodwin, 1796. (Facsimile edition produced by Dover Publications, New York, 1958, under the title *The First American Cookbook*.)

Slover, John. "Narrative." In *Indian Atrocities: Narratives of the Perils and Sufferings of Dr. Knight and John Slover, Among the Indians, During the Revolutionary War*. Cincinnati: U. P. James, 1867; repr. (as *Captivity Tales*). New York: Arno, 1974

Sonneck, O.G. *Early Concert Life in America (1731-1800)*. Leipzig, Germany: Brietkopf & Hartel, 1907.

Symonds, Craig L. *A Battlefield Atlas of the American Revolution*. Mount Pleasant, S.C.: Nautical and Aviation, 1986.

Tebbel, John. *The American Magazine: A Compact History*. New York: Hawthorn Books, 1969.

Tebbel, John and Mary Ellen Zuckerman. *The Magazine in America, 1741-1990*. New York: Oxford University Press, 1991.

Thacher, James. *The American Revolution: from the commencement to the disbanding of the American army; given in the form of a daily journal*. Cincinnati: M. R. Barnitz, 1856.

Trumbull, John. *M'Fingal: An Epic Poem*. Intro. Benson J. Lossing. New York: G. P. Putnam; Hurd & Houghton, 1864.

Tyler, Moses Coit. *The Literary History of the American Revolution, 1763–1781*. New York: G. P. Putnam's Sons, 1897.

Warren, Mercy Otis (attributed). "The Blockheads; or, the Affrighted Officers" (1776). In Norman Philbrick, *Trumpets Sounding: Propaganda Plays of the American Revolution*. New York: Arno, 1976.

———. *History of the rise, progress and termination of the American Revolution*. Boston: n.p., 1805; repr. Indianapolis: Liberty Classics, 1988.

——— (attributed). "The Motley Assembly" (1779). In Norman Philbrick, *Trumpets Sounding: Propaganda Plays of the American Revolution*. New York: Arno, 1976.

Willis, Eola. *The Charleston Stage in the Eighteenth Century*. New York: Benjamin Blom, 1968.

Wolf, Edward C. "Peter Erben and America's First Lutheran Tunebook in America." In *American Musical Life in Context and Practice to 1865*, ed. James Heintze. New York and London: Garland Publishing, 1994.

Wood, James Playsted. *Magazines in the United States*. New York: The Ronald Press Company, 1971.

Woolman, John. *The Journal and Other Writings of John Woolman*. London and Toronto: J.M. Dent & Sons, 1922.

Index

Commander-in-chief, xii, xix, 75, 94, 170; dancer, 6, 40, 149; false teeth, 36; freemasonry, 116; Mt. Vernon, 80; portraits, 202, 203; Society of Cincinnati, 117; tavern renamed in his honor, 54; tea, 114; theater, 6, 159; travels, 174; western land, 14

Water: abundant, 33, 105, 188; fear of contagion from, 10, 98; fetched for kitchen use, 12–13

Water power, 11, 173

Wayne, Anthony, xx, xxi

Weapons. *See* Guns

West, Benjamin, 199, 201

West Point, 75

Wet nurse, 62

Whaling, 5, 10, 36, 91, 107, 192–93

Wheatley, Phillis, xviii, 140–41

Whist, 122

Wigs, 89

Willard, Archibald, 152, 196

Williamsburg, 73, 80

Windmills, 11

Wine, 10

Witches, 78

Wool, 11, 33, 92

Woolman, John, xviii, 84, 174, 177; anti-slavery, 134–35, 141, 182; pro-Indian, 166, 180–81, 183

Word-of-mouth advertising, 53

Workman's compensation, 8

Wrestling, 31, 57–58, 125, 126

"Yankee Doodle," 150–51

Yellow fever, 8, 26, 118

Yorktown, Virginia, xx, 95, 105, 120, 130, 155, 188, 189

About the Author

RANDALL HUFF is Assistant Professor at Drake University.